As Philip Sassoon was, Damian Collins is the Member of Parliament for Folkestone and Hythe. Damian read Modern History at the University of Oxford and served as a Parliamentary Private Secretary to the Foreign Secretary in the coalition government. His business career before politics was at the M&C Saatchi advertising agency, and he is the Chair of the House of Commons select committee for Culture, Media and Sport.

Damian Collins

CHARMED LIFE

The Phenomenal World of Philip Sassoon

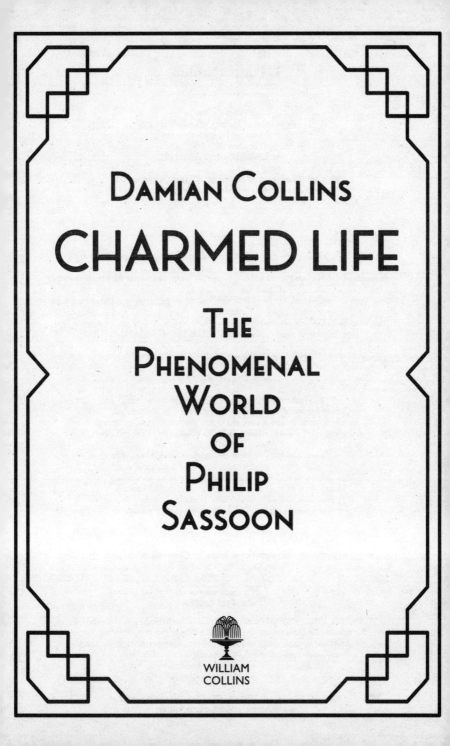

WILLIAM
COLLINS

William Collins
An imprint of HarperCollins*Publishers*
1 London Bridge Street
London SE1 9GF
www.WilliamCollinsBooks.com

First published in Great Britain by William Collins in 2016
This William Collins paperback edition published 2017

1

A catalogue record for this book is available from the British Library

ISBN 978-0-00-812763-3

Typeset in Minion by Palimpsest Book Production Ltd, Falkirk, Stirlingshire

Printed and bound in Great Britain by Clays Ltd, St Ives plc

MIX
Paper from
responsible sources
FSC® C007454

For Sarah,
and her love, support and inspiration
in all things

• CONTENTS •

• PROLOGUE •

At dawn, long before the guests arrive, a cavalcade of horse-drawn carts makes the 14-mile journey from the flower market at Covent Garden, to the edge of north London and the gates of the Trent Park estate. Legions of gardeners are waiting to receive its colourful potted cargo ready for immediate planting, while the staff collect enough azaleas, roses and lilies to fill every room in the house. By noon there is a new procession, of Rolls-Royces arriving and departing in rapid succession. Everywhere along the approach there are signs with arrows guiding the drivers 'To Trent'. Children and their parents line the route, hoping to catch a glimpse of a royal prince or a Hollywood star. The house and gardens have been profiled by *Country Life*, and the society columns regularly highlight the comings and goings of weekend guests. The Trent Park garden parties each June and July are considered the last word in elegance and luxurious informality.

Trent Park nestles in the ancient royal hunting ground of the Enfield Chase, where a broad, gentle valley is watered by a stream, creating a lake which divides the estate in two. The mansion is a fine Georgian-looking building with rose-coloured bricks and honeystone cornicing. It is a fantasy of a perfect eighteenth-century country estate, but supported by every modern convenience. In the drawing room, paintings by Gainsborough and Zoffany hang alongside Flemish tapestries. The floors are decorated with silk carpets from Isfahan, and Chinese lacquerwork sits alongside Louis XV furniture. In the Blue Room with its pale walls and accents of hot red, the contemporary artist Rex Whistler has just finished creating a mural above the fireplace which perfectly brings together the colours and elements of its surroundings.

The guests gather on the terrace, which is the heart of the party, and from where you can see right across the estate. People come and go as they please and white-coated footmen wearing red cummerbunds serve endless courses created by the resident French chefs. There is a restless atmosphere of constant activity. Winston Churchill is at the centre of the conversation, arguing with George Bernard Shaw about socialism, discussing art with Kenneth Clark and painting with Rex Whistler.

Flamingos and peacocks have been released from cages and move effortlessly between the gardens, terrace and house, mingling with the guests while Noël Coward plays the piano. And the host, the millionaire government minister and aesthete Sir Philip Sassoon, is in the midst of it all. He is a touch under 6 foot, with a handsome face, dark aquiline features and a smooth olive skin which makes him appear younger than his mid-forties. He is the creator of this tableau, and with meticulous attention to detail obsesses over every part of his production. Sassoon has an idiosyncratic and infectious style, always on the move, and is seen mostly in profile as he flits from guest to guest like a bee in search of honey.

Queen Mary and Philip's sister Sybil, the Marchioness of Cholmondeley, lead the party in the formal gardens adjacent to the swimming pool and the orangery. Wide borders, laid out to the last square inch by the fashionable garden designer Norah Lindsay, lie in pairs on a gentle slope with broad grass paths on either side so that the eye can rove easily up this glade of brilliance. The incandescent orange and scarlet of the furthest beds give way to rich purples and blues in the middle distance, and the soft assuaging creams and pastel shades in the foreground. After the long borders are pergolas of Italian marble covered with vines, wisteria and clematis, where Winston Churchill likes to sit and paint on quieter afternoons.

The Prince of Wales arrives by aeroplane, landing at the Trent airstrip, and heads to the terrace where the American golf champion Walter Hagen is waiting to play a round with him on Sir Philip's private course. The Duke of York and Anthony Eden, dressed for tennis, stride off with the professional to Trent's courts. There is an air display by pilots from the RAF's 601 Auxiliary Squadron, swooping and flying low over the estate. In the late afternoon, after the Queen has departed, the airmen join guests at the blue swimming pool, cavorting in the walled garden that surrounds it, filled with delphiniums and lilies, which deliver an almost overpowering scent.

The overnight guests withdraw to change for dinner, finding cocktails and buttonhole flowers waiting on their dressing tables as they put on their black tie. Philip Sassoon invites them to dine on the terrace, where Richard Tauber sings later by moonlight, and at the end of the evening there is a display of fireworks over the lake.

For guests reminiscing in the years to come, Philip's lavish hospitality would seem like a dream of a lost world, the like of which would never be seen again. Yet even on this 1930s summer evening, amid the elegance and luxury of Trent Park, there is concern for the future. Among the politicians there is hard talk about Mussolini, Baldwin's government, Germany's threat and British rearmament. And this was not unusual. Almost every major decision taken in Britain between the wars was debated by those at the heart of the action while they were guests of Philip Sassoon.

Their host was more than just a wealthy patron and creative connoisseur. From the First World War through to 1939, Philip worked alongside Britain's leaders and brought them together with some of the most brilliant people in the world. He exerted influence by design, while surrounded by an air of personal mystery.

I

• SON OF BABYLON •

One day, Haroun Al Raschid read
A book wherein the poet said: –

'Where are the kings, and where the rest
Of those who once the world possessed?

'They're gone with all their pomp and show,
They're gone the way that thou shalt go.

'O thou who choosest for thy share
The world, and what the world calls fair,

'Take all that it can give or lend,
But know that death is at the end!'

Haroun Al Raschid bowed his head:
Tears fell upon the page he read.

Henry Wadsworth Longfellow,
'Haroun Al Raschid' (1878)[1]

The first thing that an English gentleman might consider about Sir Philip Sassoon was that he was foreign – an 'oriental'[2] in thought and action. His friend the art historian Kenneth Clark thought him to be 'a kind of Haroun al Raschid, entertaining with oriental magnificence in three large houses, endlessly kind to his friends, witty, mercurial and ultimately mysterious'.[3] The diarist and Sassoon's fellow MP Henry 'Chips' Channon also observed, 'Philip and I mistrust each other; we know too much about each other, and I can peer into his oriental mind with all its vanities.'[4]

To some extent Philip played up to this, and like the great Persian King Haroun Al Raschid from the tales of *One Thousand and One Nights*, he surrounded himself with beauty, luxury and the most interesting and successful people. No matter that he was also a baronet, the brother-in-law of a marquess and a Conservative Member of Parliament, his eastern heritage marked him out.

Philip Albert Gustave David Sassoon was born in Paris on 4 December 1888 at his mother's family mansion in the Avenue de Marigny.* He was the first child of Edward Sassoon and Aline, the daughter of Baron Gustave de Rothschild. His great-grandfather James Rothschild had been born into the Jewish ghetto in Frankfurt in 1792, and at the age of nineteen was sent by his father and brothers to establish the family business in France. When he died in 1868, James was one of the wealthiest men in the world. Ten thousand people attended his funeral and Parisians lined the streets to pay their respects when his coffin was taken for burial at the Père Lachaise cemetery.

The Sassoons were often referred to as the 'Rothschilds of the east'. The family claimed that they were descended from King David, and that their ancestors had been transported to Babylon by

---

* Philip Sassoon was born at the Hôtel de Marigny, at 23 Avenue de Marigny. This vast townhouse was commissioned by his grandfather Baron Gustave de Rothschild. In 1972 it was purchased by the French government and is now used to provide accommodation to visiting heads of state.

Nebuchadnezzar when he sacked Jerusalem, 600 years before the birth of Christ. They had kept their faith, and over the centuries established themselves as leaders in the exiled Jewish community, while also making money trading in the souks of Baghdad.

Young Philip Sassoon would grow up with the stories of how in 1828 his paternal great-grandfather David had been imprisoned in Baghdad by Dawud Pasha* during the suppression of the city's Jews. David's father Sasson ben Surah had been treasurer to the governor of the city and his wealth and connections helped him to buy his son's freedom. David knew that his liberty would be short lived and so fled with only a money belt and some pearls sewn into the hem of his cloak. He went first by boat down the River Tigris to Basra, the port of the fabled Sinbad, and then secretly crossed the Persian Gulf to Bushire, safely beyond the reach of Pasha. Once established he sent for his family, including his eldest son, the ten-year-old Abdullah, future grandfather of Philip Sassoon. The town was the main trading post in Persia of the British East India Company, but it was a backwater compared with Baghdad. In one of Bushire's dusty courtyards, with just a canopy to protect the congregation from the glare of the sun, Abdullah's bar mitzvah was held among the traders, money-changers and pedlars of the local Jewish community. The Sassoon family's good name and the trading skills they had acquired over the generations helped David to start to rebuild their fortunes, but he could see that greater opportunities existed further east in the emerging commercial centre of Bombay. It was there he moved in 1832, the year before the end of the East India Company's monopoly on commerce in India, and established his business David Sassoon & Co., which grew into a major international trading empire – making the family, within his lifetime, one of the wealthiest in the world. As one contemporary remarked, 'Silver and gold, silks, gums and spices,

---

* Dawud Pasha was the last of the Mamluk dynasty of rulers of Iraq, which was at that time a largely autonomous region of the Ottoman Empire.

opium and cotton, wool and wheat – whatever moves over sea or land feels the hand or bears the mark of Sassoon & Co.'[5]

David Sassoon was an exotic figure in this boomtown of the British Raj. He continued to dress in the turban and flowing robes favoured by the great merchants of Baghdad. His wharfs and warehouses at the docks of Bombay were a veritable network of Aladdin's caves holding the goods of the world: Indian cotton for Manchester, Chinese silks and furnishings for the mansions of Europe, and British manufactures for distribution throughout Asia. Twice married and with eight sons in total, David followed the model of the Rothschilds in Europe, using his children to keep close control of the expanding family business. Abdullah was initially sent back to Baghdad, now safe after the fall of Dawud Pasha in 1831, to manage the firm's contacts in the Arab world. Elias would open the first Sassoon office in Shanghai, and their half-brothers Sassoon David (S. D.), Reuben and Abraham established themselves in Hong Kong.

David Sassoon was fluent in many Arab and Indian languages but never conducted business in English. However, he could see how vital Great Britain was to global trade, particularly in cotton and textiles, so in 1858 the twenty-six-year-old S. D. Sassoon, grandfather of the First World War poet Siegfried, was sent to open an office in London. England may have held no great appeal for the Sassoon patriarch, but his sons would become enthralled with life in the global centre of the British Empire. S. D. Sassoon took up residence in a fine fifteenth-century estate at Ashley Park in Surrey, where Oliver Cromwell was said to have lived during the trial of King Charles I. He opened the firm's head office at 12 Leadenhall Street in the heart of the City of London, the same street where the great East India Company had based itself. Sassoon offices were also opened in Liverpool, the gateway for trade with America, and in 'Cottonopolis' itself – Manchester – at 42 Bloom Street. The family's decision to come to England was made at exactly the right moment. The outbreak of the American Civil War in 1861 created an enormous demand from England for bales of cotton from India, as the traditional markets in the southern United States were closed by naval blockade. Bombay boomed and the fortunes of the Sassoons rose with it. When the American Civil War ended, and the cotton markets opened up again, many Indian traders went bust as prices fell. The Sassoons, though, had protected themselves, using their profits to make shrewd investments in property and developing trade with China. They were further strengthened by the comparative weakness of their Bombay competitors, many of whom had overextended themselves and were forced to sell up at rock-bottom prices when their loans were called in.

David Sassoon marked his new wealth by building a great palace for the family in Poona, about 100 miles inland from Bombay, where the British took up residence during the monsoon season. He called it Sans Souci, after the estate created by Frederick the Great near Potsdam in Germany. He also became one of the leading philanthropists of Poona and Bombay, endowing hospitals, schools and synagogues.

As David Sassoon started to draw back from his day-to-day involvement in the business, his sons began to dress as British gentlemen, rather than in the traditional Arabic costume their father favoured. Abraham Sassoon encouraged people to call him the more English-sounding Arthur. Abdullah also preferred to be addressed as Albert, and named his son Edward, after the Prince of Wales. When David Sassoon died in 1864, Albert took over as chairman of the company but much of the day-to-day running of the business was left to his brothers. Fate played a further part in the direction followed by members of the family when in 1867 S. D. Sassoon collapsed and died in the lobby of the Langham Hotel in London. Albert sent Reuben from Hong Kong to take over affairs in England, and to look after S. D.'s young family at Ashley Park. In 1872 Reuben was joined in London by Arthur and his beautiful new wife Louise, and the brothers soon made their mark on society. In addition to homes in the capital and on the coast at Hove, Arthur took possession of Tulchan Lodge, the Speyside estate in Scotland where he entertained the Prince of Wales at shooting parties. The loyalty, discretion and generosity of the Sassoon brothers won them the favour and friendship of the Prince, who was a man of great appetites, though without the necessary resources to supply them.

Back in India, Albert Sassoon pursued his chief interest of consolidating the family's position in political society, a path that both his son Edward and grandson Philip would also follow. Albert created the 'David Sassoon Mechanics Institute and Library' which still stands in the city, served on the Bombay Legislative Council and was made a Companion of the Order of the Star of India for his philanthropic works in the city, the highest British order of chivalry in India.

In 1875 Albert Sassoon was central to business and official life in Bombay. He opened the vast Sassoon Docks, the first commercial wet dock in western India, and threw a magnificent ball at Poona for Edward, the Prince of Wales to honour his official visit. Afterwards Albert presented to Bombay a 13-foot-tall equestrian statue of the Prince. It was placed in front of the David Sassoon Library and became known as the Kala Ghoda, meaning Black Horse in Hindi, a title which was subsequently used to describe that neighbourhood of the city.*

However, the success of Edward's visit, combined with the letters back to Bombay from his brothers, made Albert increasingly keen to join them permanently in England. London promised a more glamorous life, and it could be justifiably argued that the chairman of David Sassoon & Co. should be based there. He took up residence in a mansion at 25 Kensington Gore and at a large summer house in Brighton, near to Arthur's home in Hove.

Brighton would be the scene of the greatest of his royal entertainments, when Albert was persuaded to take over the arrangements for a grand reception for the state visit of the Shah of Persia,

---

* The statue was removed in 1965 and now stands with others from the colonial era, in the gardens of the Byculla Zoo in Mumbai. Kala Ghoda is still the name used to refer to the area of the city where it originally stood.

Nasr-ed-Din, in July 1889. His mansion on the Eastern Terrace was not large enough to accommodate everyone, so the Empire Theatre was hired for the occasion. He spent liberally on the decorations, on refreshments and on a programme of ballet to entertain the guests, who included members of the royal family. For Albert, it was a long way from his bar mitzvah, as a young immigrant in that dusty town on the Persian coast, nearly sixty years before.

Nasr-ed-Din was a difficult man, but Albert's hospitality had been a triumph for which his reward from a grateful British state was a baronetcy. The College of Heralds helped Sir Albert Sassoon to create a coat of arms comprising symbols appropriate to the family's heritage: the lion of Judah carrying the rod that was never to depart from their Jewish tribe; a palm tree representing the flourishing of the righteous man; and a pomegranate, a rabbinical symbol of good deeds.

On 24 October 1896, Philip Sassoon, just a few weeks short of his eighth birthday, would learn of the sudden death of his grand-father, and would then see him interred in the domed mausoleum which Albert had recently constructed for the family, close to his Brighton mansion.* Philip's father inherited the chairmanship of the family firm, as well as Albert's title, and so became Sir Edward Sassoon, second baronet of Kensington Gore. Free from the expec-tation that he would devote himself to the family business, Edward had been brought up to be an English gentleman. He had studied for a degree at the University of London, went shooting with the Prince of Wales at Tulchan and became an officer in a Yeomanry regiment, the Duke of Cambridge's Hussars. In October 1887 Edward's marriage to the French heiress Aline de Rothschild was conducted at the synagogue on the Rue de la Victoire in Paris by the Chief Rabbi of France. Twelve hundred guests attended the

---

* The mausoleum can be found today at 83 St George's Road, Brighton. It was closed in 1933 by Philip, who moved the family remains interred there to Willesden Jewish cemetery in London. Since 1949, the building has been used as a venue for bars, restaurants and cabarets.

reception at the Rothschilds' palatial home on the Avenue de Marigny, and this great dynastic union further consolidated the Sassoons' standing in European society. The Prince of Wales was often a guest of the Rothschilds at the Avenue de Marigny during his frequent trips to Paris, and Edward and Aline Sassoon became established as part of his circle of close friends known as the Marlborough House set.

Edward Sassoon was tall and handsome, with a 'sharp grim look which vanished when he smiled'.[6] He was an enthusiastic sportsman, who took particular pleasure in shooting, ice skating at St Moritz and playing billiards. Aline combined beauty and elegance with great intelligence. She brought from Paris her love of art and literature, a passion that she would share with their children, Philip and his younger sister Sybil, born six years after him in 1894. Edward and Aline created their own salon, selling Albert's Kensington Gore house and purchasing a larger mansion at 25 Park Lane, which had originally been built for Barney Barnato, the London-born Jewish diamond magnate.* Aline became a popular society hostess in England and France and the children would grow up around the parties thrown for her wide circle of friends, who included Arthur Conan Doyle, H. G. Wells and John Singer Sargent, who painted her. Aline was also one of the 'Souls', an elite social group for political and philosophical discussion whose members included the politician Arthur Balfour, Margot Asquith, the wife of Herbert Asquith, and another great hostess of the period, Lady Desborough.

The Sassoon family interest in politics was as strong for Edward as it had been for his father, and in 1899 an opportunity came to stand for election to the House of Commons as the Unionist candidate in a by-election for the Hythe constituency. His selection for

---

* Barney Barnato was a billionaire in today's money and the business partner of Cecil Rhodes at De Beers. He never actually took possession of the Park Lane property and drowned in mysterious circumstances on his return passage to England. The house was renumbered in the 1920s and became 45 Park Lane.

the seat was easier because it was considered to be a 'pocket borough' of his wife's family. Her father's cousin Mayer de Rothschild had been its MP for fifteen years until his death in 1874 and the family still made generous annual contributions to the local party funds.*

This south Kent constituency consisted of the ancient Cinque Port towns of Hythe and New Romney, as well as the fashionable resort of Folkestone, which was also a favourite of the Prince of Wales. The district embraced the wide, flat Romney Marsh, farmed since the Middle Ages when it was recovered from the sea, and which in centuries past had harboured gangs of smugglers. Following his successful election campaign Edward bought Shorncliffe Lodge as a home for his family in the constituency, a fine white-stuccoed house which stood on the Undercliff in Sandgate, a village along the coast from Folkestone. The house commanded views around Hythe Bay, and on a clear day you could see across the English Channel to France. Philip and Sybil's childhood would be spent between Park Lane and seaside holidays on the Kent coast, with frequent visits to their mother's family at the Avenue de Marigny and the Rothschild Château de Laversine near Chantilly.

Sir Edward Sassoon did not shine as a parliamentarian. He became an established backbench MP who took an interest in trade, improving international telegraph communications and the idea of building a Channel tunnel. His place in the House of Commons, the mother parliament of the British Empire, may have enhanced his standing in political society, but it was not somewhere he needed to be. He was paving the way for his children so that they could go on and attain the heights of power and prominence in the British establishment that for him were out of reach. Like all parents, he was ambitious for his children, and he clearly hoped that Philip would use the wealth, title and connections he would inherit to launch his own great career in British public life.

---

* Mayer Rothschild's daughter Hannah had married Lord Rosebery, who briefly became Prime Minister after William Gladstone's retirement in 1894.

The formal education Edward and Aline chose for Philip was one they hoped would equip him to be a leading member of the British ruling class. He attended a boarding prep school in Farnborough, before being sent to Eton College. Fathers put their sons down for a place at Eton on the day or at least in the week of their birth. In the early 1900s the purpose of the school's entrance exam was not to select the best students, but to determine into which form a boy should be placed. After Eton Philip would spend four years at the University of Oxford, where many of the young undergraduates would attend the same college as previous generations of their families, often inhabiting the same set of rooms. This was the tried and tested production line designed to mould the future elite, one that had produced in good order prime ministers, generals and colonial governors. When Philip started at Eton in spring 1902, the then Prime Minister Arthur Balfour was among the school's alumni, as had been his immediate three predecessors going back over twenty years. Edward wrote to tell his son as he embarked upon his school life that 'You will find diligence in studies particularly helpful when you join the Debating Society at Eton, an institution in which excellence means a brilliant career in Parliament later on.'[7]

Philip was the first generation of his line of the Sassoon family to receive his schooling in England, although he did have five cousins at Eton, all members of the Ashley Park branch, and grandsons of S. D. Sassoon.* There were other boys he knew from his mother's circle, particularly Julian and Billy Grenfell, and Edward Horner, the sons respectively of Lady Desborough and Frances Horner. Eton would not be a complete leap into the unknown for Philip, but nor was he a native of his new habitat.

Arriving for his first term, the thirteen-year-old Philip Sassoon was an exotic figure to those English schoolboys. He had a dark complexion, as a result of his eastern heritage, and a French accent from the great deal of time he had spent with his mother's family.

---

* Siegfried Sassoon attended Marlborough, rather than Eton with his cousins.

In particular he rolled his 'r's and at first introduced himself with the French pronunciation of his name: 'Pheeleep'. Philip had a slight build which did not mark him out as a future Captain of Boats or star of the football field; Eton was a school which idolized its sportsmen, and they filled the ranks of Pop, the elite club of senior boys. For Philip, just being Jewish made him unusual enough in the more conservative elements of society, as it aroused suspicion as a 'foreign' religion.

While it was well known that Philip's family had great wealth, this was not something that would necessarily impress the other boys, particularly when it was new money. Any sense of self-importance was also strictly taboo, and likely to lead only to ridicule. To be accepted, Philip would need to master that great English deceit of false modesty.

He was placed in the boarding house run by Herbert Tatham, a Cambridge classicist who had been a member of one of the university's secret societies of intellectuals, the Young Apostles. The house accommodation was spartan, and certainly bore no comparison with Philip's life in Park Lane and the Avenue de Marigny. Lawrence Jones, a contemporary at Eton, where his friends called him 'Jonah', remembered that in his house:

> no fires might be lit in boys' rooms till four o'clock, however hard the frost outside, and since the wearing of great coats was something not 'done' except by boys who had house colours or Upper Boats, we shook and shivered from early school till dinner at two o'clock . . . we snuffled and snivelled through the winter halves . . . If there is anything more bleak than to return to your room on a winter's morning, with snow on the ground to find the door and window open, the chairs on the table and the maid scrubbing the linoleum floor, I have not met it.[8]

Unlike many other English boarding schools of the time, boys at Eton had a room to themselves from the start, which gave them a place to escape to and a space which they could make their own. This was one definite advantage and Jones recalled that 'For sheer cosiness, there is nothing to beat cooking sausages over a coal fire in a tiny room, with shabby red curtains drawn, and the brown tea-pot steaming on the table.'[9] There were dangers too in these cramped old boarding houses, and in Philip's first year at the school a terrible fire would destroy one of them, killing two junior boys.

One of the senior boys in Philip's house was the popular Captain of the School, Denys Hatton, who took him under his wing when he started. Denys would not allow Philip to be bullied, and in return he received overwhelming displays of gratitude and admiration which at times clearly disturbed him. On one occasion when Denys was laid up in the school infirmary with a knee injury, Philip rushed to his side with lavish gifts including a pair of diamond cufflinks and ruby shirt studs. Denys received them with disgust, throwing them on to the floor, but he later made sure to retrieve them.[10] Philip remembered Denys's kindness, and when he had himself risen through the school's ranks he was similarly considerate to the junior boys. At Eton it was the tradition for the juniors to act as servants or 'fags' for senior students. Osbert Sitwell, the future writer and poet, fulfilled this role for Philip and they remained friends thereafter. Sitwell remembered that Philip was 'very grown up for his age, at times exuberant, at others melancholy and pre-occupied, but always unlike anyone else . . . And extremely considerate and kind in all his dealings.'[11]

Among Eton's unwritten rules was that, to become one of the club, you first had to become clubbable. Philip sought to gain favour with his contemporaries by throwing generous tea parties in his room, with the help of Mrs Skey, the house matron.* There he would amuse his guests with his great gift as a mimic and

---

* As a sign of Philip's lifelong affection for Mrs Skey, he remembered her in his will, leaving her an annuity of £100 for life. It was the only such bequest he made outside of his household staff and close family.

storyteller, making full use of London gossip from his parents' social circle. He was an enthusiast of the energetic cross-country sport of beagling, he rowed for his house, and he enjoyed tennis and the school's traditional handball game, Eton Fives. In his last year Philip would also receive the social distinction of rowing on the *Monarch* boat in the river pageant for the school's annual celebrations on 4 June, in honour of the birthday of Eton's great patron King George III.

Later in life Osbert Sitwell would state in his entry in *Who's Who* that he was educated during the Eton school holidays. The education of English gentlemen at that time was traditional, limited in its curriculum and designed to mould and shape, rather than to inspire and encourage. Senior Eton masters responded to such occasional criticism by pointing out that the school regularly produced brilliant and inspirational young men, so it couldn't be all bad. In the early 1900s, the Eton classrooms were even older and more basic than the boys' accommodation. The future leaders of the Empire were educated in facilities that any school inspector would today close down on sight without a moment's hesitation. Junior boys were taught in a dark, low-ceilinged, gas-lit schoolroom, with the view of the master interrupted by blackened oak pillars. It was not heated in winter, and was airless in summer. Their small wooden desks were too narrow to write at, and were carved with innumerable names of generations of boys.

The main subjects in the curriculum were Latin and Greek, with the boys required to spend many hours each week learning off by heart great tracts from Ovid and Horace, Virgil and Homer. History and maths were taught well, but science was limited and any kind of study of English poetry and literature was rare before the students' final year. For most boys French was largely taught as a dead language, with the students undertaking written translation but not speaking French. Philip, though, was already bilingual and would twice win the school's King's Prize for French. As such he was included in the special conversational French classes for exceptional students, given by Monsieur Hua, a bald-headed Frenchman with a black beard who had also been called to Windsor Castle to teach King Edward VII's grandsons.* In the evenings he would invite small groups of the boys to his rooms where they would learn to talk and gossip in French.

If the French language was a gift from his mother, so was Philip's passion for art. Art education at Eton was generally limited to the lower boys taking drawing lessons with old Sam Evans, who would direct the pupils to sketch copies of plaster casts of classical figures. Philip took up these classes but was more fortunate to come to the attention of Henry Luxmoore, the 'grand old man' among Eton's masters and a 'lone standard bearer for aesthetics'.[12] Philip would join small groups of boys for Sunday teas with Luxmoore in the famous garden he had created at Eton, where they would discuss art. These informal sessions for students whom Luxmoore regarded as potential kindred spirits was the only education the boys had in the works of the great artists. Philip could contribute with knowledge acquired from his family's extensive collection, and of course drop into conversation the news that John Singer Sargent was painting his mother's portrait.

Having grown up around beautiful things it is not surprising that he should have developed a strong appreciation of the value of art for its own sake. At Eton, Luxmoore would help to develop Philip's intellectual curiosity in the attempts of great artists to understand and capture beauty. Luxmoore's own particular interest was in the works of the seventeenth-century Spanish painter Bartolomé Murillo, whose realist portraits of everyday life, including flower girls, street urchins and beggars, may have influenced Philip's own later interest in the English 'conversation piece' paintings of Gainsborough and Zoffany, depicting the details of life in the eighteenth century. Murillo's work also showed that real beauty could be found anywhere, not just in great cathedrals and palaces.

---

* These were Philip's future friends, Princes Edward, Albert, George and Henry.

Luxmoore's passion for the art of gardening was something else that Philip would share in adult life, with both men appreciating its power to define space and create an experience of beauty.*

When Luxmoore died in 1926, the *Spectator* magazine recalled that 'his knowledge and sense of art and architecture made him an arbiter of taste. But his most abiding mark will be on the characters of innumerable boys and, we venture to say, of masters too. He inspired high motives and principles by expecting them. No one with a mean thought in his heart could come before Mr Luxmoore's eye and not feel ashamed.'[13] Philip Sassoon's education in aesthetics was energetic rather than passive. He developed not just an appreciation of art, but an idealized vision for life. He believed, as Oscar Wilde did, that 'by beautifying the outward aspects of life, one would beautify the inner ones', and that an artistic renaissance represented 'a sort of rebirth of the spirit of man'.[14] Eton suited Philip Sassoon, because despite the strictures of Edwardian English society it was a place where 'you could think and love what you liked; only in external matters, in clothes or in deportment, need you to do as others did'.[15]

Philip was not one of Eton's star scholars; those prizes were taken by boys like Ronald Knox and Patrick Shaw Stewart, who would go on to scale the academic heights at Oxford. He sat the examination for Balliol College, which had something of a reputation as an academic hothouse, but was not awarded one of the closed scholarships that were at Eton's disposal. Instead he took the traditional path to Christ Church, to read Modern History.

Leading statesmen like William Gladstone and the Marquess of Salisbury had previously made the journey from Eton to Christ Church, but it also had a reputation as the home of Oxford's more creative students. It had been the college of Lewis Carroll and of the great Victorian art critic John Ruskin; and Evelyn Waugh would later

---

* Luxmoore would visit the mansion and garden Philip created for himself at Port Lympne in August 1922.

choose Christ Church's Meadow Building, constructed in the Venetian Gothic style, as the setting for Lord Sebastian Flyte's rooms in *Brideshead Revisited*, published in 1945. Fortunate students living in the beautiful eighteenth-century Peckwater Quad could have a fine set of high-ceilinged rooms in which to live and entertain with style.

Life at Oxford in those seven years before the First World War is now seen as the high summer of the British Empire, coloured by the glorious flowering of a lost generation. It is a view inevitably shaped by the immense sense of loss at the deaths of so many brave and brilliant young men in battle. Oxford was still governed, though, by a pre-First World War social conservatism and, as at Eton, Philip could not help being somewhat 'other'. It was less than forty years since the university had first accepted students who were not members of the Church of England, and he was one of no more than twenty-five undergraduates of the Jewish faith, out of a total of three thousand at the university.

Philip had grown in confidence and stature since his early Eton days. He was sleek, athletic and always immaculately attired in clothes tailored in Savile Row. He continued to enjoy robust outdoor pursuits like beagling and was an avid swimmer and tennis player. He went out hunting with the Heythrop and Bicester, and members recalled that he always 'looked like a fashion plate even in the mud'.[16] Philip was not a varsity sportsman, so would not earn the Oxford Blue that would guarantee acceptance into Vincent's Club, but he was invited to join the renowned dining club, the Bullingdon, which was then popular with Old Etonian undergraduates who hunted.

At Oxford he also enjoyed the independence of having his own allowance to spend, and his own rooms to live in. He arranged for furniture from his parents' Park Lane mansion to decorate his quarters at Christ Church, and once gave a seven-course dinner party with the food specially brought up by train in heated containers from a restaurant in London. Despite his father's hope that Philip would start to mark out a future for himself in politics, he did not trouble the debaters at the Oxford Union Society, the training ground for generations of would-be leaders of nations. Although a confident performer in private company he remained a nervous public speaker and could not hope to compete with the Union's leading lights, such as fellow Old Etonian Ronald Knox.

At Oxford, Philip's circle of friends was drawn not from his own college, but mainly from his Old Etonian contemporaries at Balliol, men like Charles Lister, Patrick Shaw Stewart, Edward Horner and Julian Grenfell. Apart from Horner, they did not fit the mould of the traditional English gentleman, whose place and role in the world was certain. Lister had caused a stir at Eton by joining the Labour Party, a genuinely radical step in the eyes of early Edwardian society. He'd also participated actively in the school's mission to the poor in Hackney Wick in the East End of London. Shaw Stewart was academically brilliant and very ambitious but, without any real family money, was required to make his own way in the world. He was fixed on making a fortune in the City, before embarking on his own career in public life. Grenfell was someone whom Philip had grown up with, even if they had not become particularly close. Philip and his family had been frequent guests at Taplow Court where Julian's mother Lady Desborough, a close friend of Aline Sassoon, was a renowned hostess. Julian's first London dinner party had been at the Sassoons' home in Park Lane, the evening before the Oxford and Cambridge University Boat Race in 1907, and his younger brother Billy had been to stay at the Avenue de Marigny earlier that year.

Yet Philip and Julian were cut from very different cloth. Julian was 6 foot 2 and made for battle. His aesthetic interests lay in the pursuit of physical perfection through the training of his own body as an athlete and boxer. Lawrence Jones, a contemporary at Eton and Balliol, remembered that

There was something simple and primitive in [Julian] that was outraged by the perfection of well-bred luxury at Taplow . . . He felt that there was something artificial and unreal in [his mother's]

deft manipulation of a procession of week-end parties, lightly
skimming the cream from the surface of life ... Julian had a
passion for red-blooded down-to-earthiness, for action and adventure, and, with youthful intolerance, fiercely resented the easy,
cushioned existence of Edwardian society.[17]

These emotions led to frequent arguments with his mother, and
were also evident in his up-and-down relationship with Philip,
whose own tastes were closer to Lady Desborough's. Julian wrote
a mocking letter to his mother from Oxford, faking a new interest
in the more refined tastes she hoped he might develop:

I went and did a soshial [sic] last night to widen my circle of
friends and my general horizon: the Bullingdon dinner – all the
pin heads there! They are such good fellows!! and now I know
what a miserable fool I've been shutting myself away from my
fellow men, but thank God it is not too late! and I believe that
last night I laid the foundations for some golden friendships which
will blossom out and change and colour the whole of my life. Do
you know a man called Philip Sassoon?[18]

Julian kept an Australian stock whip, and once used it after a party
in Philip's luxurious rooms to chase him around Christ Church's
Tom Quad, cracking the whip to within inches of Sassoon's head,
crying out, 'I see you, Pheeleep,' mocking his French accent. Julian
would also call out 'I see you, Pheeleep' if he spotted him in the
Balliol Quad, causing Philip to scurry for the gatehouse or a nearby
staircase entrance. Their friendship, which developed at Oxford,
was largely based on their mutual interest in rigorous outdoor
pursuits. Lawrence Jones remembered that they 'both had a passion
for beauty, as well as for getting things done'.[19] Julian and Philip
were complex personalities who defied preconceived ideas of their
characters. Julian was the rough man who was also developing into
an increasingly accomplished poet. Philip was the aesthete who

jumped fences and muddy ditches in perfectly tailored buckskin breeches, and played opponents into the ground at tennis.

In July 1908, at the end of Philip's first year at Oxford, he attended a large summer party at Taplow Court given by Lady Desborough, to mark the final appearance by Julian's brother Billy in the Eton versus Harrow cricket match, with guests including the new Liberal Prime Minister, Herbert Asquith, and the Conservative leader, Arthur Balfour. Philip then departed to spend part of the vacation in Munich to improve his German. He lodged with a baron who provided rooms for young gentlemen, often those aspiring to work in the diplomatic service and looking to perfect their languages. Sassoon shared his quarters with John Lambton, who was just a few years older than him but already much the same as the rather staid Earl of Durham that he would become.

Lambton was friendly with the American novelist Gertrude Atherton, who was living in the city at the time, and Philip joined their group. There could not have been a greater contrast between the irrepressible Philip and the stolid Lambton. Gertrude remembered that Philip was 'as active as Lambton was Lymphatic; he might indeed have been strung on electric wires, wanted to be doing something every minute ... To sleep late was out of the question with that dynamo in his room at nine in the morning demanding to be taken somewhere.'[20]

Along with Gertrude's niece Boradil Craig, they embarked on an energetic tour of the sights and treasures of Bavaria, including Ludwig II's extraordinary Romanesque Revival castle of Neuschwanstein. Ludwig had created a romantic fantasy of pre-Raphaelite splendour high in the rugged hills above Hohenschwangau. It was inspired by the world of German knights, honour and sacrifice captured in the works of Richard Wagner, whom Ludwig worshipped. Philip Sassoon toured every corner of the castle, devouring in detail the architecture and decor, and admiring the personal artistic statement that Ludwig had made. Philip's great-grandfather David had similarly built his own palace at Poona, and the young Sassoon would later fashion a new estate in Kent at Port Lympne, which would be his greatest creative legacy.

In the evenings the group would often attend Munich's Feldherrnhalle opera house, and on one occasion Philip and Boradil danced in the open air in Ludwigstrasse, on a platform before a replica of Florence's Loggia di Lanza. Gertrude recalled that Philip 'in an excess of high spirits kicked off [Lambton's] hat and played football with it [and] he was highly offended. Despite his lazy good nature he could be haughty and excessively dignified, and all his instinct of caste rose at the liberty. But Young Sassoon was irrepressible. Hauteur and aristocratic resentment made no impression on him.' Gertrude thought Philip 'a nice boy and an extremely brilliant one, the life of our parties'.[21]

Philip returned to his studies at Oxford, working diligently if not with huge distinction, and graduated after four years with a second-class honours degree in Modern History, specializing in eighteenth-century European studies. He'd also signed up at Oxford, with his father's encouragement, as a junior officer in the East Kent Yeomanry, which was the local reservist regiment for Edward's parliamentary constituency of Hythe. Edward, always thinking of a future career for his son in public life, told Philip that such a move would be 'useful in other ways later on'.[22]

A number of Philip's Oxford friends joined various respectable institutions after graduating. Julian Grenfell became a professional soldier, Charles Lister went to the Foreign Office, and Patrick Shaw Stewart followed his first-class degree with a fellowship at All Souls and a position at Baring's Bank. It was not clear what Philip would do next. He did not need to make money, and there was no requirement that he should take an active interest in the family firm. He would accompany his father on occasional visits to the office of David Sassoon & Co. in Leadenhall Street, and also to some political meetings and speaking engagements in the constituency.

However, from the summer of 1909, halfway through Philip's Oxford career, and for the next ten years, death did more than anything to shape the course of his life. Philip would lose in succession his parents, his surviving grandparents and then, in the First World War, a great number of his friends. With death as his constant companion, he could not have been blamed for being imbued, as he would later remark, 'with a fatalism purely oriental'.[23] By this he meant the idea that life is preordained, and that nothing can be done to avoid the fate for which you are destined. Philip would certainly follow the path his parents had set out for him, but his response to each of the blows which death delivered shows a determination to rise to the challenges they presented, and not to be cowed by them.

In early 1909, Philip's beloved mother Aline was diagnosed with cancer, and her health failed fast. On 28 July, aged just forty-four, she died at her family's home in the Avenue de Marigny and was buried alongside her grandfather in the Rothschilds' family tomb at Père Lachaise. The whole family was devastated, and Aline's friends tried to rally around the children. Frances Horner wrote to Philip in Paris immediately after her friend's death to remind him that 'You will return to a country that loved her and will always love her children.'[24] Philip was given the string of pearls that Edward had presented to Aline on their wedding day, in the expectation that he would one day give them to his own bride. Instead he often kept them in his pocket, rubbing them occasionally – in order, he would tell friends, 'to keep them alive'.* Philip believed, as he would later tell Lady Desborough, that the greatest burden of sorrow was felt for those who had to live on without Aline, rather than for his mother herself, whose life had been so tragically cut short.[25]

Edward Sassoon never recovered from the loss of his wife, and became a withdrawn figure, remote even from other members of the family. In the winter of 1911 he was involved in a collision with a motor car on the Promenade de la Croisette in Cannes and remained badly shaken by the accident. His health further deteriorated in the

---

* Charlie Chaplin remembered Philip doing this when he stayed with him in 1921, and recalls it in his autobiography.

new year, as a result, it was discovered, of the onset of cancer. Just as with Aline, the end came all too rapidly and he died at home in Park Lane on 24 May 1912, a month short of his fifty-sixth birthday. His coffin was enclosed in the Sassoon mausoleum in Brighton, alongside that of his father, Albert. The twenty-three-year-old Sir Philip, now the third baronet, and his seventeen-year-old sister Sybil were left with the grief of having lost both parents in less than three years. Their maternal grandparents had also both died, in 1911 and 1912, first Baron Gustave de Rothschild and then their grandmother, to whom Sybil had been particularly close. Frances Horner again wrote to Philip: 'You have both been so familiar with grief and suffering these two years [that it] must have [made] a deep mark on your youth.'[26]

Philip did not receive the normal orphan's inheritance, as tragic circumstances had contrived to make him one of the wealthiest young men in England. Along with his title, he received an estate from his parents worth £1 million, including the mansion at 25 Park Lane, a country estate and farmland at Trent Park, just north of London, and Shorncliffe Lodge on the Kent coast at Sandgate. There was also property in India, including his great-grandfather's house at Poona, and Edward's shares in David Sassoon & Co. These came with the request in his father's will that he should never sell them to outsiders and thereby weaken the family's control of the business. He honoured Edward's request and remained a major shareholder, although he never took much of an interest in the business. Philip took up residence alone at 25 Park Lane. It was felt that brother and sister should not live together, so Sybil moved in with their recently widowed great-aunt, Louise Sassoon, at 2 Albert Gate near Hyde Park.*

Edward left one further gift for Philip, for whom he had such high hopes, stating in his will that it was his 'special wish' that his

---

* Louise's husband Arthur, the younger brother of Philip's grandfather Albert, had also died that year. The mansion at 2 Albert Gate is currently the Kuwaiti Embassy.

son should 'maintain some connection with my parliamentary constituency'. This request merely emphasized an undertaking that he had sought from Philip before he died. Sybil remembered that when their father was 'very ill and they knew he was not going to recover, they asked my brother to take his place'.[27] It was also reported in the newspapers the day after Edward died that 'it is freely stated that Mr Philip Sassoon ... will be put forward' as parliamentary candidate for Hythe.[28]

It was not unusual for sons to follow their fathers into politics, but the final decision on the candidate would be made by the party leader, Andrew Bonar Law. The former MP Sir Arthur Colefax was also staking a claim to the seat and his experience was much greater than Philip's, who had made his first public political speech just a few weeks previously, an address to the Primrose League* in opposition to Home Rule for Ireland. Bonar Law was advised, however, to give the young Sassoon the chance to stand. This was not purely down to sentiment, but was chiefly because of the large financial contributions that the Sassoon and Rothschild families had made to the local constituency party funds over many years. Both Philip and Colefax addressed the meeting at Folkestone town hall where the local Conservative Party adopted their candidate, but it was clear that the overwhelming majority were with Sassoon.

Philip's selection meant that there was no time to grieve for his father, as the by-election was to be held on 11 June. He threw himself into the campaign, building on the goodwill people felt towards Edward, and working hard to fulfil his father's final wish that he should be elected. In his election address Philip set out his credentials as the Conservative and Unionist candidate: opposing home rule as something which would in his opinion cause grave troubles in Ireland, supporting tariff reform to give preference to goods imported from the British Empire, and calling for further investment

---

* Founded in 1883, the Primrose League was a grassroots political organisation named after Disraeli's favourite flower.

in new battleships for the Royal Navy.[29] He could certainly rely on the support of the Folkestone fishermen, who had carried Edward Sassoon's banner and party colours on their boats moored in the harbour at the general election in 1910, and did the same during Philip's campaign. They were set against the Liberal government's free-trade policies that allowed French fishermen to land their fish in Folkestone tariff free, while British vessels were charged if they brought any of their catch into French ports. Philip also received backing from the licensed victuallers in the constituency, continuing the traditional support the Tories enjoyed from the drinks industry.[30] He upset some of the more traditionalist Conservative MPs during the by-election by supporting the suffragette campaign for votes for women. At his first public meeting of the campaign, he was accused by some in the audience of being too young, but the newspapers reported that he 'promised to grow out of that if they gave him the chance'.[31] His performance at the meeting was also reported by the local newspapers as an 'amazing success'.

On polling day the weather was fine, which was good for encouraging voters to turn out and, just in case, Philip's campaign used motor cars to drive their supporters to the polling stations. The voters of the Hythe constituency safely returned to Parliament the young man they had known since he was a boy, with a majority almost exactly the same as his father had enjoyed at the previous general election. At the age of just twenty-three, Philip also had the distinction of being the 'baby of the House'.* Contemporaries of Philip's such as Patrick Shaw Stewart were working to make their fortune, with the hope later of taking a seat in Parliament. Sir Philip Sassoon had now secured both through inheritance. Edward Sassoon's vision of the life that was to open out for Philip had come to pass, but while the efforts of his ancestors could help to deliver him to the House of Commons, he would have to make his own reputation once there.

---

* An informal title reserved for the youngest MP.

Max Beerbohm, the well-known satirist of the politicians of the day, depicted a sleek and impassive Philip Sassoon sitting cross-legged in the lotus position on the green benches, between two large, booming and red-faced Tories.[32] He called the caricature *Philip Sassoon in Strange Company*. Philip was very different in appearance and manner from the knights of the shires and veteran soldiers of colonial wars who adorned the House of Commons. There were also very few Jewish MPs, and over 90 per cent of the Conservatives were practising members of the Church of England. But Parliament was starting to change with more businessmen and middle-class professionals, as well as the growing representation of workers and trade unionists from the Labour Party. The House of Commons Philip entered in June 1912 featured some of the greatest names in the history of that chamber, including statesmen like David Lloyd George, Arthur Balfour and Winston Churchill. It was also a time of political uncertainty as the Liberal government led by Prime Minister Herbert Asquith, whose wife Margot had been a close friend of Philip's mother, was beginning to run into trouble. There had been Lloyd George's great and controversial 'People's Budget' in 1909, followed by the constitutional crisis over reform of the House of Lords, and the ongoing and intractable problems of the government of Ireland. The Conservatives had been in opposition for over six years, but they had high hopes of getting back into power at the next election.

Philip waited until November 1912 to make his maiden speech, speaking against the government bill on Irish home rule. Max Aitken (later Lord Beaverbrook*), the Canadian businessman, MP and newspaper proprietor, remembered that 'It was an indifferent performance but it brought forth a flood of notes of congratulations not because he had made a good speech but because he had big houses and even bigger funds to maintain them.'[33] Philip looked to put

---

* Beaverbrook was the owner of the *Daily Express* and the role model for Lord Copper in Evelyn Waugh's great satirical novel on the press, *Scoop* (1938).

these to good effect as well, by hosting a grand lunch at Park Lane before the great Hyde Park demonstration in support of Ulster loyalism, with guests including the Unionist leader, Sir Edward Carson, and senior Conservatives like Lord Londonderry, F. E. Smith and Austen Chamberlain. Philip's Unionist credentials were further established when it was reported that at a speech in Folkestone he had suggested that he would pay for a ship to take local army reservists to Ireland to support the cause of Ulster remaining free from the interference of home rule government in Dublin – although it was a promise that he later denied having made.[34] These actions may reflect his early ambitions in politics and a desire to make a good impression, rather than a genuine conviction on his part. He was trying to be helpful in aligning himself with issues close to the heart of the leadership of the Conservative Party, but he otherwise made no great impression in Parliament in his first two years in the House of Commons. He certainly became much more liberal in his views on issues like Irish home rule after the war.

The years 1912 and 1913 marked a turning point in Philip's life, and that of his sister Sybil. With their parents gone, youth had ended and adult life had been thrust upon them. This also brought them closer together. Sybil had been educated in Paris, while Philip was at school in England. Now they would both live in London. In 1913 Philip and Sybil had individual portraits painted by the family friend, John Singer Sargent, who captured their beauty and poise, presenting them both on the brink of fulfilling their youthful promise. More interesting was a second portrait Philip commissioned from his friend the young artist Glyn Philpot. In this darker painting Philpot depicts Sassoon dressed in the same formal clothes as in the Sargent portrait, but instead of looking away and into the distance, Philip's head is turned and lowered a fraction to look at us. While still elegant, he appears a more human, lonely and less certain figure, carrying the weight of the responsibilities that have been placed upon him.

On 6 August 1913 Sybil, at nineteen, was married after a brief courtship to George, Earl of Rocksavage, the dashing heir of the Marquess of Cholmondeley. Philip had introduced Sybil to 'Rock'; they had known each other through their mutual friend Lady Diana Manners. Sybil's marriage added to Philip's relative isolation at this time. She would depart on a honeymoon of almost a year in India, and when they returned set up home at Rock's family estate in Norfolk, Houghton Hall, and their townhouse at 12 Kensington Palace Gardens. The marriage also caused a severe rift with many of their Jewish relations, particularly the Rothschilds, who took exception to Sybil marrying outside their religion. Philip gave his sister away, and their great-aunt Louise Sassoon and cousin David Gubbay were witnesses, along with Rock's father, the Marquess of Cholmondeley. None of Sybil's Rothschild relations attended the ceremony and they would have no contact with her for many years. The wedding was a quiet affair, and took place at Prince's Row register office, off Buckingham Palace Road in central London. The ceremony lasted only a quarter of an hour and there were no more than ten guests, who were themselves outnumbered by the pressmen and photographers waiting for them outside.[35]

Before her marriage, Sybil had often accompanied Philip to parties and West End first-night performances. She had also supported him at dinners and the entertainments he gave at home at Park Lane. Philip never married, and would often insist that he had been so spoilt by his charming sister that no other woman could match up to her. However, while there is no definitive proof either way, the suspicion has always been that the real reason why Philip Sassoon never married was that he was gay.

Homosexuality remained illegal in the United Kingdom until 1967, and even the word itself was considered taboo during Philip's life-time.[36] He was in any case a very private man who did not like to discuss his personal affairs, but for it to have been generally known that he was gay would have caused a scandal. The writer Beverley Nichols recalled that 'there were still a large number of people – particularly in high places – to whom the whole of this problem was so dark, so difficult and so innately poisonous, that they instinctively shut their eyes to it'.[37] In 1931, when King George V was confronted with the news that Earl Beauchamp, a friend who had carried the Sword of State at his coronation, was in danger of being exposed as a homosexual, he exclaimed, 'I thought men like that shot themselves.' The Earl escaped prosecution but was required to live most of the rest of his life in exile from England.*[38]

Yet the trial of Oscar Wilde for 'gross indecency' in 1895 showed that just because homosexuality was illegal, that didn't mean it was unheard of, even if it was 'the love that dare not speak its name'.† In fact after the First World War in 'university circles' Oscar Wilde was considered to be something of a 'martyr to the spirit of intolerance'.[39] The writer Robert Graves, seven years Philip's junior and a friend of his distant cousin Siegfried Sassoon, believed that at that time 'Homosexuality had been on the increase among the upper classes for a couple of generations,'[40] and in part he blamed the public school system. Graves also discussed homosexual experiences in a very matter-of-fact way in his memoir *Goodbye to All That*. Eton was considered to be 'perhaps the most openly gay school of the era',[41] but Philip Sassoon's contemporary Lawrence Jones believed that at Eton 'homosexuality [was] a mere substitute for heterosexuality. It would not exist if girls were accessible. It was not carried beyond that leaving day.'[42] This idea was also expressed by another Old Etonian friend of Philip's, Lord Berners, who wrote in his memoirs:

There can be no denying that in the Eton of my time a good deal of this sort of thing went on, but to speak of it as homosexuality would be unduly ponderous . . . I can only say that, in all cases of which I have been able to check up on the subsequent history, no irretrievable

---

* The story of Earl Beauchamp and his exile from his ancestral estate of Madresfield was used by Evelyn Waugh as a model for the Marchmain family in *Brideshead Revisited*.

† The phrase came originally from the poem 'Two Loves' by Lord Alfred Douglas, and was used against Oscar Wilde in his trial.

harm seems to have been done. Some of the most depraved of the boys I knew at Eton have grown into respectable fathers of families, and one of them who, in my day, was a byword for scandal has since become a highly revered dignitary of the Church of England.[43]

Many of Philip's friends in the inter-war period were, however, either gay or bisexual, including Berners himself, Glyn Philpot, Philip Tilden, Bob Boothby, Cecil Beaton, Rex Whistler, Noël Coward and Lytton Strachey. During a First World War military service tribunal, when Strachey was asked, 'Tell me, Mr Strachey, what would you do if you saw a German soldier trying to violate your sister?', he famously replied, 'I would try to get between them.'[44] Sassoon was certainly at home in the private and bohemian world these men enjoyed, but he also had many close friendships with women, in particular with the writers Marie Belloc Lowndes and Alice Dudeney, and the garden designer Norah Lindsay. These relationships were not romantic, mostly based on mutual interests and an easy personal rapport. Alice Dudeney did note one occasion in her diary while staying with Philip in Park Lane, when he was 'very restless', and told her, 'I'm one of those people who can't say things. I want helping out.' Alice recalled that, at the end of their conversation, Philip 'just laughed and stooping kissed me – for the first time. I was very much stirred as – clearly – was he.'[45] There was certainly no affair between Philip and Alice, who was by her own admission old enough to be his mother, but this episode gives an insight into the difficultly that he had in expressing his feelings towards others. This could have been the result not just of his Edwardian childhood, but also of the loss of his parents before he had reached emotional maturity.

Philip Sassoon's surviving personal papers provide little concrete evidence of his private life. In 1919 he kept a travel diary of a tour of Morocco and Spain he made with a friend referred to only as 'Jack', who had apparently been a fellow staff officer at General

Headquarters during the First World War. There are also a few undated letters to Jack, with one including this passage, heavy with romantic overtones, 'So you waited all the day & all the evening to ring me up . . . But I'll be even with you. I'll ring you up tomorrow morning – very early . . . before even the rosy fingered dawn has caused your white pyjamas to blush . . . I'll wait until you are weak unwoken & at my mercy.'[46]

Whatever the truth about Philip's personal life, the one thing we can say with certainty is that while he had close and loyal friends, there was no one whom he shared his life with romantically over any meaningful period. There was no special partner whose relationship with him could be understood, if not acknowledged. His personal life was something that he shut away from the world; it was a part of himself that he sought to hide. One of the lessons he had learnt at Eton was that, while you could be whoever you wanted to be, there were still expectations of external conformity in Edwardian England. However, in private, and particularly at the estate he created for himself at Lympne, Philip, according to Bob Boothby, 'gave freer rein to the exotic streak that was in him'.[47]

Philip began work on the estate shortly after his father's death, when he sold Shorncliffe Lodge and purchased 270 acres of farmland at Lympne, commanding excellent unbroken views of Romney Marsh and the English Channel beyond. The location was probably the best on the south Kent coast, and the whole estate was set into a secluded natural amphitheatre, created by an ancient cliff line. Philip was attracted not only to the topography of Lympne, but to its history as well. The estate marked the site of an old Roman port, Porta Lemanis, that had slowly transformed over the last thousand years into a hilly bank, as the sea had withdrawn and the wide flat marshes formed below. Philip loved the idea of his new estate having such old foundations, rather like the history of his own family.

He appointed a fashionable architect to design the mansion, Herbert Baker, who was best known at the time for his work for

Cecil Rhodes in South Africa* and had only just moved his practice to London. Sir Herbert chose a Dutch colonial style, similar to designs he had used in South Africa, with the house gable-ended and facing the sea. Philip requested that older bricks be used to give softer tones to the appearance of the house and also to make it look longer established in its setting. Years later, when the gardens had been created and Philip opened up the estate to occasional public tours to raise money for deserving charities, he delighted in retelling the remark about Port Lympne he had overheard from one of the guides, that it was 'All in the old world style, but every bit of it sham.'[48]

Although the main structure of the mansion was completed in 1913, further design work on the house and grounds would be interrupted by the approaching war in the summer of 1914.

---

* Most notably Baker designed Union Buildings in Pretoria, the seat of the government of South Africa. He was knighted in 1926 and is buried in Westminster Abbey.

2

• THE GENERAL'S STAFF •

Fighting in the mud, we turn to Thee
In these dread times of battle Lord,
To keep us safe, if so may be,
From shrapnel snipers, shells and sword.

Yet not on us – (for we are men
Of meaner clay, who fight in clay) –
But on the Staff, the Upper Ten,*
Depends the issue of the day.

The Staff is working with its brains
While we are sitting in the trench;
The Staff the universe ordains
(Subject to Thee and General French).

---

* The phrase comes from an American expression referring to the 'upper ten thousand', the higher echelons of New York society in the mid-nineteenth century. It was first used in Britain by William Thackeray in his novel *The Adventures of Philip*, published in 1861–2. The work became popular again during the First World War.

God help the staff – especially
The young ones, many of them sprung
From our high aristocracy
Their task is hard, and they are young.

O Lord who mad'st all things to be
And madest some things very good
Please keep the extra ADC
From horrid scenes, and sights of blood.

See that his eggs are newly laid
Not tinged as some of them – with green
And let no nasty drafts invade
The windows of his limousine.

Julian Grenfell,
'A Prayer for Those on the Staff' (1915)[1]

The First World War thundered into the summer of 1914 from a clear blue sky. On the morning of 28 June the heir of the Emperor of Austria, the Archduke Franz Ferdinand, and his wife Sophie, the Duchess of Hohenberg, were assassinated in Sarajevo by a young 'Yugoslav nationalist', Gavrilo Princip.[*2] In thirty-seven days Europe went from peace to all-out war at 11 p.m. on 4 August. People at that hour had little comprehension of the magnitude of the decision that had been made, and how it would shatter the lives of millions of people.

Doom-mongers in the press and the authors of popular fiction had, however, been predicting war for years. The growing military

---

* 'Yugoslav nationalist' was the term that Princip used to describe himself at his trial, stating that his goal was the separation of the Slavic peoples from the Austrian Empire.

rivalry between the powers and the ambition of Germany in particular, they believed, would inevitably lead to conflict. H. G. Wells, a friend and near neighbour of Philip Sassoon's in Kent, had also made this prediction in his 1907 novel *War in the Air*.

As relations between the nations of Europe deteriorated in late July, people started to prepare for war. On 28 July, the day Austria declared war on Serbia, Philip Sassoon's French Rothschild cousins sent a coded telegram to the London branch of their family asking them to sell 'a vast quantity' of bonds 'for the French government and savings banks'. The London Rothschilds declined to act, claiming that the already nervous state of the financial markets would make this almost impossible, but they secretly shared the request with the Prime Minister, Asquith, who regarded it as an 'ominous' sign.[3]

On 3 August Philip Sassoon sat on the opposition benches of a packed House of Commons to listen to the Foreign Secretary, Sir Edward Grey, update Parliament on the gravity of the situation in Europe. Britain stood ready to honour its commitments to the neutrality of Belgium, and to support France if it were to be the victim of an unprovoked attack. Sir Edward argued to cheers in the House that if a 'foreign fleet came down the English Channel and bombarded and battered the undefended coasts of France, we could not stand aside and see this going on practically within sight of our eyes, with our arms folded, looking on dispassionately, doing nothing'. It was a scene that Philip could all too easily envisage, as it was one that might be observed standing on the terrace of his new house at Lympne. The prospect of a naval conflict near the Channel, and fighting on land, of the kind that the Foreign Secretary described would also place his own parliamentary constituency in south-east Kent almost exactly on the front line. For Britain to fight in defence of France, the home of his mother and where he had spent so much of his own life, would be for Philip a just cause.

His first thought following the outbreak of war was for the safety of his sister Sybil and her husband who were in Le Touquet, on the return journey from their honeymoon in India. They had stopped off there so that Rock could play in a polo match, but now there were reports of chaos at Channel ports like Boulogne, where people were trying desperately to get home. So Philip's first act of the war was to dispatch his butler Frank Garton to France with a bag of gold sovereigns to ensure their safe passage home.

Conscription into the British army would not be introduced until 1916, but Philip was not faced with the dilemma of when or whether to volunteer for the armed forces. As an officer in the Royal East Kent Yeomanry reserve force, he received his mobilization orders the day following the declaration of war; Philip was one of seventy Members of Parliament who were called up in this way. There was no question of MPs who volunteered to fight being required to give up their seats. Philip believed that as a young man he was better placed to serve the interests of his constituents in wartime by joining up with the armed forces than by working in Westminster.

Philip's Eton and Oxford friends, such as Patrick Shaw Stewart, Edward Horner and Charles Lister, volunteered. Julian Grenfell was already a professional soldier as a captain in the Royal Dragoons. Lawrence Jones, who also served as a cavalry officer, remembered that 'whereas Julian went to war with high zest, thirsting for combat, and Charles with his habitual selflessness to a cause, Patrick had it all to lose . . . but knowing the risks, let go his hold of them and went cheerfully to war'.[4]

Philip also went cheerfully, and even as late as 1915 he wrote to Julian Grenfell's mother Lady Desborough from France, telling her, 'It is so splendid being out here. The weather is foul – the climate fouler and the country beyond words and nothing doing – but it is all rose coloured to me.'[5] Philip did not have the swagger of a natural soldier. A fellow officer recalled walking into a French town with him when they met a young woman with bright-red hair. 'Philip wishing to pay her a compliment said to her "vous avez de très jolies cheveux Mademoiselle". But as he said it he tripped up over his silver spurs and fell on his face on the pavement.[6] Men like Julian Grenfell were, however, in their element at the front. Grenfell wrote to his mother, 'I adore war. It is like a big picnic without the objectlessness of a picnic. I've never been so well or so happy. Nobody grumbles at one for being dirty. I've only had my boots off once in the last ten days; and only washed twice.'[7]

Philip did not join this band of brothers fighting at the front. He was held training with his regiment until February 1915, when he was transferred to St Omer to work as a staff officer at the headquarters of Field Marshal Sir John French, the Commander in Chief of the British Expeditionary Force. The British were fighting in alliance with the forces of France along a united front, and so coordination and understanding between the commanders was a necessity. Philip Sassoon's family and political connections in London and Paris, as well as his perfect command of the French language, made him an excellent choice to serve on the British staff.

The staff soon became the focus of resentment among the soldiers serving at the front. While the latter endured the mud, wet, cold and death in the trenches, the staff officers operated from headquarters based at French chateaux many miles behind the lines. In the *Blackadder* version of the history of the First World War, staff officers like Captain Darling are characterized as being rather arrogant and effete, leading a life of relative comfort and security. Similarly in the 1969 satire *Oh! What a Lovely War* the immaculately dressed staff officers play leapfrog at General Headquarters (GHQ) while the men die at the front. As the war went on the soldier poets came to curse the 'incompetent swine'[8] on the staff whom they blamed for the failures of military strategy, and Julian Grenfell in one of his poems went as far as to accuse some of the young officers of being too 'green' to fight.[9]

Yet many staff officers lost their lives during the war, and they were at risk from direct fire, particularly from enemy shells, both when they visited advanced positions closer to the front and on the occasions when they were targeted at GHQ itself. Philip worked long hours, but while the small wooden hut at GHQ that served as his personal quarters was not at all luxurious, it was not the trenches. It was a distinction he recognized, writing to Lady Desborough during a period of particularly bad weather, 'I can't imagine how those poor brutes in the trenches stick it out. I simply hate myself for sleeping in a bed in a not so warm house.'[10] But other men of similar status had opted to serve at the front, and twenty-four MPs would be killed in action during the war. Raymond Asquith, the son of the Prime Minister, had refused a transfer to a position on the staff, and would later die leading his men in battle. Philip had simply obeyed his orders; he was mobilized at the start of the war, and until February 1915 was preparing to fight at the front. He had never sought to avoid combat, and it was his skill as an accomplished staff officer that kept him at GHQ. Nonetheless, some would later question his war record, with the Conservative politician Lord Winterton wondering in his diary after dining with Philip, 'which is more disgraceful, to have no medals like [the Earl of] Jersey* who has shirked fighting in two wars, or to have them like Philip Sassoon without having earned them'.[11]

After his initial placement on Sir John French's staff, Philip was promoted to serve as aide-de-camp (ADC) to General Rawlinson, the commander of IV Army Corps. The IVth was part of the British Expeditionary Force and had seen heavy fighting in Belgium at the first Battle of Ypres, and in early 1915 would take the lead at the Battle of Neuve Chapelle. Philip had Eton in common with Rawlinson, but otherwise their lives had been completely different; the general was a professional soldier who had passed out from Sandhurst before Sassoon was born, and he had served in Lord Kitchener's campaign in the Sudan in 1898–9. In August 1914 optimists had predicted that the war might be over by Christmas,

---

* George Child Villiers, eighth Earl of Jersey·

but as the stalemate of trench warfare became established on the Western Front, the generals had to plan for a long campaign. Rawlinson believed that the war would be won only by attrition, and by early 1915 Philip agreed that the Germans would have to be driven back trench by trench until the Allies reached their border, rather than by some great breakthrough that would deliver a knockout blow. He was also concerned that any eagerness for an early peace settlement before Germany had been clearly defeated would leave it strong enough to start another war in fifteen or twenty years.[12]

The day-to-day reality of this strategy of attrition was found in the death toll at the front. Philip would anxiously look for the names of his friends, as each morning he went through the lists of the dead and missing. In May 1915 Julian Grenfell received a head injury from a shell fragment at Railway Hill near Ypres. The initial prognosis was positive, but his condition deteriorated and he died on 26 May at the military hospital at Boulogne. When the notice of his death was placed, The Times printed a poem he had recently completed and sent to his mother in the hope she might be able to get it published. Entitled 'Into Battle', it extolled the honour and glory of the fighting, with Mother Nature urging on the soldiers with the words, 'If this be the last song you shall sing, / Sing well, for you may not sing another.'

Philip was greatly affected by the loss of Julian, but it was nearly a month before he wrote to Lady Desborough. 'I have tried to write to you every day since Julian died, but have been fumbling for words . . . ever since I had known him in the old Eton days I had the most tremendous admiration for him and always regretted that circumstances and difference of age had prevented our becoming more intimate.' Julian had been only a few months older than Philip, although he was a more senior figure in the hierarchy at Eton, and almost the epitome of the heroic Edwardian English schoolboy. Philip's choice of words reflected the distance in their relationship, but underlined how he looked up to Julian and desired his approval.

It was as if for Philip that personal acceptance by Julian represented the broader appreciation of English society of his character and ability. Philip continued his letter to Lady Desborough by quoting from the war poet Rupert Brooke, who had himself died just the month before, telling her that Julian had left a 'white unbroken glory, a gathered radiance, a width, a shining peace, under the night'.[13] Julian had seemed so indestructible, it was barely credible to Philip that he could be gone. 'Such deaths as his', he told Lady Desborough, 'strengthen our faith – it is not possible that such spirits go out. We know that they must always be near us and that we shall meet them again.'[14]

There was a curious epitaph to Julian's death a few weeks later, during the Battle of Loos. One of the reservist cavalry regiments was saddled up, night and day, in the grounds of General Rawlinson's chateau, ready in case a breakthrough in the line was achieved and the cavalrymen would be called on to gallop through the gap. Lawrence Jones, who was among their number, recalled:

> After a sleepless night spent attempting to get some shelter under juniper bushes from the incessant rain, we were gazing, chilled and red-eyed, at the noble entrance of the chateau from which we expected our orders to come forth, when a very slim, very dapper young officer, with red tabs in his collar and shining boots, began to descend the steps. It was Philip Sassoon, 'Rawly's' ADC. I have never been one of those to think that Staff Officers are unduly coddled, or that they should share the discomforts of the troops. Far from it. But there are moments when the most entirely proper inequality, suddenly exhibited, can be riling. Tommy Lascelles, not yet His or Her Majesty's Private Secretary, but a very damp young lieutenant who had not breakfasted, felt that this was one of those moments. Concealed by a juniper bush he called out, 'Pheeleep! Pheeleep! I see you!' in a perfect mimicry of Julian's warning cry from his window when he spied Sassoon, who belonged to another College, treading delicately through Balliol Quad. The beauteous

ADC stopped, lifted his head like a hind sniffing the wind, then turned and went rapidly up the steps and into the doorway. Did he hear Julian's voice from the grave? . . . We shall never know.[15]

Julian's younger brother Billy was killed in action on 30 July leading a charge at Hooge, less than a mile from where Julian had been wounded. Billy's body was never found, and without a known grave he was remembered after the war on the Menin Gate memorial at Ypres. Philip had grown up with Billy at Eton and at numerous weekend parties at Taplow, and he sat down in his quarters once again to write the most painful of letters to Lady Desborough:

It was only about a fortnight ago that I had a letter from him saying that he was so bored at being out of the line and aching to get back into the salient – I rushed up to Poperinge – but he had left that morning for the trenches – now I shan't ever see him. This has taught me not to look ahead – but I had allowed myself somehow to look forward to Billy's friendship as something very precious for the future – and he has left a blank that can never be filled. I look back on all the pleasant hours we spent together. I have that possession at any rate. How I shall miss him.[16]

Philip's words reflect the more conventional friendship he had enjoyed with Billy, compared to that with Julian, one that was not marked by the need for acceptance.

In late August 1915, Charles Lister, a lieutenant in the Royal Marines, died in the military hospital at Mudros from wounds sustained in the fighting at Gallipoli. Lister had sailed out to the eastern Mediterranean with Rupert Brooke and Patrick Shaw Stewart, and while Shaw Stewart survived this doomed campaign he would later succumb at the Battle of Cambrai in 1917 along with Edward Horner. 'Would one ever have believed before the war', Philip wrote to a friend, 'that one could have stood for one single instant the load of pain and anxiety which is now one's daily breath. I find that, although I can study the casualty list without ever seeing a name I know – for all my friends have been killed – yet nevertheless one feels as much for others as for oneself – just a blur of grief: and one wakes every morning feeling one can hardly bear to live through the day.'[17]

The deaths of these young men led to a series of publications to commemorate their short, heroic lives. Ronald Knox quickly produced a biography of Patrick Shaw Stewart, and another book, E. B. Osborn's *The New Elizabethans*, included essays on the Grenfell boys, Charles Lister and others. The title was inspired by Sir Rennell Rodd's vision of Lister as belonging to the 'large-horizoned Elizabethan days, and he would have been in the company of Sidney and Raleigh and the Gilberts and boisterously welcomed at the Mermaid Tavern'.*[18]

Not all of their contemporaries recognized these romantic portraits of their friends. Lawrence Jones recalled:

> A legend has somehow grown up, that Julian was one of a little band of Balliol brothers knightly as they were brilliant who might, had they survived, have flavoured society with an essence shared by them all. As far as [Charles Lister, Patrick Shaw Stewart and Edward Horner] and Julian are concerned, the legend is very wide of the mark. Apart from their delight in each other's company, and common gallantry in the exacting tests of the war, few men could have been less alike in temperament, character and outlook.[19]

Duff Cooper, another Eton and Oxford contemporary, wrote to Knox to protest about his biography of Shaw Stewart. In his diary he complained, 'He never consulted me . . . nor asked either me or

---

* Lister had worked for the British Ambassador Sir Rennell Rodd at the Embassy in Rome.

Diana for letters. This irritates me. The book as it stands is bad and dull.'*[20]

Yet one of these testaments to the doomed youth of the war would remain beyond reproach – Lady Desborough's tribute to her sons, *Pages from a Family Journal*. This great book, running to over six hundred pages, published in 1916, was an intimate portrait of their lives from early childhood. It was, in the words of Lord Desborough, 'intended for Julian and Billy's brothers and sisters and for their most intimate friends'. Upon receiving his copy, Philip Sassoon told Lady Desborough that 'it will be a tribute for all time to those two splendid joyous boys whose loss becomes more unbearable every day. One would like to have included every letter they ever wrote . . . I keep rereading their letters and your accounts of them until I cannot believe that they are gone.'[21]

For many people, this belief that their loved ones could not really be gone took them in search of the intervention of spiritualist mediums. The number of registered mediums in England would more than double by the early 1920s, compared with pre-war figures.[22] Shortly after the end of the war, following the death of a pilot friend in a plane crash, Philip Sassoon approached an old family friend, Marie Belloc Lowndes,† and begged her 'to write to Sir Oliver Lodge . . . to ask for the address of a medium'.[23] Lodge was a Christian spiritualist who had come to particular prominence following the publication in 1916 of his sensational book *Raymond, or Life and Death*.‡ The book detailed his belief that his son Raymond, who had been killed in action in Flanders in 1915, had

---

* Lady Diana Manners, the future Diana Cooper, was also a close friend of Patrick Shaw Stewart's

† Marie Belloc Lowndes was a prolific English novelist whose best-known work, *The Lodger*, was based on the Jack the Ripper murders. She was the sister of the writer Hilaire Belloc, and was much admired by Gertrude Stein and Ernest Hemingway.

‡ Twelve editions of the book were published between November 1916 and December 1919.

communicated with him through séances that he and his wife had attended with the medium Gladys Osborne Leonard. Marie Belloc Lowndes secured the details from Sir Oliver of a medium in London and she accompanied Philip on the visit. She recalled that they

> drove to a road beyond Notting Hill Gate, and stopped in front of a detached villa. We were admitted by a middle-aged woman, who led us into a room which contained some shabby garden furniture . . . after a few moments, the medium went into a trance, and from her lips there issued a man's voice, describing a fall from a plane, and the instant death of the speaker. The same voice then made a strong plea concerning the future of a group of children he called the 'kiddies', and who, he was painfully anxious, should not be parted from their mother. Meanwhile Philip remained silent, staring at the medium. After a pause the same man's voice as before issued from the sleeping woman's lips. Again the accident was decried and there then followed an allusion to a pair of flying boots, which the speaker hoped Philip would find useful. When we were back in his car, Philip Sassoon turned to me and exclaimed, 'The voice which spoke to me was the voice of the man who was killed flying in Egypt.' Did you understand the allusion to his flying boots? He said, 'Of course I did. I bought his flying boots after his death.'[24]

On 29 October 1915 Philip was in Folkestone harbour, ready to return to France after a brief period of home leave. He waited to board his ship at the simple café on the harbour arm, which catered for service personnel. It was run by two sisters, Margaret and Florence Jeffery, and Mrs Napier Sturt, who dispensed free refreshments and kept visitors' books which they asked all their guests, servicemen and statesmen of all ranks, to sign. Philip was happy to oblige along with the group of staff officers with whom he was travelling.[25] Looking around, he could see how Folkestone had been transformed by the war. It had been an elegant resort town from where the wealthy had journeyed to the continent on the Orient

Express, which had descended with its passengers into the harbour station. Now it was the major embarkation point for servicemen to France, and over ten million soldiers would pass through the town on their way to and from the trenches of the Western Front. In addition to this the town was home to tens of thousands of Canadian servicemen stationed at Shorncliffe Barracks, and thousands of refugees from Belgium who had fled from the advancing Germans in August 1914.

The pre-war world was gone for ever and in October 1915 it wasn't clear when peace would return, or if Britain and its allies would be victorious. The Germans were winning against the Russians in the east, and in the west they were fighting in French and Belgian territory, not on their own soil. The British attempt to open up the war in the east at Gallipoli had failed and in November 1915 brought about the resignation from the cabinet of Winston Churchill, whose idea it had been. A further setback on the Western Front at the Battle of Loos created pressure for a change in the direction of the war effort, and on 3 December General Sir Douglas Haig replaced Sir John French as commander of the British forces in France. This change of leadership would have a sudden and profound impact on Philip Sassoon. Haig, upon taking up his new post, invited Philip to work for him as his private secretary at GHQ. The war had now given Philip something he had sought in peacetime – a chance to perform a meaningful role at the centre of great events.

On 31 March 1916 Haig established his personal headquarters at the Château de Beaurepaire, in the hamlet of Saint Nicolas, a short distance from the beautiful town of Montreuil-sur-Mer, and about 20 miles south of Boulogne. The communications nerve centre of GHQ was based in the historic Citadel at Montreuil, but the whole town became an English colony for the remainder of the war. The Officers' Club in the Rue du Paon was believed to have one of the best wine cellars in Europe,[26] and tennis courts were constructed between the ramparts that surrounded the Citadel.

Montreuil was chosen because it was centrally placed to serve as the communications centre for forces across a front stretching from the Somme to beyond the Belgian frontier. It was also a small town of only a few thousand inhabitants, and no great distractions for the officers and men stationed there.

Montreuil and the Château de Beaurepaire would be Philip's principal base for the rest of the war, although for the launch of new battle offensives GHQ could move to an advanced position, often in a house closer to the front line, or in some railway carriages parked in a nearby siding. Philip would also accompany Haig to conferences of the British and French leaders and represent him at meetings in London and Paris. There was a dynamism to working for Haig that suited Philip's energetic personality: cars and drivers on standby to rush between meetings, special trains and steamships ready to convey the 'Chief' at any hour, the King's messenger service available for the express delivery of important messages or specially requested luxury items for an important dinner.

Philip's working routine was set around Haig's. He would be at his desk before 9 a.m. each morning, breaking at 1 p.m. for lunch, which lasted for half an hour. In the afternoon, Philip would typically accompany Haig to meetings at GHQ or to visit 'some army or corps or division' in the line.[27] After returning to Beaurepaire they worked up to dinner at 8 p.m., then went back to the office at 9, until about 10.45 p.m. Brigadier-General John Charteris, who was Haig's Chief Intelligence Officer, remembered that 'At this hour [Haig] rang the bell for his Private Secretary, and invariably greeted him with the same remark: "Philip – not in bed yet?" He never changed this formula, and if, as did occasionally happen, Philip was in bed, he always used to say to him next morning: "I hope you have had enough sleep?" There were only rare occasions when this routine of the Commander-in-Chief's day was broken by even a minute.'[28]

Sassoon and the general developed a good working relationship, and Haig came to regard Philip as a 'very useful private secretary'.[29]

Robert Blake, who would later edit Douglas Haig's private papers, noted that 'Haig did not talk much himself but he enjoyed gaiety and wit in others, and he appreciated conversational brilliance. This partly explains his paradoxical choice of Philip Sassoon as his private secretary.'[30] There was criticism from some of the other staff officers of Haig's decision. Philip was in their eyes a politician who had not been trained at Sandhurst like the rest of them, or seen any military service, yet he was now to have privileged access to the Commander in Chief at all hours. According to Blake, they saw Philip as a 'semi-oriental figure [who] flitted like some exotic bird of paradise against the sober background of GHQ'.[31] Some also felt he had been preferred because his uncle Leopold Rothschild was a friend of Haig's. Leopold, with Philip's assistance, would certainly make sure that Haig was kept well supplied with food parcels from his estate, which may have added credence to these mutterings.

Philip's appointment was due in part to the reputation he had earned during the war as an efficient and effective staff officer; but there were plenty of those for Haig to choose from. As a fluent French-speaker, and a relative of the French Rothschilds, Philip was also able to assist in the liaison between Haig and the military commanders and senior politicians of France. His contacts in Westminster and the London press were similarly invaluable. Douglas Haig had learnt from the removal of Sir John French as Commander in Chief that the position of a general in the field could soon become vulnerable without powerful supporters at home.

But while Philip knew the leading politicians in London, he had not yet established himself as a figure in their world. In January 1916 Winston Churchill visited Haig at GHQ, which he found deserted, except for Sassoon sitting outside the Chief's office, 'like a wakeful spaniel'.[32] As a former serving officer in the Hussars, Churchill, free from ministerial responsibility, now wanted a command on the front line in France. A few days after Churchill's visit, Philip wrote to H. A. Gwynne, the editor of the *Morning Post*, informing him that 'Winston is hanging about here but Sir D. H. refuses to give him a Brigade until he has had a battalion several months. It wouldn't be fair to the others and besides does he deserve anything? I think not, certainly not anything good.'[33]

Philip was now in the front line of the war within the war – that between Britain's leading politicians and the military commanders in France over the direction of the conflict. At its heart was an argument that continues to this day: whether it was poor generalship or poor supply that was prolonging the war. One of Philip's allies in this new front was Lord Esher, a member of the Committee for Imperial Defence, who had been an éminence grise in royal and military circles for many years. Regy Esher ran an informal intelligence-gathering network based on gossip and insight collected from his well-connected friends in London and Paris. His style and experience suited Philip perfectly. Esher was also a sexually ambiguous character, who made something of a habit of befriending young men like Philip Sassoon. There is no romance in their letters, which while full of gossip were largely focused on the serious matter of winning the war. However, Philip certainly opens up to Regy, suggesting a strong mutual trust, and a relationship similar to those he formed with other older friends, who became a kind of surrogate family for him. One letter in particular to Esher is full of melancholic self-reflection. 'To have slept with Cavalieri [Michelangelo's young male muse], to have invented wireless, to have painted Las Meninas, to have written Wuthering Heights – that is a deathless life. But to be like me, a thing of nought, a worthless loon, an elm-seed whirling in a summer gale.'[34]

Esher advised Philip on the importance of his role as a gatekeeper and look-out for the Chief against the interference of government ministers in Whitehall. He told him in early 1916 that the 'real crux now is to erect a barbed wire entanglement round the fortress held by K,* old Robertson† and the C[ommander] in C[hief] ... But subtly propaganda is constantly at work.'[35]

This 'propaganda' was emanating from Churchill, F. E. Smith‡ and David Lloyd George, who had started to question the strategy of the generals; in particular they shared a growing concern at the enormous loss of life on the Western Front for such small gains, and debated whether some other means of breaking the deadlock should be found. The generals on the other hand firmly believed that the war could be won only by defeating Germany in France and Belgium, and were against diverting resources to other military initiatives. Churchill in this regard blamed Lord Kitchener and the generals in France for the failure of his Gallipoli campaign, because he felt they had not supported it early enough and with the required manpower to ensure success.

These senior politicians also believed that the generals were seeking to undermine confidence in the government through their friends in the press, so that any blame for military setbacks fell on the ministers for their failure to supply the army with sufficient trained men, ammunition and shells. Churchill was highly critical of what he saw as

> the foolish doctrine [that] was preached to the public through the innumerable agencies that Generals and Admirals must be right on war matters and civilians of all kinds must be wrong. These erroneous conceptions were inculcated billion-fold by the newspapers under the crudest forms. The feeble or presumptuous politician is portrayed cowering in his office, intent in the crash of the world on Party intrigues or personal glorification, fearful of responsibility, incapable of aught save shallow phrase making.

---

* Lord Kitchener, the Secretary of State for War.
† Field Marshal Sir William Robertson, Chief of the Imperial General Staff.
‡ Rt. Hon. F. E. Smith MP, Attorney General. He was ennobled as Lord Birkenhead in 1919.

> To him enters the calm, noble resolute figure of the great
> Commander by land or sea, resplendent in uniform, glittering
> with decorations, irradiated with the lustre of the hero, shod
> with the science and armed with the panoply of war. This stately
> figure, devoid of the slightest thought of self, offers his clear
> far-sighted guidance and counsel for vehement action, or artifice,
> or wise delay. But this advice is rejected; his sound plans put
> aside; his courageous initiative baffled by political chatterboxes
> and incompetents.[36]

In 1916 Philip Sassoon would be the most significant of those
'innumerable agencies', taking on the responsibility for liaising with
the media on behalf of Douglas Haig. His most important relationship was with the eminent press baron Lord Northcliffe, owner of
The Times and the *Daily Mail*, whose regard for military leadership
was as great as his general contempt for politicians. Northcliffe had
started from nothing to become the greatest media owner of the
day, and could boast that half of the newspapers read every morning
in London were printed on his presses. He was at this time,
according to Lord Beaverbrook's later account, 'the most powerful
and vigorous of newspaper proprietors'.[37]

Philip had the emotional intelligence to understand that the
great press baron expected to be appreciated. He would facilitate
Northcliffe's requests to visit the front or for his journalists to have
access to interview Haig. Philip would also write to thank him for
reports in his papers that had pleased GHQ. The great lesson that
Philip would learn from Northcliffe was that even people who hold
great office cannot fully exercise their power without the consent
of others, and that consent is based on trust and respect. The
press had the power to apply external pressure which could lead
people to question the competences of others. In this way they
had helped to bring down Sir John French, and forced Prime
Minister Asquith to bring the Conservatives into the government.

Northcliffe had complete faith in the army and in the strategy of the generals to win the war on the Western Front. He wanted to deal directly with Haig's inner circle, and he knew that when he was talking to Philip Sassoon he was as good as talking to the Chief. Philip had good reason as he saw it to give his full support to Haig, and this was not just motivated by personal loyalty. Lloyd George had a reputation as a political schemer who had been the scourge of many Conservatives.* Churchill was also hated by many Tory MPs for leaving their party to join the Liberals (in 1904), a decision that seemed to them to have been motivated by opportunism and desire for government office rather than by any high principle. After the failure of Gallipoli and Churchill's resignation from the cabinet, Philip was also clear with Northcliffe that he was no Churchill fan, and was against his return to any form of influence over the direction of the war, 'with his wild cat schemes and fatal record'.[38]

In early June 1916 Philip stepped ashore at Dover with Haig after a stormy Channel crossing from Boulogne which had left him terribly sea sick. On seeing the news that was immediately handed to the Commander in Chief, any remaining colour would have drained from his complexion. Lord Kitchener, the hero of the Empire and the face of the war through the famous army-recruitment posters, was dead. He had drowned when the armoured cruiser HMS *Hampshire*, which was conveying him on a secret diplomatic mission to Russia, sank after striking a mine off the Orkney Islands. Philip had got to know Kitchener only since joining Haig's team and found him to possess, 'apart from his triumphant personality – all those qualities of sensibility and humour which popular legend has persistently denied him. He dies well for himself but how great his loss is to us the nation knows well and some people in high places will learn to realise.'[39] Kitchener's death blew a hole in the 'barbed wire entanglement' Lord Esher wanted to see

---

* Philip Sassoon's father Edward, for example, refused to leave any money to charity in his will in 1912, in reaction to Lloyd George's inheritance taxes, introduced in the 1909 budget.

protecting the military command from the politicians. Worse still, as far as GHQ was concerned, he was replaced as Secretary of State for War by Lloyd George.

The Battle of the Somme, which started on 1 July, brought further heavy losses on the Western Front: there were 60,000 casualties on the first day, with 20,000 soldiers killed. This was the worst day of casualties in the history of the British army, yet Haig was determined to press on with his campaign. Later in the month GHQ decided to mobilize press support for Haig ahead of any attempt by the new Secretary of State to interfere in military strategy. Philip Sassoon arranged for Lord Northcliffe to stay at GHQ, and he set up a meeting for him with Haig. The success of this encounter, Philip told Lord Esher, 'will prove as good as a victory . . . One must do all one can to direct press opinion in the right channel.'[40] Although he was sometimes baffled by the interest of the press in the day-to-day trivia of Haig's life at GHQ, he remarked to Esher that 'Apparently the British public have much more confidence in him now they know at what time he had breakfast.'[41] Haig was more than happy with the initial results, noting with pleasure in a letter to his wife that his name was 'beginning to appear in the papers with favourable comments! You must think I am turning into an Advertiser!'[42]

Northcliffe wanted Philip to stay in contact with him over the summer while he was holidaying in Italy and told him to send messages via the British Embassy in Rome and his political adviser in London, Geoffrey Robinson. He encouraged Philip to stay close to Robinson and to allow him to come and visit out at the front. He told him that Robinson was his closest adviser on the thoughts and actions of members of the cabinet: 'It is our system that he should know them and I should not, which we find an excellent plan. They are a pack of gullible optimists who swallow any foolish tale. There are exceptions among them, and they are splendid ones, but the generality of them have the slipperiness of eels, with the combined vanity of a professional beauty.'[43]

The opening barrage from the politicians was delivered by Winston Churchill, who after leaving the cabinet had served at the front in early 1916, but by the summer had returned to London to speak up in the House of Commons as the champion of the soldiers serving in the trenches.* On 1 August he prepared a memo for the cabinet, which was circulated with the help of his friend F. E. Smith. Churchill argued that, following the start of the Battle of the Somme, the energies of the army were being 'dissipated' by the constant series of attacks which despite the huge losses of life on both sides had failed to deliver a decisive breakthrough.[44] This memo immediately captured the attention of Lloyd George. Robertson, the Chief of the Imperial General Staff, tipped off Haig that 'the powers that be' were beginning to get a 'little uneasy' about the general situation, and Haig prepared a note in response to Churchill's criticisms which was circulated to the War Committee, the cabinet committee that oversaw the national contribution to the war effort.[45] The King visited GHQ on 8 August and discussed Churchill's paper with Haig in detail. Haig recalled in his diary that he had told King George 'that these were trifles and that we must not allow them to divert our thoughts from the main objective, namely "beating the Germans". I also expect that Winston's head is gone from taking drugs.'[46]

Philip Sassoon heeded Northcliffe's request to keep him informed of developments at GHQ and wrote to tell him that 'We have heard all about the Churchill Cabal from the King and his people who are out here this week . . . The War Committee are apparently quite satisfied now at the appreciation of the situation which the Chief had already sent them and proved a complete answer to Churchill's damnable accusations.' Philip then added suggestively, 'Lloyd

---

* Churchill's return to politics was also necessitated by his being required to give evidence to the Dardanelles Commission on his role in the Gallipoli campaign.

George is coming to dine here Saturday night. I shall be much interested to hear what he has to say. I do trust that he and Carson* will be made to realise how damaging any flirting with an alliance with Churchill would be for them. Do you think they realise this? Sufficiently?'[47]

On 14 August Lord Esher wrote to reassure and warn Philip that

No combination of Churchill and F. E. can do any harm so long as fortune favours us in the field. These people only become formidable during the inevitable ebb of the tide of success. It is then that a C in C absent and often unprotected by the men whose duty it is to defend him, may be stabbed in the back. It is for this reason that you should never relax your vigilance and never despise an enemy, however despicable.[48]

Philip certainly had complete faith in Haig's strategy and the ongoing Battle of the Somme, writing to his uncle Leopold Rothschild the same day, 'Everything is going very satisfactorily here and the whole outlook is good. If we can, as I hope, keep up combined pressure right into the autumn, the decision ought not to be far off.'

During Lloyd George's visit to GHQ he reassured Haig that he had 'no intention of meddling'.[49] Yet, the following month, news reached Haig directly from the French commander General Foch that Lloyd George had been asking his opinion about the competence of the British commanders. Haig could not believe that 'a British Minister could have been so ungentlemanly as to go to a foreigner and put such questions'.[50] Philip Sassoon was given a full debrief on Lloyd George's visit to see Foch, which could only have come directly from Haig, and he immediately set to work on Northcliffe. His response was designed to be personally wounding, saying that Lloyd George's visit to both the British and French

---

* Sir Edward Carson, effectively Leader of the Opposition.

headquarters had been a complete 'joy ride from beginning to end'. He also told Northcliffe that Lloyd George had been discourteous by keeping General Foch waiting an hour and a half for lunch, without giving an apology, and then he had asked him why the French guns were more effective than the British, which Foch refused to answer. Lloyd George also found only fifteen minutes of private time for Douglas Haig during his visit. 'If this is the man some people would like to see PM,' Philip told Northcliffe, 'I prefer old Squiff* any day with all his faults. It is my private opinion that he has neither liking nor esteem for the C in C. He has certainly conveyed that impression to all. No doubt Churchill's subtle poison has done its deadly work.'[51]

Philip's intervention led to a series of articles in Northcliffe's newspapers praising Haig and the work of the British army in France, and sniping at the 'shirt-sleeved politicians' who were interfering with the war. Philip's efforts on behalf of his Chief were also coming to the attention of Lloyd George's advisers, who warned him that Haig was 'trying to get at the press through that little blighter Sassoon'.[52]

The growing pressure on GHQ for a real success in the field led to the use of tanks for the first time during the later stages of the Battle of the Somme, at Pozières. The idea of an armoured trench-crossing machine had first been suggested in October 1914 by Major Ernest Swinton, who was the official British war correspondent on the Western Front. It captured the imagination of Winston Churchill, who in early 1915 urged Asquith to allow the Admiralty to develop a prototype for a 'land ship'. To help keep the programme secret, designs were developed under the misleading title of 'water-carriers for Russia'. When it was pointed out that this could be abbreviated to 'WCs for Russia', that name was changed to 'water-tanks', then to 'tanks'.[53]

---

* Asquith was known as 'Squiff' or 'Squiffy' in parliamentary circles on account of his heavy drinking.

Churchill had begged Asquith not to allow the machines to be used until they could be perfected and launched in large numbers and to the complete surprise of the Germans. Haig, however, was agitating to get them into the field as soon as possible, and their initial deployment in September 1916 met with limited success. Nevertheless, they caused yet more intrigue between the politicians and GHQ over who should take the credit for them. Northcliffe wrote to Philip on 2 October:

> You may have noticed that directly the tanks were successful, Lloyd George issued a notice through the Official Press Bureau that they were due to Churchill. You will find that unless we watch these people they will claim that the great Battle of the Somme is due to the politicians. That would not matter if it were not for the fact that it is the politicians who will make peace. If they are allowed to exalt themselves they will get a hold over the public very dangerous to the national interests.[54]

Lord Esher's advice to Philip earlier in the summer, that all would be well for Haig as long as there was success in the field, was true not just for the generals but also for the politicians. The Battle of the Somme had not produced the decisive breakthrough that Philip had hoped for, and there was concern that Britain might actually be losing the war. Northcliffe decided that Asquith had to be replaced as Prime Minister, and his papers led the calls for change at the top of government. He did this not out of support for Lloyd George, who would be the main beneficiary of this campaign, but because he believed that the Asquith government was weak and a peril to the country.

There was little trust between Lloyd George and Northcliffe, and the War Secretary regarded the press baron as 'the mere kettledrum' of Haig.[55] Northcliffe would remain firmly in the camp of the generals, and the day after Lloyd George took up office as Prime Minister, he informed Philip Sassoon that he had 'told the *Daily*

Mail to telephone you every night at 8pm, whether I am in London or not'.*[56]

Philip was in London on a week's leave during the political crisis and wrote to Haig with updates as Lloyd George's new government took shape: 'I think by now all the appointments and disappointments have been arranged ... I think Derby's is a very good appointment. Northcliffe said, "That great jellyfish is at the War Office. One good thing is that he will do everything Sir Douglas Haig tells him to do"! I think the whole week has been satisfactory.'†[57]

Philip also made good use of his London leave by arranging to meet the leading novelist Alice Dudeney, whose books he had long admired, having been introduced to her works by his friend Marie Belloc Lowndes. Alice Dudeney was well known for her romantic and dramatic fiction, often based on life near to her home in East Sussex, and would publish fifty novels in the course of her writing career. Philip managed to get her address from Marie, and wrote out of the blue to her: 'I am such a great admirer of your books that I know it would be the greatest pleasure to me to talk to you. Would you not think it impertinent of me to introduce myself in this manner and to say how much I hope you may be able to come to lunch [at Park Lane].'[58] Alice duly came to lunch with Philip and Sybil the following week, and it was the start of a great friendship between them that would last the rest of his life.

Throughout the war, in what spare time he had, Philip read contemporary novels, taking up suggestions from Marie Belloc Lowndes, and getting his London secretary, Mrs Beresford, to send them out to him at GHQ. The one book that he kept constantly by his side, reading it again and again, was Marcel Proust's *Du côté de chez Swann*, the first volume of À *la recherché du temps perdu*, which had been published in 1913. The novel's narrator opens the story by recounting how as a boy he missed out one evening on

---

* 8 p.m. was the exact time that Haig left the office every day for dinner.
† Lord Derby had just been appointed Secretary of State for War.

his mother's goodnight kiss, because his parents were entertaining Mr Swann, an elegant man of Jewish origin with strong ties to society. In the absence of this kiss he gets his mother to spend the night reading to him. The narrator says that this was his only recollection of living with his family in that house, until other sensations, like the taste of a madeleine, brought back further memories of that time. For Philip, alone in his hut at GHQ, the world before the war had become a distant memory. Perhaps as he read Proust's lines he was trying to remember his mother's kiss, or a weekend party at Taplow with friends who now lay dead in Flanders. Even a loud cracking noise outside, like the sound of a stock whip, might be enough to bring Julian Grenfell vividly back to life.

The British entered the new year of 1917 with little confidence that the end of the war was in sight. Philip Sassoon remained steadfast in his support for Haig (who was now a field marshal) and in a well-reported public speech during a visit back to Folkestone in January he told his audience:

> They could trust their army and trust their generals. For them [the generals] the days of inexperience and over-confidence were gone. They knew their task, and they knew they could do it . . . the Battle of the Somme had opened the eyes of Germany, and she saw defeat in front of her. We must not be trapped by any peace snare. We had the finest army our race had produced, a Commander in Chief the army trusted, and a government they believed capable of giving vigour and decided action.[59]

The new Prime Minister, however, had the generals in his sights. Lloyd George had formed a new government in response to growing concerns about the direction of the war, and he wanted to have some influence on the conduct of operations on the Western Front. In this regard he was determined to sideline or remove Robertson as Chief of the Imperial General Staff, and Haig as Commander in Chief in France.

Philip would accompany Haig to a series of conferences in Calais, London and Paris, where Lloyd George's plan unfolded: to create a new supreme command for the Western Front that would remove power from Haig and transfer it to the French generals above him, as well as give more autonomy to the divisional commanders in the field. Lloyd George also brought Lord Northcliffe inside his tent by appointing him to represent the government in the United States of America, on a special tour to promote the war effort. Northcliffe was delighted with his new role, and the Prime Minister then felt emboldened to perform a further *coup de main* by bringing Churchill back into the cabinet as Minister for Munitions.

The War Secretary, Lord Derby, wrote to Philip to complain that he 'never knew a word about [Churchill's appointment] until I saw it in the paper and was furious at being kept in ignorance, but you can judge my surprise when I found that the war cabinet had never been told . . . Churchill is the great danger, because I cannot believe in his being content to simply run his own show and I am sure he will have a try to have a finger in the Admiralty and War Office pies.'[60]

Philip could all too clearly see the dangers of Lloyd George's initiatives for Haig and GHQ. After the Calais conference where the Prime Minister had first set out the idea of a combined French and British supreme command, Philip warned Esher that despite the personal warmth of the politicians towards Haig, his position remained vulnerable. He wrote, 'Everyone – the King, LG, Curzon etc. – all patted DH on the back and told him what a fine fellow he was – but with that exception, matters remained very much as Calais had left them and the future may be full of difficulties.'[61]

It was not just the continued heavy casualties being sustained at the front; now German bombing raids on England from aerodromes in Belgium were inflicting terrible loss of life at home as well. On 25 May 1917, on a warm, clear late afternoon, German Gotha aeroplanes dropped bombs without any warning on the civilian population in Folkestone, in Philip's parliamentary constituency. One fell outside Stokes's greengrocer's in Tontine Street, killing sixty-one people, including a young mother, Florence Norris, along with her two-year-old daughter and ten-month-old son. Hundreds more were injured, and other bombs fell on the Shorncliffe military camp to the west of the town, killing eighteen soldiers. The raid shocked the nation and led to calls for proper air-raid warning systems to be put in place in towns at risk of attack.

There was further controversy over Douglas Haig's brutal offensive in the late summer and autumn of 1917 at Passchendaele in Flanders. In June GHQ had suggested to the cabinet that 130,000 men would cover the British losses that would be sustained during the course of the battle. Instead, the total number of British casualties across the whole of the front by December was 399,000. When it became clear that no significant breakthrough had been achieved, Lloyd George resumed his agitation for Haig's removal, but a victory at the Battle of Cambrai in late November initially seemed to secure the Commander in Chief's position. Cambrai was the first successful use of tanks on a large scale, but there was criticism that the level of success had been exaggerated by the military intelligence staff at GHQ, and then more seriously that they had tried to cover up failings on their part which had allowed the Germans to counter-attack successfully, retaking most of the territory they had lost. Two of Philip Sassoon's Eton and Oxford friends, Patrick Shaw Stewart and Edward Horner, lost their lives in the battle.

The outrage at the missed opportunity of Cambrai, and the further unnecessary loss of life that seemed to be a direct result of poor planning on the part of the generals, shook even Northcliffe's belief in the military leadership. *The Times* reported that 'The merest breath of criticism on any military operation is far too often dismissed as an "intrigue" against the Commander-in-chief.' It demanded a 'prompt, searching and complete' inquiry into the fiasco of Cambrai.[62]

Lord Esher discreetly briefed Lloyd George at the Hôtel de Crillon in Paris on the full extent of what had happened at Cambrai, which produced a furious reaction from the Prime Minister. Esher recalled in his diary that Lloyd George

> launched out against 'intrigues' against him. Philip Sassoon was the delinquent conspiring with Asquith and the press. I expressed doubt and said that Haig had no knowledge of such things if they existed, but Lloyd George replied that every one of the journalists etc. reported interviews and letters to him. He was kept informed of every move. He then used most violent language about Charteris . . . Haig has been misled by Charteris. He had produced arguments about German 'morale' etc. etc. all fallacious, culled from Charteris. The man was a public danger, and running Haig. Haig's plans had all failed. He had promised Zeebrugge and Ostend, and then Cambrai. He had failed at a cost of 400,000 men. Now he wrote of fresh offensives and asked for men. He would get neither.[63]

Philip Sassoon shared the growing disillusion over the reliability of Charteris, and after being told by Esher about his meeting with the Prime Minister wrote back that he had 'never agreed with these foolish optimistic statements which Charteris has been putting in DH's mouth all year but what they [the war cabinet] ought to know is that morale is a fluctuating entity and there is no doubt that events in Russia and Italy have greatly raised the enemy's spirits'.*[64]

Lord Derby told Haig that the war cabinet had no confidence in Charteris and wanted him to be removed from his position. He

---

* The Russian Revolution in November 1917 had brought the Bolsheviks to power. German victory on the Eastern Front would be confirmed with the Russian armistice in December 1917 and the signing of the Treaty of Brest-Litovsk on 3 March 1918. Germany and Austria also won a decisive victory in November on the Italian front at the Battle of Caporetto.

added that in his opinion practically the whole army considered Charteris to be 'a public danger'.[65] The following day Lord Northcliffe weighed in against him as well. He warned Philip Sassoon, 'I ought to tell you frankly and plainly, as a friend of the Commander in Chief, that dissatisfaction, which easily produced a national outburst of indignation, exists in regard to the Generalship in France . . . Outside of the War Office I doubt whether the High Command has any supporters whatever. Sir Douglas is regarded with affection in the army, but everywhere people remark that he is surrounded by incompetents.'[66] The message was duly delivered to Haig, who acknowledged that it was impossible to continue to support Charteris when he had 'put those who ought to work in friendliness with him against him'.[67] Charteris was gone the same day. Philip had little sympathy for him, telling Lord Esher that 'rightly or wrongly he was an object of odium and his name had become a byword even at home. I hear that he has been heading a faction against me for developing the position of private secretary too much. I am diverted. I went to see DH but you know the length of my material ambitions and I would not stay on a second longer than I was wanted.'[68]

Haig survived the crisis, but in February 1918 Robertson was replaced as Chief of the Imperial General Staff, and the following month Lloyd George achieved his aim with the creation of a supreme Allied command for the armed forces on the Western Front under the French general Ferdinand Foch.

The various Anglo-French conferences during the war also gave Philip an opportunity to broaden his own circle of contacts in Paris, and one such opportunity presented itself at the Hôtel Claridge. He was attracted to successful people from a wide range of backgrounds, although the sporting, media and cultural worlds were firm favourites. One morning during a break in the conference proceedings Philip spotted across the lobby the handsome French flying ace Georges Carpentier. As Carpentier recalled:

A slim distinguished-looking gentleman with fine features came up to me and chatted to me in excellent French though with a slight English accent . . . Realising that he was a member of the British delegation I took out my cigarette case and said, 'Do you know what I'd like very much? To get the autographs of Admiral Beatty, Winston Churchill and the other gentlemen on this case.'

'That is a perfectly simple matter,' he replied with a smile. 'Let me have the case and I'll give it back to you here tomorrow. Unless you would like me to leave it at your place?'

I left it with him and arranged that I should come back to Claridge's the next day to pick it up. My unknown friend was as good as his word and when he returned my cigarette case it bore the signatures of Admiral Beatty, Winston Churchill, Lloyd George, Lord Birkenhead and Lord Montagu – and a sixth signature Philip Sassoon. 'I took the liberty of adding my own,' he said with a smile.[69]

Their chance meeting was the start of another great friendship. Like Julian Grenfell, Carpentier was a boxer, and he would go on to have considerable success as a heavyweight champion after the war. He and Philip shared a passion for flying, an activity that was exhilarating, increasingly effective as a weapon of war, but also extremely dangerous. Carpentier had won the Croix de Guerre for his war exploits as a pilot, a decoration that Sassoon, along with other members of Haig's staff, had also received from the French commander Joseph Joffre during a visit to GHQ in 1916. Philip had not flown in combat, but used aeroplanes to travel between meetings, and marvelled that he could get from GHQ in Montreuil back to his home in Kent in just forty minutes.

It was as recently as 1909 that Louis Blériot had made the first Channel crossing in an aeroplane, and there were frequent crashes even for experienced pilots. Winston Churchill was also a great enthusiast; he would often fly out to the front from London and return to Westminster that same evening to give an update to the House of Commons based on what he had seen. He considered the air to be a 'dangerous mistress. Once under its spell, most lovers are faithful to the end, which is not always old age.'[70] In 1918, after his third plane crash, and the death of airmen in aircraft that he had previously piloted himself, Churchill gave in to the pressure from his family and friends to abandon his mistress. Philip, free from such domestic pressures, remained faithful to the air throughout his life, and not just because of its speed and convenience, but because in the skies he didn't suffer from the motion sickness that made journeys by sea such an ordeal for him. Air travel also demonstrated just how close normal life was to the horrors of the Western Front. Folkestone was less than 100 miles from Ypres, and from his house at Lympne Philip could hear the guns during heavy artillery bombardments at the front.

Working alongside the high command gave Philip the opportunity to bring forward ideas of his own. One of these was encouraging famous artists to come and use their creative perspective to capture aspects of life at the front. He shared the idea with Northcliffe, who was excited by the prospect of these works capturing the everyday nobility and heroics of the men. Northcliffe credited himself with having conceived of it but praised Philip for making it happen. For Philip it was the perfect marriage of his military duties and his artistic instincts. He obtained permits for friends like John Singer Sargent and William Orpen to spend time in Belgium and France, with the freedom to paint whatever they chose. Sargent evoked a haunting beauty in his depiction of the ruins of the cathedral at Arras and great dignity in his tableau *Gassed*, which showed a line of men supporting each other after suffering the temporary blindness caused by a mustard-gas attack. In bad weather Philip fixed it for Sargent to tour the trenches in a tank, 'looping the loop generally'.[71] He also arranged for him to meet with Douglas Haig to show him some of his work, and was greatly entertained by the juxtaposition of these two strong if mildly eccentric personalities. Philip would recall that 'Sargent cannot begin his sentences and starts them in the middle with a wave of his hand for the beginning, while Haig cannot finish his and often concludes with hand work instead of words. In consequence, the meeting between the two was quite amusing – a series of little pantomimes.' He also remembered taking Haig to see a remarkable picture by Sargent showing a train full of men going up to the front at twilight. Haig looked at it intently for some time and then, turning to Sargent, remarked, 'I see – one of our light railways,' to which the artist just smiled back in response.[72]

William Orpen was one of the greatest portrait painters of the day; his 1916 painting of a haunted Winston Churchill after the failure of Gallipoli was Clementine's favourite portrayal of her husband. He had also previously painted Philip Sassoon and his sister Sybil. Philip arranged for him to paint a number of the generals; in May 1917 he telephoned to invite him to paint the Chief and to come and meet him at an informal lunch at advanced HQ. Haig made a positive impression on Orpen. In the artist's view:

Sir Douglas was a strong man, a true Northerner, well inside himself – no pose. It seemed it would be impossible to upset him, impossible to make him show any strong feeling and yet one felt he understood, knew all, and felt for all his men, and that he truly loved them; and I knew they loved him . . . when I started painting him he said 'why waste your time painting me? Go and paint the men. They're the fellows who are saving the world, and they're getting killed every day.'[73]

Although Philip was increasingly confident in using his position to develop his personal networks, there was one man of growing reputation he studiously avoided – his second cousin, the decorated army officer and poet Siegfried Sassoon. Siegfried was the grandson of S. D. Sassoon, the half-brother of Philip's grandfather. While Philip was the principal male descendant of their great-grandfather David Sassoon, and the holder of the family's baronetcy, Siegfried's branch

had become somewhat estranged from the rest of the Sassoon clan.*
At that time the two cousins had never met,† but they had mutual
friends, including the writer Osbert Sitwell and the painter Glyn
Philpot. Philip had been an early patron of Philpot's and, as already
noted, had had his portrait painted by the artist in 1914. Philpot
then painted Siegfried in June 1917, after the publication of his first
volume of war poems, *The Old Huntsman*, had brought him to public
attention. This was just before his statement calling for an end to
the war was read out in the House of Commons, an episode that
gave him even greater notoriety. His declaration would have come
to the particular attention of Philip at GHQ, as Siegfried was not
just some pacifist poet, but an officer who had been awarded the
Military Cross for his bravery in battle. Siegfried's fame grew in June
1918 when a second volume of his poems, *Counter-Attack*, was
published. Lord Esher asked Philip, 'By the way, who is Siegfried
Sassoon? Tell me, and do not forget. He is a powerful satirist. Winston
knows his last volume of poems by heart, and rolls them out on
every possible occasion.'[74] Philip initially ignored Esher's question
but, when he wrote asking again, confirmed that Siegfried was a
distant relation. Philip would have found the war poet's work embarrassing, with its constant references to the bravery of the men, the
brutality of the military commanders and the incompetence of their
staff officers. One poem in particular that Churchill had committed
to memory was 'Song-Books of the War', with its lines:

> And then he'll speak of Haig's last drive,
> Marvelling that any came alive
> Out of the shambles that men built
> And smashed to cleanse the world of guilt.

---

* Siegfried Sassoon's father, Alfred Ezra Sassoon, had married a Catholic against
the wishes of his Jewish family, which led to his estrangement from them.
† Philip would not meet Siegfried at all until a chance encounter at Lady
Desborough's home, Taplow Court, in 1925.

Yet Siegfried was just as damning of the politicians as he was of the generals, exclaiming in his poem 'Great Men':

> You Marshals, gilt and red,
> You Ministers and Princes, and Great Men,
> Why can't you keep your mouthings for the dead?
> Go round the simple cemeteries; and then
> Talk of our noble sacrifice and losses
> To the wooden crosses.

The sacrifices had been great and the losses terrible. There was no doubt by 1918 that the world had grown weary of the war, but there was still no obvious end in sight. In early 1918 the British were instead bracing themselves for a massive German assault on their lines. The Russian Revolution of 1917 had heralded victory for the Germans on the Eastern Front, which would allow them to move large numbers of men and munitions over to France and Belgium. The United States had entered the war in support of the western Allies, but its troops were only just starting to arrive at the front. On 4 a.m. on 21 March, Operation Michael, the first phase of the great German spring offensive, or Kaiserschlacht (Kaiser's Battle), was launched. Its objective was simple: to smash the British, drive them back to the sea and then force the French to surrender.

Philip and GHQ would be in the firing line of the German attack and its significance was clear to him. As he wrote to Lord Esher after the offensive had started:

This is the biggest attack in the history of warfare I would imagine. On the whole we were very satisfied with the first day. There is no doubt that they lost very heavily and we had always expected to give ground and our front line was held very lightly. We have had bad luck with the mist, because we have got the supremacy in the air, fine weather wd. have been in our favour . . . The situation is a very simple one. The enemy has fog, the men, and we haven't. For two years Sir DH has been warning our friends at home of the critical condition of our manpower; but they have preferred to talk about Aleppo and indulge in mythical dreams about the Americans . . . We are fighting for our existence.*[75]

The British were being driven back, but the Germans were sustaining heavy losses. Nevertheless, when the King visited GHQ on 29 March, Philip reflected to Esher that 'This is the ninth day of the attack. It feels like nine years. There have been times in every day when one might have thought the game was up.'[76] Haig told the King of his concern that, while the British army had held up well, its position had been compromised by decisions made by the politicians. They were fighting a German army vastly superior in size with 100,000 fewer of their own men than the year before, and over a longer section of front line. This was a result of Lloyd George's agreement that Britain would take over some sectors that had previously been held by the French. The following day Philip wrote to Esher again: 'We have been promised 170,000 men from home of which 80,000 are leave men. The remainder will not fill our losses and then basta [i.e. 'enough', from the Spanish]. Nothing to fall back on. It is serious.' [77]

On the morning of 11 April, Haig was at his desk early, writing out in his own hand a special order for the day, which he gave to Philip with the instruction that it should be sent to all ranks of the British forces serving at the front. Two days earlier, the Germans had launched Operation Georgette, the second phase of the Kaiserschlacht, and there was no doubting that this was the critical moment of the war. Haig wrote:

---

* Philip's letter references two common complaints of GHQ: that they do not have enough manpower at their disposal; and resources have been diverted to secondary theatres of war, like the campaign in the Middle East against the Ottoman Empire, hence the reference to Aleppo.

Many amongst us now are tired. To those I would say that Victory will belong to the side which holds out the longest. The French Army is moving rapidly and in great force to our support.

There is no other course open to us but to fight it out. Every position must be held to the last man: there must be no retirement. With our backs to the wall and believing in the justice of our cause each one of us must fight on to the end. The safety of our homes and the freedom of mankind alike depend upon the conduct of each one of us at this critical moment.

The lines held, and on 24 April the great offensive was halted by British and Australian forces in defence of Amiens. The Germans would launch a final attack in July, but essentially their forces were spent, and with the arrival of growing numbers of fresh American reinforcements, it would just be a matter of time before victory would be delivered.

Philip came down with a dose of Spanish flu in July while on leave in London, and after resting made it to his home at Lympne for the weekend, before returning to GHQ. He was fortunate to have contracted a milder form of the virus that spread across the globe in a more virulent form in the autumn and winter of 1918–19. Over 200,000 people in Britain alone would be killed by the flu that claimed the lives of 50 million around the world.

Following the summer successes against the Germans he allowed himself to start to look forward to peace. He wrote to his friend Alice Dudeney about Lympne, 'It was lovely there. I do want to show it to you. I am on the lip of the world and gaze over the wide Pontine marshes that reflect the passing clouds like a mirror. The sea is just far enough off to be always smooth and blue.'[78]

At 4.20 a.m. on 8 August, having withstood all that the Germans could throw at them over the previous months, the Allies launched their own offensive. This campaign, known as the Hundred Days Offensive, commenced with the Battle of Amiens, which pushed the Germans away from their positions to the east of the town. Philip Sassoon was with Douglas Haig at advanced HQ, a train parked in the station at Wiry-au-Mont, about 40 miles west of the front line at Albert. The British broke through the lines, advancing 8 miles on what the German commander Erich Ludendorff called 'the black day of the German army'.[79] Haig told his wife, 'Who would have believed this possible even 2 months ago? How much easier it is to attack, than to stand and await the enemy's attack!'[80] The Allied advance continued through the rest of the summer and by late September the Oberste Heeresleitung, the supreme German army council consisting of both the Chief of the General Staff Paul von Hindenburg and his deputy Ludendorff, told the government that the position on the Western Front was close to collapse. On 4 October the new German Chancellor Max von Baden approached the Allies with a view to agreeing an armistice to end the war, appealing in particular for the intervention of the American President, Woodrow Wilson, to act as an honest broker. As talks between the Allies and Germany continued, Philip travelled to London with Douglas Haig later that month for discussions with the French on the terms to be offered for the armistice. He told Lady Desborough after the talks, 'We saw Foch today, he says "peace approaches". This would certainly be the best solution of all. If only we knew and could state our peace terms we could then calmly await the day of Germany's acceptance of them. Meanwhile Wilson über alles is the Saxon chant. Everyone is furious, but helpless. We do the fighting – America reaps the harvest.'[81]

At 5 a.m. on 11 November 1918, in a railway carriage parked in the Compiègne forest, General Foch signed the armistice agreement with Germany on behalf of the Allied forces. At 11 a.m. that day, the moment the agreement came into effect, Philip was with Haig and the army commanders at Cambrai, to share in the moment of celebration. The news of the pending armistice had reached Folkestone in Philip's constituency, no doubt with his help.

Reporting on the events of 11 November the *Folkestone Express* noted that

> There had been quite an electric feeling about the townspeople from early morning. Folkestone was one of the first towns, although not officially, acquainted of the fact that the war was at an end. Consequently in the vicinity of the Town Hall crowds began to gather as early as nine o'clock all full of the news. The townspeople were augmented by soldiers from every part of the British Empire, and representatives of practically all our gallant Allies.

In the drizzling rain of a November morning, the town's mayor, Sir Stephen Penfold, announced the news of the armistice 'in a voice trembling with joy and maybe with grief at the thought of those who had gone never to return . . . Pandemonium reigned for some minutes, for motor horns and anything that could make a noise were used for the purpose of spreading the glad tidings. The bells of the Parish church rang out their joyous song. At once flags and bunting were exhibited.'[82]

Philip Sassoon would have little time for rejoicing as three days after the armistice David Lloyd George called a general election for 14 December. The Prime Minister wanted an immediate mandate for the coalition government that had won the war to negotiate the peace. The Conservative leader Andrew Bonar Law agreed that candidates from his party who supported the coalition should receive a joint letter of endorsement, from both himself and the Liberal leader Lloyd George. It was the first time that such an electoral pact between parties had been organized. The endorsement letters were dismissed as a 'Coupon' by Herbert Asquith (now leader only of a splinter group of Independent Liberals), but it proved to be a highly effective tactic. This wasn't the only revolutionary change to be rushed through for the election. The 1918 Representation of the People Act gave the vote for the first time to all men over the age of twenty-one, and to some women as well. Philip Sassoon had supported votes for women when he first stood for Parliament in 1912, and this reform, so long campaigned for by the suffragettes, had finally been achieved, if not yet on a fully equal basis to men.* The new Act of Parliament expanded the electorate from 7.7 million to 21.4 million; and three-quarters of these had never voted before.

The election campaign was famous for its promises that Germany would be made to pay for the war, and that there would be rewards for the people in return for their sacrifice and forbearance, most notably homes 'fit for heroes'. Philip was still on active service with Douglas Haig at GHQ, but the Chief gave him leave to make flying visits home to campaign in his constituency. His first trip back was on Thursday 21 November, and he addressed a series of public meetings before returning to France the following Monday.

Philip was 'enthusiastically received' at his first election rally at a packed Folkestone town hall. Some pride was expressed by his supporters in the role he had played supporting Douglas Haig during the war. Philip, now returning to the stage of the civilian politician, set out his wholehearted support for the coalition: 'no government', he said, 'but a coalition government could have won the war and I am convinced that nothing but a coalition government can secure a satisfactory peace and start the country wisely, safely and prosperously on a new path. That is why I am a coalition candidate. On some points I may not, perhaps, see eye to eye with the Prime Minister, but I leave my personal views behind.'[83]

This speech also demonstrated the impact of the war on Philip as a politician, and his belief that things could not just go back to the way they had been in 1914. 'The lesson of this war', he told his listeners, 'is that all sections of the community are dependent on one another, and why only by unselfish desire to help the common-good

---

* Only women who were aged over thirty and who met the minimum property qualifications had the vote at this time. It would not be until 1928 that there would be equal voting rights for men and women over the age of twenty-one in the United Kingdom.

can happiness come.' It was a message that his Eton friend Charles Lister, who had died of his wounds fighting at Gallipoli, would have appreciated. Charles, who had devoted much of his time to the school's mission to the poor in Hackney Wick, would have noted the change in Philip, from the student who seemed to care only for beautiful things to the champion of opportunity for all.

In particular, Philip focused on education, care of children and their mothers, and his belief that 'every child born should be given a chance to become a fit and useful citizen of the Empire'. He also told his audience in the town hall that housing was 'one of the most important questions before them. It has always been important and should have been taken up before the war.'

Even on the question of home rule for Ireland, something he had campaigned against when he first entered Parliament, the war would seem to have softened his position. The *Folkestone Express* reported him as stating at the meeting that

He had always held very strong views and he had not abandoned them but he realised the need of a solution which would allow Ireland to build up her industrial and political prosperity. Mr Lloyd George said he would have nothing to do with any settlement which involved the forcible coercion of Ulster and on that basis he would support any measure which would bring peace and prosperity to that much troubled land.

On the Saturday after this speech at the town hall, Philip addressed an open-air meeting in the cobbled Fishmarket in Folkestone harbour. He was again given a rapturous reception and the crowd sang 'For he's a jolly good fellow' as he stood on the podium. Here, from the harbour that had sent millions to fight on the Western Front, he turned his fire on the Germans. He declared that the Allies 'had given the Germans a damned good hiding, although he thought they had not given them the hiding they deserved', at which there were cries of 'hear, hear' from the crowd. He stated that Germany should be made to pay towards the cost of recon-struction following the damage it had brought about during the war.[84] At an eve-of-poll public meeting at the Sidney Street School in East Folkestone,* he told the audience that 'He wanted the Germans from the Kaiser down to be punished.'[85] He also advocated that Germany should be permanently deprived of its colonies.

The election was held on 14 December, but the result was not declared until 28 December, to allow time for the counting of postal votes from soldiers still on active service. Philip Sassoon safely defeated his Labour Party opponent, Robert Forsyth, by 8,809 votes to 3,427.

Immediately after the election Philip went back to GHQ, where he would stay until he was demobilized on 1 March 1919. His last service for Douglas Haig would bring him to the positive attention of Lloyd George. In February he was sent to London to negotiate the terms of Haig's retirement settlement; it was not uncommon for military leaders to receive a generous pension for winning a war. Haig was prepared to accept a peerage as part of his settlement, most probably an earldom, but would need the means to afford the estate that would be expected to go with it. Sassoon proposed to Lloyd George that Haig should receive a cash settlement of £250,000, a relatively modest sum to a millionaire like himself, and equivalent to what he had spent on Port Lympne. The Prime Minister countered with £100,000, which was the amount that was eventually agreed, plus the earldom, and the purchase of Bemersyde House in the Scottish Borders. It was a much better deal than the settlement for generals like Edmund Allenby, who received £30,000 and a peerage.[†] Philip had also insisted at Haig's request that the settlement for the generals should be granted alongside the

---

* The Sidney Street School became known as George Spurgeon Primary School in 1928. Its buildings are now part of Castle Hill Community Primary School

† Allenby had led the Egyptian expeditionary force in its conquest of Palestine and Syria in 1917 and 1918, a campaign made famous by the role played by T. E. Lawrence.

agreement on the war pensions for all servicemen. Lloyd George accepted this in principle, but the delivery of that end of the bargain took longer to realize.

GHQ had been Philip's home for more than three years, and he had been a serving army officer for over four. He was returning to his half-finished estate at Port Lympne and a House of Commons from which he had been largely absent since war was declared. 'I am demobilising on March 1st – but with a rather heavy heart,' Philip wrote to Alice Dudeney,

> yet there is something corpse like about GHQ now . . . the ashes of last night's fire . . . if it had not been for the sickening conscious- ness of casualties I should have been very happy during the war. Soldiers are so delightful and hard work a continual interest & away from all the rumours and intrigues of the home front! But – I shall certainly not be happy in peace – and in the House of Commons with those 700 mugs to look at – ugh!! Worse than any prison.[86]

• BRAVE NEW WORLD •

All the arts and science that we used in war are standing
by us now ready to help us in peace . . . Never did science
offer such fairy gifts to man. Never did their knowledge
and organisation stand so high. Repair the waste. Rebuild
the ruins. Heal the wounds. Crown the victors. Comfort
the broken and broken-hearted. There is the battle we
have now to fight.

Winston Churchill, speech in Dundee,
26 November 1918

Philip Sassoon's Avro 504K aeroplane charged back across the
English Channel towards home.[1] In bright sunlight and with low
cloud, it was hard to distinguish between the sea below and the
sky above. With the landscape barely changing there was almost
no sense of movement, as if despite the noise of the engines you
were floating suspended between heaven and earth. As the pilot
brought the plane down towards the airfield at Lympne the clouds
cleared; below were the elegant Edwardian buildings on the
clifftops at Folkestone and the steamers chugging into the harbour;
ahead Hythe Bay curved away from them to the point at

Dungeness. From the air at least the scars of the war at home were barely visible.

Philip's growing passion for flying led him to purchase his own aircraft in 1919,* the same year in which the world's first commercial air passenger service started. According to the London society column in the *Evening Standard*, Philip was the first man in England 'to venture on buying and keeping an aeroplane as other people buy and keep a motor car'.[2]

His aeroplanes carried his adopted symbol of the cobra. A bronze statue of a coiled cobra, rising to strike, also decorated the bonnet of his Rolls-Royce motor cars, in place of the flying lady known as the Spirit of Ecstasy. In ancient Egypt the cobra offered protection to the pharaohs, and in eastern mythology symbolized good fortune, new life and regeneration – the serpent could change its skin and each time emerge new and whole. Now that he was out of his khaki uniform, 1919 would be a year of regeneration for Philip Sassoon; he had just turned thirty, with seemingly limitless funds at his disposal, no personal ties and a seat in the House of Commons.

Harold Macmillan, another Eton and Oxford survivor of the war, remembered, 'To a young man . . . with all the quick mental and moral recovery of which youth is capable, life at the end of 1918 seemed to offer an attractive, not to say exciting, prospect.'[3] Looking back on this period, Evelyn Waugh wrote, 'Everyone was agog for youth – young bishops, young headmasters, young professors, young poets, young advertising managers. It was all very nice and of course they deserved it.'[4]

As a surviving member of the lost generation, Philip Sassoon was also determined to make the most of the life given to him but denied to so many of his friends by the war. The strictures of Edwardian society had been replaced by new social freedoms. People had grown used to mixing freely with people of all ranks and stations in life during the war, and women in particular now had much more

---

* He did not learn to fly until 1929.

independence. Philip would not subscribe to the view first expressed
by the American writer Gertrude Stein that the lost generation were
not the young men who had been killed in the war, but those who
had returned to a life of drink, drugs and directionlessness.[5] Philip's
life was driven by energy and purpose, and he would become one
of those singular young men who suddenly rose to prominence both
as a society host and as a politician.

In March and April 1919, Philip marked his new freedom from
the army with a holiday in Spain and Morocco, accompanied by a
fellow staff officer from GHQ named Jack. Together they experienced the cultural treasures of these two countries and Philip was
particularly moved by the works of Velázquez* at the Prado museum
in Madrid. In his travel journal he declared Velázquez to be 'the
most wonderful artist in the world. Best of all is the "Las Meninas"
[Maids of Honour]. If by a miracle we mean an event in which the
effect is beyond measure out of proportion with the seeming
simplicity of the cause, then we may say that of all the great pictures
of the world this may most precisely be called miraculous.'[6]

Philip Sassoon was not alone in his regard for *Las Meninas*. His
friend William Orpen later wrote, 'It is hard to conceive of a more
beautiful piece of painting than this – so free and yet firm and so
revealing . . . Like all of the great artists Velázquez takes something
out of life and sets it free.'[7] *Las Meninas* had also been an inspiration for the composition of works by John Singer Sargent, and
Sir John Lavery's 1913 portrait of King George V and his family.

Las Meninas has been a mystery to the centuries of admirers who
have stood before it. The scene is set in the Alcazar Palace in Madrid,
and the central figure is the five-year-old daughter of King Philip
IV of Spain, the 'Infanta' Margaret Theresa. She is accompanied by
her two maids of honour, her dog, and two court dwarfs, Maribarbola
and Nicolasito. To the left of this group stands Velázquez himself,

---

* Diego Velázquez (1599–1660), Spanish painter and leading artist at the court
  of King Philip IV.

looking towards us as he works at a large canvas, but we cannot see what he is painting. Facing us on the far wall in the picture is a mirror reflecting back the shadowy images of King Philip IV and Queen Mariana, suggesting that they might have been standing next to the viewer. Next to the mirror is an open door, and through it stands a nobleman, perhaps arriving with news for the King.

The art historian Kenneth Clark wrote of the painting that 'Our first feeling is of being there.'[8] It not only transports you back to the court of Philip IV of Spain, but invites you to look at it through his eyes. For Philip Sassoon, standing before *Las Meninas* in March 1919, after the fall of the Emperors of Austria, Germany and Russia, he might have considered the precarious position of rulers, and how quickly they can pass from being the centre of attention to becoming peripheral figures, like the king in the painting. Looking at the beautiful but vulnerable Infanta, Philip might have also reflected on his own gilded childhood at the Avenue de Marigny, in that lost pre-war world of Paris in the time of his parents and grandparents.

On his tour of Spain, Philip was greatly impressed with the Alhambra, the palace and fortress complex in Granada. It provided 'a lot of ideas for Lympne . . . The Alhambra . . . must remain for all time the crowning glory, the seal, the apogee, in a word the supreme consummation of Moorish Art.'[9]

It was a timely inspiration, as back in England Philip Sassoon's great project in 1919 was the completion of his house and estate in Kent. Port Lympne was more than just a building project designed to provide him with a comfortable home in his constituency; it was a work of art in its own right and a statement of Philip's flair, style and ambition.* His friend the writer Osbert Sitwell thought that Lympne captured his 'fire and brilliance as a young man'.[10] Sybil also recalled that Philip 'loved [Lympne] very much because he had built it himself'.[11]

---

* The house was originally called Belcaire, and the name was changed to Port Lympne in the early 1920s.

Sir Herbert Baker had designed and built the mansion before the war, but was unavailable to continue the project as he was working with Sir Edwin Lutyens in India on the construction of New Delhi. Instead Philip brought in the fashionable young architect Philip Tilden to complete the interior and external works on the estate. Tilden is now better known for his work for Winston Churchill at Chartwell, but Philip Sassoon was his main patron in the early 1920s; and it was he who introduced Churchill to Tilden when Winston was in the process of purchasing his Kent estate. Sassoon and Tilden were kindred spirits – dynamic and creative, of similar age and shared artistic tastes. There was also a strong mutual respect: Tilden thought that no more 'brilliant man existed for this age than Philip. I do not mean necessarily brilliant in scholarship, but in effect; intensely amusing and amused, full of knowledge concerning many things that others care not two pence for; imaginative, curious and above all intelligent to the last degree.'[12]

Tilden believed that Port Lympne should be 'all new and forceful, pulsing with the vitality of new blood'.[13] Everything inside the mansion house would be entirely modern. Philip didn't bring any of the antique furniture or artworks from his other homes to Lympne; nearly all of the contents were commissioned from contemporary artists and designers. The *Country Life* profile of Lympne exclaimed that 'to be blasé has become a pose, almost an accepted virtue. Today most of us think, some of us even like to think, that we are prepared for everything – at least nearly everything. For everything except say a visit to Port Lympne . . . there it is possible to feel some inkling of true wonder.'[14]

Philip had learnt at Eton the importance of external conformity in behaviour, whatever the true nature of the emotions that lie within, and the same principle was applied to Lympne. The mansion was a modern building, but made to look more established by being built from old bricks. As you approached the entrance to the house from the east, it presented the stylish yet conservative appearance of an old English manor. Philip also bought old garden statues from the country house sale at Stowe to add to the impression of the property's longevity.* Yet from the south side Port Lympne had an Italianate feel, with curved loggias extending from the house and a series of terraces below. As a final external feature Tilden created a great stone staircase to the west of the house which climbed the slope to the rear, seemingly rising like Jacob's ladder to infinity. The staircase was decorated with fountains and pavilions supported by classical pillars, an homage to Lympne's ancient heritage as a Roman port. It provided a sense of drama and ambition more akin to the golden age of Hollywood than to the Home Counties of England.

The greatest transformation came once you had crossed the threshold. As you went through the green bronze front door, you were transported into what Marie Belloc Lowndes called 'a strange and beautiful house – a house which might have come right out of the pages of Hajji Baba of Ispahan'.[†15] The oriental appearance of the interior gave free rein to Philip Sassoon's more exotic creative ambitions and was completed at seemingly limitless expense. The drawing room had given him particular trouble. Just before the war, while watching the *Josephslegende* ballet, choreographed by Nijinsky for Sergei Diaghilev's Ballets Russes, Philip had fallen in love with the sets designed by the Catalan artist Josep Maria Sert.[‡] He commissioned Sert to paint a mural for the drawing room at Lympne, and the artist created a work which was an allegorical depiction of Germany's defeat in the war. France was shown as a draped and crouching female figure being attacked by two German

---

* One statue of King George II still stands in the grounds of Port Lympne at the end of the lime walk.

† The reference is to the hero of the novel *The Adventures of Hajji Baba of Ispahan* by James Justinian Morier (1824).

‡ The *Josephslegende* ballet is based on the story of the dreams of Joseph in Egypt described in the Old Testament. It was commissioned for the Ballets Russes and premiered in Paris in May 1914. There were appropriately seven performances in Paris followed by a further seven in London. The music was composed by Richard Strauss.

eagles. She was assisted by a flock of children representing the Allies, each wearing a headpiece from their national costume. The Indian Empire was portrayed by elephants which were shown on the broad breast of the fireplace in the centre of the room carrying all before them. The story ends with the German eagle being torn asunder, feathers flying.*

At that time Sert favoured painting in a monochrome style, but at Lympne he used tones of black and gold, rather than black and white, which while impressive were somewhat overbearing in the drawing room. Philip came to have grave doubts about Sert's work. 'Personally I think it monstrous,' he wrote to his friend Sir Louis Mallet, adding that the work was

> Of course ingenious in imagination and drawing – but so fright-fully heavy that although the room is beautifully proportioned you feel impelled to throw yourself down on your belly and worm yourself through the door as the only alternative to battering out one's brains against the ceiling – and from being a light sunny room brighter than the inside of an Osram bulb it is now so pitchy that you have to whip out a pocket electric torch even at midday or you're as good as lost. And an awful cooked celery colour which gives you a liver attack before you can say knife. Unless Sert can alter it past all recognition it will have to go.[16]

In an attempt to salvage the situation Philip asked John Singer Sargent's advice on how to complete the room. Sargent's only comment on being introduced to Sert's work was that the remaining uncovered walls should be 'slabbed with marble the colour of chow'. Philip Tilden, who was given the task of executing the command,

---

* Sert's mural at Port Lympne no longer exists, but his 1913 work *The Triumph of Apollo*, which is held as part of the collection of the Fundación Banco Santander in Madrid, offers a good comparison for its style and colour scheme. Sert's work can also be seen in New York at the Waldorf Astoria Hotel and the Rockefeller Center.

recalled that 'this remark was typical for Sargent; he was never a man of many words, and no doubt we should have known what he meant. But there are many chow coloured dogs of many colours, and a whole day's argument could not elucidate his meaning.' By a process of elimination they settled on a warm, moss-brown marble, streaked with gold, which had to be created synthetically by a firm at the back of Marylebone Station in London.[17]

The drawing room was connected to a small library which looked over the terrace and out to the sea beyond. From the dark brooding colours of Sert's room you were transported to a bright space with books lining the walls, all bound in a pinkish-red morocco leather and housed in wooden bookcases sheened with 'gilver' – silver with a tinge of gilt. The carpet was green and pink, with pink also used in the lining of the bookshelves and in the marble of the mantelpiece. Passing through the library you arrived in the dining room, with its walls lined with marble-effect lapis lazuli, producing an undulating and moving cover of cobalt blue. Set against this were golden chairs around the central table, with arms carved to resemble the wings of an eagle. The artist Glyn Philpot created a frieze depicting a scene from ancient Egypt of near-naked black men, described by Philip Tilden as 'gesticulating and attitudinising figures',[18] working with animals.* Looking back from the dining room, through the doors into the library and then on to the drawing room, you could enjoy the contrast of colours, tones and textures – the cobalt blue of the lapis lazuli giving way to the red, gold and pink of the library and leading to the brooding gold, black and mossy tones of the drawing room.

The most talked-about feature of the internal works was the creation of a Moorish patio in a courtyard at the centre of the mansion buildings, perhaps inspired by Sassoon's visit to the Alhambra Palace. It was to be accessed from the first half-landing of the main staircase at the centre of the house through a sliding plate-glass electric door.

---

* This frieze is still at Port Lympne, although now located in a different room.

The structure included white marble columns, white-stuccoed walls and brilliant green pantiles. The courtyard was decorated with fountains and running streams, orange trees and cypress hedges, and behind columns at the far end of the patio were two free-standing pink marble baths in an area that had the appearance of a Turkish hammam. The overall scene was reminiscent of Sir John Lavery's painting of a Moorish harem, and was most certainly the feature of Port Lympne that Lady Honor Channon, the wife of Chips Channon, was referring to when she compared the house to a Spanish brothel.[19]

Port Lympne was not a place for sitting around; the interior stimulated rather than relaxed its guests. For this reason Philip Tilden added an additional library standing to the right of the main entrance to the mansion. It was a domed octagonal room, modelled on the Radcliffe Camera at Oxford, and designed to be a sanctuary from the rest of the house. Philip Sassoon's private quarters were on the ground floor adjoining the front terrace, and his restless pace would dictate the rhythm of life at Lympne. He would go running in the grounds in the morning, and there were two tennis courts set at right angles to each other, so that as the sun moved through the sky you could still play without it being in your eyes. Tilden also designed a large marble swimming pool which was built below the terrace. The pool comprised three square sections making one rectangular-shaped bathing area. A fountain in the central pool required its own water supply after it was discovered that when fully operational it drained the resources for the whole area; a wave machine had also been built for the pool. Eventually they found that the weight of the marble pool was too great and it was in danger of sinking into the garden below, which led to it being redesigned around the single central pool which remains to this day.

Lympne was for entertaining, and particularly for summer parties. Philip wanted it to be a place, as Taplow Court had been for Lady Desborough, where his friends would choose to gather.

The estate would also be a home to his small court of close friends who since the war had become like an extended family to him. In addition to Tilden, who was in semi-permanent residence while the works on the estate were completed, there was Sir Louis Mallet,* who had rented a house from Philip on the edge of the estate called Bellevue. Sir Louis was a bachelor and retired diplomat who had been close to Philip's parents and in their absence took on a mentoring role, somewhat similar to the relationship that Philip had enjoyed with Lord Esher during the war. Louis had sold his own home at Otham in Kent to move to Lympne, an act that Philip Tilden referred to as a 'capitulation to Philip Sassoon's selfishness'. Tilden said that he did not mean this in an unkind sense, but as an expression of 'the fact that Philip needed someone of experience near him as a dumping ground for confidences'.[20] Louis also kept rooms at 25 Park Lane when he was in London. Other frequent guests included older friends like Marie Belloc Lowndes and Alice Dudeney, as well as his cousin David Gubbay, who had taken over the running of the London office of David Sassoon & Co., and his wife Hannah. Alice Dudeney recorded her first visit to Lympne in the summer of 1919 in her diary: 'The house most lovely and luxurious. I seem to be staying with a fairy prince. While I was in my bath before dressing for dinner he came knocking at the door. "Mrs Dudeney, are you in your bath? Get dressed and come down quick. I am dying to see you." All very boyish and gay and much emphasised.'[21]

The estate was also conveniently located, less than 70 miles from London and close to the Channel ports, and Philip particularly encouraged friends to stay when on their way to or from the continent. Duff Cooper, a contemporary of Philip's at Eton, and his wife Diana spent the first two nights of their honeymoon at Port Lympne before continuing their journey to France. Patrick Shaw Stewart

---

* Mallet had been British Ambassador to Turkey before the war, as well as an adviser to the then Foreign Secretary, Sir Edward Grey.

had been Duff's rival for Diana's affections before he was killed at Cambrai in 1917, and under different circumstances Philip would no doubt have welcomed his lost friend to Lympne. Duff thought the house 'charming – almost ideal for a honeymoon . . . the decorations are ultra modern – might not perhaps do to live with but perfect to stay in. The luxury and comfort are beyond reproach.'[22]

Although much of Philip's attention was taken up by the works at Port Lympne, he did not neglect his political career at Westminster, despite his misgivings about returning to the House of Commons at the end of the war. Upon his return to Parliament after demobilization, he was offered a place on the most junior rung of the government ladder, as a parliamentary private secretary (PPS) to the new Minister for Transport, Eric Geddes. A businessman turned politician, Geddes had been a strong ally of Lloyd George's during the war. Haig congratulated Philip on the appointment, stressing that this would be a vital department in the reconstruction of the post-war economy. The PPS acts as the eyes and ears of his or her minister in Parliament, and is expected to report back on gossip in the Members' Tea Room and Smoking Room, gauge the mood of colleagues at private dinners and pick up the discussions in the voting lobbies. Although Philip had been absent from the House of Commons for most of the war, he knew the senior members of the government from his work for Douglas Haig at GHQ. The role of PPS also suited his natural talents as a networker.

In November 1919 Philip hosted a dinner party for Eric Geddes at his mansion in Park Lane, and also invited Lloyd George along with his private secretary and mistress Frances Stevenson. The Prime Minister's relationship with Frances was an open secret among senior figures in Westminster, but it was only at private dinners like these, away from Downing Street, that the couple could socialize publicly together. Philip could see that Frances was politically influential with the Prime Minister, and the two of them particularly hit it off.

A couple of weeks after the dinner Frances noted in her diary that Philip had 'just dropped in for a chat. He has been very attentive lately, I think probably because he wants to get an undersecretaryship, or something of the kind. Nevertheless he is an amusing person and as clever as a cartload of monkeys.' She also observed that Philip 'is quite good company. Very ambitious though, which he admits. D [Lloyd George] has asked him to come to Paris with us after Xmas purely D says because he has been nice to me! He certainly has and very attentive – almost embarrassing, in fact. He seems to be fabulously rich, but is clever also and can be most amusing. But one of the worst gossips I have ever come across.'[23]

Philip and Lloyd George shared a passion for golf and started playing together, often with Lord Riddell, the Prime Minister's informal media adviser and the managing director of the *News of the World*. At the end of 1919 Philip hosted a New Year's party at Port Lympne, where the guest of honour was the Prime Minister, and in February he invited Frances to join him for a weekend party at his other country estate at Trent Park, on the north-west outskirts of London, while Lloyd George was away on government business. Frances recalled that it was a most 'interesting and enjoyable weekend',[24] with a group of the younger royals adding to the excitement. Philip had got to know the three eldest sons of King George V during the war, particularly Edward, Prince of Wales, whom he had met on the latter's visits to GHQ. Philip's father and grandfather had been friends of King Edward VII, and his family was used to mixing in intimate royal circles. Frances Stevenson played tennis with Princes Henry and Albert,* whom she thought 'great fun'. She had also come with a gift for her host from the Prime Minister. Lloyd George wanted her to ask Philip if he would like to become his parliamentary private secretary. So within a year of

---

* Prince Henry was later the Duke of Gloucester, and Prince Albert became Duke of York and then King George VI.

leaving Douglas Haig's GHQ he would move to the centre of the government's operations at 10 Downing Street.

It was extraordinary that Lloyd George and his circle were so accepting of Philip, a man they had dismissed during the war as a 'delinquent' and Haig's 'spaniel'. He had impressed them as an efficient and effective aide to Sir Douglas, and his great wealth and magnificent homes certainly made him a useful friend to have. But there was more to their relationship than that. During the 1918 election campaign Philip had demonstrated not just his political support for Lloyd George and the coalition, but a shared determination to construct a new world from the old one that had been so shattered by the war. Philip's ostentatious style, so often frowned upon by more conservative members of society, and overwhelmingly displayed at his new estate in Kent, also attracted Lloyd George. In their different ways they were both outsiders to the English establishment: the Welsh non-conformist and the oriental Jew.

The attraction to Philip of working with the Prime Minister was clear enough. In 1919 David Lloyd George was 'the most powerful man in Europe'.[25] In June, when he had returned in triumph from the signing of the Treaty of Versailles, he was greeted by the King and the two men rode through the streets of London in an open carriage. Looking back on this time, the press baron Lord Beaverbrook recalled that 'it is now not possible to realise the immense position of this man Lloyd George'.[26] Philip found that in the post-war world of Westminster he had more in common with the instincts of men like Lloyd George and Winston Churchill to create a new style of politics than with the more diehard Conservatives who resisted change. Philip had even established some credentials of his own as a social reformer, fulfilling the promise he had made during his 1918 re-election campaign in Folkestone to improve the quality of housing available to the people. In one of his first appearances back in the House of Commons after the war he reiterated that he was 'anxious to see a great many more houses built than already exist',[27] and decided to set a personal example to show how this could be done. He created a public utility society to build new homes in Folkestone, and financed the project with a combination of private investment and a government grant. Two acres of land were purchased for the development at the Durlocks, an area above the harbour. In total thirty-three dwellings were created, including cottages and flats, which were considered something of an innovation at the time. Another novel feature for the period, although commonplace today, was Philip's requirement that the tenants should participate in the management of the estate. According to the local newspaper, the accommodation was 'well above the minimum of the Ministry of Health', which then set the government standards for social housing. The cottages in the scheme included a 'living room, kitchen and scullery, three bedrooms and bathroom'.[28]

Philip's housing project was also favourably reviewed by *Architect* magazine, which praised it for being 'immune from the charge of monotony so frequently levelled at state-aided housing schemes'.[29] One element of the design personally requested by Sassoon was the introduction of a Dutch gable, similar to those built by Herbert Baker for Port Lympne. In the new world after the war, he believed people of all classes should benefit from good design.

Working for Lloyd George, Philip turned the role of PPS to the Prime Minister into something much more closely resembling his position as private secretary to Douglas Haig. He described his role as 'political secretary' to the Prime Minister, and this more wide-ranging term is a better description of his office. Rather than being confined to Parliament, as PPSs traditionally are, he accompanied Lloyd George to international conferences and would also make his homes available to the Prime Minister as places he could work from; Port Lympne would often become Lloyd George's general headquarters.

Foreign affairs dominated Philip's first months working for Lloyd George, as international conferences continued to take up a large part of the Prime Minister's time, even after the signing of the Treaty of Versailles. There were still critical issues to be resolved, including the break-up of the former Ottoman Empire territories in the Middle East, and the level of reparations that were to be paid by Germany to the Allies, following Berlin's acceptance in the peace treaty of responsibility 'for causing all the loss and damage to which the Allied and Associated Governments and their nationals have been subjected as a consequence of the war imposed upon them by the aggression of Germany and her allies'.[30]

Philip's first international conference with Lloyd George was at San Remo on the Italian Riviera in April 1920. He benefited from speaking perfect French, then the international language of diplomacy, and also knew France's military leaders and politicians, such as Foch, Briand and Poincaré, from the various meetings he had accompanied Haig to during the war. The San Remo conference reached an agreement on the dissolution of the Ottoman Empire and the new borders for Syria, Iraq, Palestine, Lebanon and Jordan. The new boundaries of Syria placed it under the mandate of France, and thus brought to an end the Arab Kingdom of Syria, created by King Faisal, the prince who had led the great Arab revolt against the Ottomans with T. E. Lawrence. At San Remo it was also concluded that the planned conference with the Germans to discuss their reparation payments, due to be held at Spa in Belgium in early June, would have to be postponed until after the forthcoming elections to the Reichstag. The hard terms of the Treaty of Versailles had led to the collapse of the post-war German government, following a putsch led in Berlin by Wolfgang Kapp and members of the recently disbanded Freikorps, the paramilitary organizations largely formed of ex-servicemen returning from the war.

The question of reparations would cause a great deal of dispute among the Allies and considerable anger in Germany. Lloyd George recalled that 'In 1919 public opinion, both here and in France, was out and out in favour of making Germany pay,'[31] a sentiment that Philip Sassoon had strongly appealed to during his re-election campaign in 1918. There were direct costs which the Allies could lay at Germany's door, like the cost of war pensions, which in Britain alone was estimated at £3 billion. The trench warfare on the Western Front had been fought in France and Belgium, and the two countries wanted compensation to pay for the restoration of these lands. This 'devastated zone' was 400 miles long and approximately 30 miles wide. Britain's equivalent to the devastated zone had been the impact on its shipping and global trade. The direct damage to British shipping from German attacks amounted to £551 million. There would also be a lasting loss of export markets through disrupted lines of supply caused by the war. This led Britain's former customers to look to other markets or start manufacturing products for themselves. By 1927, for example, while worldwide trade would be 120 per cent of the pre-war level, British exports were only 83 per cent of their pre-war height.

For Britain, getting trade going again was the key to recovery. That might mean that imposing a less punitive financial settlement on Germany would pay dividends in the long run if it helped the general recovery of the European economy. France, however, wanted cash now. Heavily in debt, and without the option of continuing to borrow more, it needed German reparations to come through in order to start the restoration of the devastated areas.

At the end of the San Remo conference, the British and French governments decided to meet again before the postponed meeting with the Germans at Spa. A location was required that was convenient for both London and Paris, so Philip Sassoon offered Port Lympne to Lloyd George and it was duly agreed as the venue for a conference which would begin on 14 May 1920. But Port Lympne would become the centre of operations for the Prime Minister even sooner than that. Returning from San Remo, Lloyd George went by train via Paris so that he could meet with the British Ambassador Lord Derby, the former War Secretary. The two men held a lengthy conversation on a chilly railway station platform, and as a result the Prime Minister caught a severe cold. The Cabinet Secretary,

Maurice Hankey, believed that he was 'really suffering from nervous exhaustion . . . this is about the fourth time I have known him beaten to a frazzle'.[32] Lloyd George was advised by his doctors to spend the three weeks before the Anglo-French summit recuperating and Philip Sassoon was happy to put Port Lympne at his disposal.

For most of the next month, Philip's estate would be the home of the ultimate executive power in the British Empire. He took personal charge of the arrangements at Port Lympne for Lloyd George, and Frances Stevenson was also installed there. Lloyd George was a seducer of colleagues and opponents, and transporting them to Lympne suited him perfectly in this regard. There, away from the real world, in Philip Sassoon's temple of luxury and informality, the Prime Minister could set to his work. Senior ministers and officials would shuttle back and forth from London on the Charing Cross train and find one of Philip's drivers waiting for them with a car at Sandling Junction to complete the journey to Lympne. Philip's French chefs catered to the Prime Minister's every need. This form of country-house government was certainly appealing; for Lloyd George it was partly reminiscent of life in Paris during the peace negotiations, and it was a model for how Winston Churchill would later use Chartwell and Chequers.

Philip Sassoon often joked that it was so quiet at Lympne you could hear the dogs barking in Beauvais.* The growing crisis in Ireland, where there had been a severe escalation in republican nationalist violence, would however shatter that peace. General Nevil Macready, who was commanding the British military forces on the island, came to Port Lympne to ask for Lloyd George's support for more resources to be put at his disposal – in particular, five more battalions and a large number of motorized armoured vehicles. This prompted the Prime Minister to write to Winston

---

* The town of Beauvais in Picardy, northern France, is about 170 miles from Lympne.

Churchill, now Secretary of State for War, asking him to 'help' and to come down to Lympne to discuss the situation. He added, 'We cannot leave things as they are. De Valera* has practically challenged the British Empire and unless he is put down the Empire will look silly. I know how difficult it is to spare men and material, but this seems to me to be the urgent problem for us.'[33] The cabinet in London under Andrew Bonar Law's chairmanship was due to consider Macready's request the following day, and Lloyd George also wrote to Bonar Law stressing that 'we are bound to give him [Macready] all the support in our powers . . . in order to crush rebellion. Unless we do any measure of home rule is in my judgement bound to fail. I beg you not to allow delays to occur.'[34]

Bonar Law wrote back to Lloyd George to confirm the cabinet's acceptance of Macready's request for supplies, and also to convey the suggestion that 'a special body of ex-servicemen here in England should be enlisted on special terms, as gendarmerie to be used in Ireland'.[35] This 'gendarmerie' would become the 'Black and Tans', who would make themselves notorious for their reprisal actions following attacks from the IRA. So while Philip Sassoon's Port Lympne was to play a part in settling the peace of Europe, its exquisite rooms and gardens also formed the unlikely location where the Prime Minister decided to support the escalation of the war in Ireland.

Maurice Hankey arrived at Lympne for the Anglo-French conference early on 14 May and found Lloyd George and Churchill in

---

* Éamon de Valera MP, Irish republican leader and President of Dáil Éireann. The Dáil Éireann (Assembly of Ireland) comprised the 76 Sinn Féin MPs who had been elected at the United Kingdom general election of 1918 but refused to their seats in the House of Commons. At its first meeting at the Mansion House in Dublin on 21 January 1919, the Dáil ratified the declaration of independence for Ireland that had been proclaimed at the Easter Rising in 1916. The Dáil was regarded as a revolutionary assembly by the British, who declared it illegal in September 1919, but to Sinn Féin it represented the legitimacy of their self-proclaimed government for Ireland.

the drawing room concluding their discussions on Ireland from the evening before. He noted that, even though it was before lunch, 'Winston was drinking and he looked very bloated and bleary.' And he thought that, despite Philip's care, the Prime Minister was 'looking old and ill, but he had just had 24 hours of Winston which is enough to make anyone look old and ill'.[36] Hankey could see the appeal of Port Lympne for Lloyd George, noting 'Everything [is] of the very best and most expensive. The best beds, linen, baths, food, wine, cigars, Rolls Royce motor cars etc.' There was a pool and fountain in the hall; a swimming bath and more fountains in the terrace.'[37] He also acknowledged that it was 'a very lovely place . . . If I were convalescent and comfortably settled here, nothing would induce me to budge,'[38] but Hankey had a 'disagreeable feeling' that Lloyd George was getting 'too fond of high living and luxury . . . though I am bound to say that though he likes it, he doesn't miss it if he has not got it'.[39]

At 7.30 on the evening before the conference opened, the French Prime Minister Alexandre Millerand arrived at Folkestone harbour on board a specially chartered ship, the *Ailette*, accompanied by his Finance Minister, Frédéric François-Marsal, and the British Ambassador to France, Lord Derby. Philip Sassoon led the receiving party with the Chancellor of the Exchequer, Austen Chamberlain, and the Mayor of Folkestone, Reginald Wood, who wore a button-hole of red, white and blue. *The Times* reported that 'outside the gates of the harbour station a great concourse of Folkestone towns-people had assembled, and as the party drove in motor cars through the gaily decorated streets of the town hearty cheers were raised'.[40] The procession of Philip's Rolls-Royces continued along the coast road, through Hythe and on to Lympne, where the Prime Minister was waiting at the front door of the house to receive them.

The French tricolore and the Union flag flew one above the other from the same flagpole at Port Lympne. Lord Riddell had carefully coordinated the media coverage of the event. The cinema newsreel cameras recorded Lloyd George welcoming Millerand, and press photographers took informal shots of the leaders walking and talking together. Police officers also patrolled the grounds of the estate to make sure the leaders were not disturbed.

Philip invited his sister Sybil to join him at Lympne to help host the conference, which had more of the character of a weekend house party than an international summit between two of the world's leading powers. In the official photographs distributed to the media, Philip and Sybil both looked notably younger and sleeker than their guests. They were the social centre of the conference, making sure everyone was at their ease and switching effortlessly between French and English as they moved from statesman to statesman. Lord Riddell remembered that Philip was 'a restless creature' during the conference and that he 'flitted about from room to room, and person to person, like a bee in search of honey'.[41]

The newspapers expressed some surprise at the informal setting for such an important conference, the like of which had not been seen in England before. The *Daily Mail* commented that 'Gossip is naturally rife as the reason for thus settling the affairs of Europe, or trying to, at an overcrowded house party'.[42] The same newspaper also ran a cartoon, with reference to the previous international conference, proclaiming 'Come to Hythe, the San Remo of England'. Riddell thought Philip's entertainments for his guests were on a 'lavish scale', and that he had 'made hospitality an art'. Port Lympne mansion was reserved for the leading members of the delegations, so they could meet and socialize in the seclusion of the house and grounds. Senior officials such as Maurice Hankey stayed at Louis Mallet's house, Bellevue, a seven-minute walk away on the edge of the estate. For the other officials and policy experts, Philip had taken over the Imperial Hotel on the seafront at Hythe. His fleet of Rolls-Royces was on standby throughout the conference to take the delegates between the locations or wherever else they needed to go. For Lloyd George and Millerand, this included being driven by Philip himself to visit Canterbury Cathedral on the Sunday of the conference.

Riddell recorded in his diary that it was 'the most informal conference I have seen. Most of the talking was done by Millerand and LG when walking about the grounds.'[43] Philip Tilden was also there in the background, though the conference had disturbed his ongoing works on the estate. He remembered the Prime Minister 'pacing up and down on the south terrace at Port Lympne, enveloped in his perennial cloak. His gleaming hair was blown about by the wind from the sea. His walk was solid and full of assurance, now halting for a moment, now proceeding, as he pressed his points home in conversation with his companion.'[44]

The main conference sessions were to have taken place in a large tent erected on one of the lawns below the south terrace of the house, looking out to the sea. Unfortunately, poor weather made this impractical and the drawing room of the mansion was used for this purpose instead. Josep Sert's great allegorical mural of the defeat of Germany in the war sat oppressively above the leaders as they gathered for these discussions. The three triumphant Indian elephants painted on to the chimney breast weren't to everyone's taste – the Cabinet Secretary Maurice Hankey remembered the 'bizarre oriental decorations all over the walls'.[45] Philip Tilden's octagonal library became the communications nerve centre, with a telephone hotline to the French Foreign Ministry on the Quai d'Orsay in Paris.

Dinner was held in the blue dining room where Lloyd George, Millerand and Chamberlain were all in 'good form' and enjoying each other's company. Hankey was next to the French Finance Minister Marsal, whom he thought a 'very poor conversationalist and [who] seemed ill at ease. He had an uncomfortable trick of rubbing his hands together all the time as though he was washing them.' Their policy discussions were no more successful, with Hankey feeling that Marsal 'was so woolly that even with the aid of an interpreter I could not make out what he meant to say'.[46] After dinner, Sybil had the novel idea of screening some Charlie Chaplin films to lighten the mood after a full day of discussions, and this proved to be a great success. At night, the *Daily Mail* reported from the conference, 'the electric light plant makes the house glitter like a liner at sea'.[47]

The conference discussions were dominated by the issues of Allied debt and German reparations. Lloyd George rejected France's some-what naked proposal not to agree a fair division of the reparations from Germany between the Allies, but rather to prioritize projects that needed urgent financial support wherever they occurred – most of which would have been in France. Instead Lloyd George got Millerand to agree that experts from their respective countries would prepare 'immediately for examination . . . a minimum total for the German debt which will be acceptable by the Allies and at the same time compatible to Germany's capacity to pay'.[48]

Millerand's opponents in France were aghast at this conclusion. Hardliners like the former President Raymond Poincaré, who was also Chairman of the Reparations Commission,* believed he had been overwhelmed by Lloyd George's persuasion and Philip Sassoon's hospitality. Poincaré resigned from the commission, believing that there should be no consideration of what the Germans thought they could pay; they should be told to pay up or accept that the Allies would otherwise seize what was owed to them by force.

If the Lympne conference had been a diplomatic success for Lloyd George, it had been a personal triumph for Philip Sassoon. As he and Philip Kerr, Lloyd George's private secretary, saw off the French delegation at Folkestone harbour, Sassoon was pursued by a *Daily Mail* journalist asking him to comment on the conference and his weekend guests. Philip replied that he had 'not a word' to say and added, with false modesty, 'Don't say a word about myself or my house and I will bless you for evermore.' But the papers were intrigued by this wealthy young man with his 'boyish smile' whom they saw 'walking briskly' up and down Folkestone harbour in the company of Europe's leading statesmen.

---

* The Reparations Commission had been established by the Treaty of Versailles to oversee the German payments.

Personal profiles of Philip were carried in *The Times* and the *Daily Mail*, both owned by his old friend Lord Northcliffe. These detailed the rise of the Sassoon family in India, and the *Mail* noted of Philip that 'The ancient and inscrutable east speaks in the dark aquiline features of this wealthy young aspirant to political honours; but his manner is that of the average good-natured young university-bred Englishman; full of sport, master of more than sufficient means to free him from care.'

The paper added that 'In truth' Philip was 'a very pleasant young man. Aladdin and his wonderful lamp are an inevitable comparison. Philip Sassoon has only to wish for a thing and lo! It comes.'[49] He was 'in the running for cabinet honours and a probable peerage. Some have said he will be "Lord Lympne" but the more knowing declare that he will do nothing that loses him the representation of Hythe, a constituency which he admires and looks upon as his own . . . He intends say the village sages to become Prime Minister and they talk of Disraeli.'

For Philip Sassoon the combination of hosting the Lympne conference and his new position working for Lloyd George had projected him into the centre of political affairs. Just as when he had worked for Douglas Haig during the war, he used his position to develop and activate his network of contacts in Britain and France. This was also useful to Lloyd George given the precarious political situation in Paris, and the seriousness of the issues the government was looking to resolve with the French. The great French leader in the last year of the war, Georges Clemenceau, had retired at the beginning of 1920 and his successor Alexandre Millerand was not thought to have a secure grip on power.

A couple of weeks after the conference, Philip Sassoon caught up again with the British Ambassador in France, Lord Derby, renewing the working relationship they had enjoyed when he was Secretary of State for War. Derby thought that Millerand was polit-ically 'shaky and will probably have to go after Spa . . . we could save him if we wished to by wiping off one third of the French debt as a contribution to the devastated areas. If Millerand goes Poincaré will probably come in.'[50]

Philip relayed the message to Lloyd George, but it could well have been a ploy by the French. They knew that Lloyd George understood that his best chance of getting the right agreement on reparations from Germany would be with Millerand, and not Poincaré. Millerand was effectively saying, Give me what I need at Spa, or face the consequences. If Derby thought Millerand was 'shaky', things were even worse for the French President, Paul Deschanel. He had only been in post since February but had suffered a complete breakdown at the end of May. Things had come to a head when, dressed only in a nightshirt, he had fallen out of a large window of the presidential train near Montargis, about 70 miles south of Paris. Derby gave Philip the whole story to pass on to Lloyd George. Deschanel 'had to be doped going down to Montargis and it was while he was being sick out of the window that he fainted and fell out'. Found wandering by the tracks, he was taken to the nearest level-crossing keeper's cottage where he apparently remonstrated with his hosts: 'Can't you see I'm a gentleman as I've got clean feet?' Philip told Lloyd George that 'All Paris revues are full of skits on him.' According to Lord Derby, Clemenceau thought it was 'not surprising that [Deschanel] had come off his head as he had after all very little brains to lose, adding "The world is divided into two clans – those who don't get what they want and those who do and find it is not what they expected."'

The Spa conference had been rescheduled for 21 June, but was moved again, to 5 July, so Lloyd George and Millerand decided to use that time to meet again at Boulogne to finalize their negotiating position with the Germans. Maurice Hankey noted that 'originally this conference [at Boulogne] was to have been a private conversation between LG and Millerand and it was intended to keep it very secret. It leaked out however and all the other nations got suspicious and announced their intention of coming.' So Lloyd George and Millerand decided to 'dodge the others and have their private conversation' at Port Lympne the day before.[51]

Despite the last-minute arrangement of these conversations at Lympne a great civic reception welcomed Millerand and the rest of the French delegation, including the supreme commander of the Allied forces on the Western Front, Marshal Foch. Philip Sassoon greeted Millerand, with the Mayor of Folkestone, accompanied once again by cheering crowds in the harbour. The excitement in the town about the conference was clear and the *Folkestone Herald* proclaimed that 'Once again Folkestone, Hythe and Lympne have received a world-wide advertisement through the meeting at Sir Philip Sassoon's house.'[52] Philip personally drove the French Prime Minister through the town's streets decorated with red, white and blue bunting, along the coast to the Hythe Golf Club,* where Lloyd George was waiting to receive them having just played a round with Philip's cousin David Gubbay. A tea was given for them by Alderman John Jeal, a former Mayor of Hythe and ex-captain of the club, who tragically collapsed and died later that evening.

Lord Riddell, who was again on duty to coordinate the media briefings about the meetings, recalled that 'Lympne presented a curious spectacle. In one room the chiefs conferring, in another the minor officials in conference, in another the secretariat at work, in a fourth a sumptuous tea, cakes, fruit, and every delicacy. In the kitchen the French chefs getting ready a magnificent dinner . . . everything done regardless of expense.' The details of the talks were supposed to be secret, but Riddell complained that 'as usual everything [was] wrapped up in mystery – hush being the order of the day. But as usual everything leaked out.'[53] The press were told that the conversations 'were more satisfactory than those of the first conference at Lympne',[54] but little was actually accomplished. The

---

* The original Hythe course was badly damaged during the Second World War and subsequently closed. Folkestone Golf Club later took over the majority of the land and Henry Cotton designed a new eighteen-hole course. This became Sene Valley Golf Club in 1965–6.

British and French agreed a tougher public line on Germany, calling for it to meet its obligations both on reparations and on disarmament, but there would be no more progress before the conference at Spa.

Philip Sassoon travelled with Lloyd George to the Spa conference, the first meeting of the Allied and German leaders since Versailles. The choice of Spa was telling; it had not only been occupied by Germany throughout the war, but was also the base for its military headquarters in 1918. The war had ended not with Germany's invasion but instead its capitulation. British and French forces would subsequently occupy German territory west of the Rhine after the armistice, but, for Philip Sassoon, Spa was a first chance to look into the eyes of their old enemy, and on land they had taken in Belgium, a country whose liberation had been the precursor to Britain entering the war.

When the British delegation arrived by steamer in Ostend, Philip observed on the quayside a line of Belgian girl guides 'carrying flags and cardboard laurel wreaths, and as our good ship drew alongside 37 men in 37 bowlers played 37 versions of the German national anthem (by mistake from force of habit!)'.[55] They motored along the coast to Zeebrugge, where they saw the 'really terrific coastal defences the Bosch had put up', and spent the night at a hotel in Brussels which, Philip noted, was 'supposed to have a bad reputation – so we were disappointed to find that we were all to dine in a private room and have no chance of inspecting the Promised Land'. Lloyd George was particularly put out and asked Sassoon to 'try to fix up something downstairs', but this was not possible. In the morning they continued their journey to Spa and en route visited the Waterloo battlefield near Brussels. Standing on the Lion's Mound monument they surveyed the site below them where the forces of Wellington and Napoleon had fought just over a century before. With the Great War so recent, and forever burnt into his memory, Philip thought it 'all very Lilliputian after the battlefields of the Somme and Flanders – and makes one realise that the warfare of Waterloo was nearer akin to Thermopylae than to Neuve Chapelle'.

The Spa conference was held in the Villa Fraineuse, where Wilhelm II of Germany had spent his last night as Kaiser before his abdication and flight to Holland. The British delegation stayed at the Hôtel Britannique which had been the General Headquarters of the German military command in the last months of the war. To complete the spirit of the storming of the Bastille, Philip inspected the 'Imperial dugout' where the Kaiser had sheltered during British bombardments of the nearby front. It was 'many feet below the surface of the earth and encased in 2 metre thick concrete and hung with chintz'.

Philip was moved to write a long letter from Spa to Lady Desborough, the mother of his lost friends Julian and Billy Grenfell. 'There is something very dramatic about the conference,' he told her. 'The Germans coming on their knees to this place which was the GHQ when their hopes were highest. This hotel was the office of Ludendorff and Hindenburg and it was in the room next to mine that the Kaiser abdicated.'

The conference itself was bad tempered and not a success. Emotions were still very raw, illustrated by an attack on a German journalist by a Belgian cavalry officer on the terrace of a café late one evening. The German delegation turned up in full military uniform, and Hugo Stinnes, the owner of much of the coal industry in the Ruhr Valley as well as a member of the Reichstag and a newspaper proprietor, lectured the Allies on the arrogant tone they had adopted in victory. The Germans stated that there should be a plan for the 'partaking of the Allied governments' in the improvement of economic and financial conditions in Germany, and that any agreement on reparations could be based 'only' on the country's ability to pay.[56]

This led to an ultimatum from the British and French that unless the deliveries of coal they had been due to receive as part of the first £1,000,000,000 of the reparations package were made up within seventy-two hours they would occupy the Ruhr and take it for themselves. The ultimatum was later withdrawn, but the crisis remained unresolved. The Germans offered a schedule for deliveries of coal for the next six months, but nothing more was agreed other than a resolution on how the reparations should be divided among the Allies.*

Philip closely observed the German delegation fighting their corner. At the end of the war, he had said that he wanted to see the Germans punished, but when face to face with the representatives of his former enemy, he seemed moved more by pity than by anger. He thought their Chancellor, Konstantin Fehrenbach, 'a very respectable old man [who] looks like the father of the prodigal son', whereas the Defence Minister, Otto Gessler, was 'very truculent'. The Germans asserted that they needed to maintain military and financial strength within their country to keep radical forces on the extreme right and left at bay. Philip had little sympathy for this argument, thinking it was just a 'bluff' and that against a 'master hand like LG they are like very poor amateurs'.[57]

Philip Sassoon's position in Lloyd George's inner circle made him a more significant member of the British government than that given by his official rank as a parliamentary private secretary. A consequence of this was Philip's developing friendship with Winston Churchill, one that would be sustained through all of the crises and challenges of the inter-war years. During the war Philip had been very critical of what he believed were Churchill's attempts to undermine the generals. Winston for his part then saw Philip as little more than an agent of Douglas Haig. Yet, in different circumstances after the war, they could appreciate the considerable number of tastes and interests they had in common. Their social circles had already overlapped for a number of years.

---

* The proportions were 52 per cent to France, 22 to Britain, 10 to Italy, 8 to Belgium and the rest to the other Allies. Belgium, in view of its sufferings during the German occupation, was to have priority up to the amount of £100,000,000.

Churchill had been a guest before the war at some of Lady Desborough's gatherings at Taplow Court, and occasionally at dinners given by Philip's parents. Winston and Philip shared a great enthusiasm for playing polo and for flying; in the last year of the war, so frequent were Churchill's trips by air to General Headquarters at Montreuil that he was given his own quarters there. Sassoon's friend the artist William Orpen had painted Churchill's portrait in 1916, and Philip would also encourage Winston's own developing passion for oil painting. He lent him some of the works from his collection, such as John Singer Sargent's painting of the ruins of Arras Cathedral, for Winston to copy. Churchill painted more than twenty pictures while staying at Philip's estates at Port Lympne and Trent Park. The no-expense-spared high living of Philip Sassoon's world was certainly to Churchill's taste. Churchill also considered himself something of an aesthete and greatly admired the works of Oscar Wilde, the person he once confessed he would most like to meet in the afterlife.[58] Churchill had a socially liberal attitude to homosexuality: his long-serving private secretary, Edward Marsh, was gay and as Prime Minister in the 1950s he privately supported relaxing the laws in Britain against homosexual relationships.[59]

Winston and Clementine Churchill joined Philip Sassoon at Port Lympne for a weekend party at the beginning of August 1920, with other mutual friends like Lady Desborough and Hugh Cecil. Philip would base himself at Lympne from the start of the parliamentary summer recess into September and encourage a constant stream of friends to come and join him there. International affairs cast their shadow over this gathering at Lympne, as the war that had broken out between Soviet Russia and the newly independent Polish state was threatening to reach a dangerous intensity. The war had started in the Ukraine, and the Red Army now clearly had the upper hand and was set to cross the Vistula and take Warsaw. At the second conference at Lympne in June, Lloyd George had suggested to Millerand that they should enter into diplomatic relations with Russia, which both governments had avoided since the Bolshevik Revolution in 1917. The French refused, principally because they wanted the Bolsheviks to agree to honour part of the debt owed to France by the former tsarist regime, which of course the Bolsheviks had no intention of doing. Yet this war could be the first real test of the Treaty of Versailles. The new state of Poland, a country regarded as the 'lynch-pin' to peace in the east,* had been created at Versailles, and if its territory was seized by Russia, without any reaction from the other world powers, could any of the other international borders created by the treaty be considered secure?

In the tranquillity of Lympne Winston Churchill sought distraction from the crisis by painting the view across Romney Marsh to the sea. As he worked, surrounded by paints and canvases, he was disturbed by another of Philip Sassoon's guests walking in the gardens, Marthe Bibesco, a Romanian princess and then a popular society and literary figure in London and Paris. She remembered that 'He was completely absorbed . . . painting that great expanse of marshland . . . Four sketches were drying in the sun, propped up against the feet of the easel. He was now slashing the fifth canvas, almost throwing the paint on; he was sighing, almost out of breath with the effort of expressing his feelings.'[60]

Churchill waved at Marthe to join him and, as she sat and watched him work, he asked her, 'Is it the first of August today?' She confirmed that it was, adding, 'You saved the fleet on that day,' referring to his decision as First Lord of the Admiralty in 1914 to put the fleet to sea in readiness for the war that came a few days later. Churchill's face instantly lit up: 'Yes, I was haunted by the thought that we would find ourselves strangled by the German submarines in the Channel. That night, six years ago, I ordered the

---

* The term 'lynch-pin' was used by Winston Churchill in his history of the First World War, *The World Crisis*, vol. IV: *The Aftermath 1918–1922* (1929).

fleet to sail under cover of darkness – eighteen miles of warships, all lights out. Next morning they were safe in the deep waters of the North Sea. If I hadn't done it the war might have taken a different course.'[61]

A few days later, on 4 August, Churchill was in the Cabinet Room at 10 Downing Street to hear Lloyd George tell the Russian representatives Lev Kamenev and Leonid Krassin, 'If the Soviet armies advanced further into Poland, a rupture with the Allies would be inevitable.' It was six years to the day since Britain had entered the Great War and Churchill recalled that, as at Lympne the previous weekend, his 'mind's eye roamed back over the six years of carnage and horror through which we had struggled. Was there never to be an end? Was even the most absolute victory to afford no basis for just and lasting peace? . . . Again it was August 4th, and this time we were impotent. Public opinion in England and France was prostrate. All forms of military intervention were impossible. There was nothing left but words and gestures.'[62]

Lloyd George was determined to make the most of the words and gestures at their disposal, and called an urgent conference with the French Premier Millerand, to agree a joint position. Philip Sassoon once again put Port Lympne at the Prime Minister's disposal, and the statesmen met there on 8 and 9 August. The issue at the meeting was neatly summed up by Philip as 'peace or war with Russia'. The British delegation consisted of military and diplomatic advisers, including Sir Henry Wilson, and from the Foreign Office Robert Vansittart and Ralph Wigram. The French team again included Marshal Foch, and also the 'brilliant but luxurious' Aristide Briand,[63] a former and future Prime Minister. In the absence of his sister Sybil, Philip asked Lady Desborough to assist in hosting the conference, and with Arthur Balfour also part of the British delegation it was reminiscent of some of the old gatherings at Taplow Court. Port Lympne was now hosting its third major international conference in twelve weeks, yet the enthusiasm of the local community had not dissipated in any way. Once again large crowds turned out at Folkestone to cheer the arrival of the French delegation.

At the conference itself, Lord Riddell recalled, Lloyd George was 'in wonderful spirits. When I arrived he was crossing the lawn to speak to Millerand. He came over to me and shielding his mouth with his hands as if he were telling me a secret, whispered, "We have decided to go to Warsaw for another conference. Will you come with us?" In the evening there was a cinema show at the villa, which produced roars of laughter from the PM, Millerand and Foch.'[64] There was to be no conference in Warsaw and the Russians also rejected the idea of a conference in London, opting instead for peace talks with Poland in Minsk. The British and French agreed at Lympne that they would not declare a 'final breach' with Russia until after these talks at Minsk, and they would intervene only if the Polish government was determined to resist the offer made by the Russians, or if an agreement reached between the two countries contravened the terms of the Treaty of Versailles. Foch was greatly concerned about the situation and told Lord Riddell at Lympne, 'It is serious. If Poland fails, Germany and Russia will combine. You will have a worse position than in 1914.' To which Riddell replied, 'Are you willing to say that publicly?' Foch answered, 'Yes, it is a serious position which the world should understand. Events are on the march.'[65] The crisis was averted by a surprise and decisive military victory for the Poles in the Battle of Warsaw. This brought to an end any chance of further Russian military operations in Poland, and a peace treaty was successfully concluded. Nevertheless, it had forced the Allies to consider how far they were prepared to go to uphold the terms of the Treaty of Versailles. They would soon face similar challenges elsewhere in Europe.

For Philip Sassoon, 1920 was the year when his position in high politics came together with his life in high society. He would become a prominent public figure as a consequence both of working for the Prime Minister and of partying with the Prince

of Wales. Philip's friends in politics, regardless of their own background, were bons vivants and challengers of the more socially
conservative orthodoxy. The Prince also represented a new generation of the royal family, conscious of his duty to serve, yet longing
to live the independent life open to other wealthy young men. He
was also the first member of the royal family to grow up in the
new media world of cinema newsreel, picture newspapers and
radio, which had helped to establish him as the greatest celebrity
of his day.

Even the way men like Philip Sassoon and the Prince of Wales
dressed marked a break from the orthodoxies of the pre-war
world. From 1919, the Prince favoured the Dutch tailor Frederick
Scholte at 7 Savile Row. Philip's tailor was the Swede Per Anderson,
from Anderson & Sheppard, then at number 13, who regarded
Scholte as his mentor. Scholte revolutionized men's fashion and
brought Savile Row into the twentieth century through the creation of what became known as the 'London cut' or 'English drape'.
They were 'civil' tailors who designed suit coats using softer fabrics
which draped naturally from the shoulders, as opposed to the
traditional tailors who made coats based on the principles of
military tailoring, with high shoulders and stiff fronts, designed
to make you stand to attention. The idea that a suit should be
comfortable would not have been a primary consideration to a
Victorian gentleman.

The Prince recalled in his memoir, *A Family Album*, 'My father
and his generation, except when in the country, remained imprisoned in frock-coats and boiled shirts. All my life [until adulthood],
I had been fretting against those constrictions of dress which
reflected my family's world of rigid social convention. It was my
impulse, whenever I found myself alone, to remove my coat, rip
off my tie, loosen my collar, and roll up my sleeves – a gesture
aspiring not merely to comfort but, in a more symbolic sense, to
freedom.'[66]

Some men may have thought it scandalous that a Dutchman

and a Swede should be allowed to rewrite the rules of Savile Row tailoring. Their new look required a certain panache on the part of the wearer, and the Prince was the perfect model to popularize it.

Philip Sassoon was often seen out with the Prince enjoying London's new nightclub scene, particularly at the Embassy Club in Mayfair, joining the dancing to Bert Ambrose's famous band. They were also enthusiastic sportsmen, sharing passions for polo and golf; Philip and Winston Churchill both played polo with the Prince in his team at Roehampton. Philip also introduced Edward to his friend the great French boxer Georges Carpentier after they'd watched him knock out the British fighter Joe Beckett at London's Olympia Arena in 1919. After their initial meeting in Paris during the war Philip had extended an open invitation for Georges to stay at Park Lane whenever he was in London. Carpentier thought his hospitality was 'very English . . . a butler was always there ready to serve me with lunch or dinner, and a valet was attached to me for my personal service'. Georges had a reputation as something of a playboy and, as well as joining Philip at the Embassy Club, would be seen at Ma Meyrick's notorious club, The 43, in Gerrard Street.* Philip organized a dinner for the Prince with Georges and Winston Churchill, where Georges found Winston 'a very gay companion and full of amusing anecdotes'. He also remembered that 'It was the first time I had seen the Prince of Wales since he had shaken hands with me at the Beckett match. He was the only guest not in evening dress and that, it seemed, was because he was leaving immediately after dinner for the provinces to play polo.'[67]

The Prince had a childlike desire for indulgence and devotion from his friends,[68] something that Philip was generally able to supply in abundance. He showered the Prince with gifts: an ancient

---

* The 43 was the model for 'Ma Mayfield's' club The Old Hundredth in Evelyn Waugh's *Brideshead Revisited*.

snuffbox was sent as a Christmas present and some 'marvellous' diamond and onyx cufflinks for his birthday which caused Edward to reflect 'how that man spoils me'.[69]

Philip was both discreet and open minded regarding his friends' affairs of the heart. With Lloyd George, he had welcomed Frances Stevenson as if she was his wife rather than his mistress, and provided the opportunity for them to be together in the company of other friends, something that would have been impossible at official events. Philip would similarly support the Prince's complicated private life. In 1918 Edward had embarked on an affair with Freda Dudley Ward, the wife of the Liberal MP William Dudley Ward. The Dudley Wards had married when she was only nineteen, and he was sixteen years her senior. By the end of the year, and only five years since their marriage, they were effectively living separate lives. William Dudley Ward made no great objection to the affair, providing it was discreetly conducted, which it was. Freda had no public profile and very few people outside the Prince's circle would have known about the relationship. Some who did thought Freda was just an ornament for the Prince, but others, including Lord Riddell, who would meet her at one of Philip's parties, thought she was 'a clever, perceptive sort of woman, always on the move, singing, dancing, smoking, talking or playing tennis'.[70]

In March 1920, the Prince was sent on a tour of Australia and New Zealand which would last seven months, and his letter to Philip Sassoon on the eve of his departure underlined the closeness of their friendship. 'No tongue can ever say', the Prince wrote, '<u>how</u> grateful I am to you or how much I have enjoyed the marvellous weekends at Trent or your delightful "intime" dinner parties at 25 Park Lane.'[71] Then, from on board HMS *Renown** between San Diego and Honolulu, the Prince wrote again to Philip, stating, 'let

---

* HMS *Renown* was a Royal Navy battlecruiser, the fastest of its kind in the world when it was launched in 1916, and was frequently used to convey royal passengers and senior politicians.

me again repeat what you already know that I can never even begin to thank you for all your great kindnesses to me or say how grateful I am.' He added, 'I've just finished *Susan Lenox*,* a marvellous book and the only novel I've ever read that really makes one think; of course it's terribly sordid the whole way through, tho' it's meant to be!!'[72]

Philip promised to look after Freda Dudley Ward while the Prince was away; he dined with her the evening Edward departed and gave her the use of a cottage on the estate at Lympne. Edward wrote to Philip during the tour, telling him that Freda thought Lympne was 'too marvellous for words'.[73] He added later, 'How I'm longing to see that marvellous place and now so <u>famous</u> for the conferences held there.'[74] Philip was so trusted by Freda that she shared with him the secret code language for her correspondence with the Prince. This 'puzzled' Edward when he received a cable from Philip in which he used the code, causing him to reflect to Freda that 'you must have worked it out for him from our little unicode book'.[75]

The Prince wrote to Philip from Government House in Melbourne on 11 June, complaining that he was feeling depressed and overworked, that he had hardly seen a pretty woman in Australia, and that they were 'a ham faced crowd and make me tired'.[76] There had also been growing pressures from home. The King had deplored the publication of a photograph of the Prince of Wales and his cousin Lord Louis Mountbatten, who was accompanying him on the tour, in a swimming pool, telling Edward, 'You might as well be photographed naked; no doubt it would please the public.'[77] It had also been suggested by Buckingham Palace that the Prince should extend his tour and visit India on his way home from

---

* David Graham Philips' *Susan Lenox (Her Fall and Rise)* (1912) was a story told from a woman's perspective of her struggle to free herself from a life of prostitution. In 1931 it was adapted into a film starring Greta Garbo and Clark Gable. Such was the notoriety of the novel that the film was initially banned from release in the UK.

Australia, something that Edward was set against. He prevailed on Philip to use his position working for Lloyd George to try to get the tour postponed. Putting aside his general feelings of gratitude to Sassoon, he told him bluntly, 'I'm rather disappointed that you haven't been able to tell me what the little P.M. thinks about it all <u>now</u> and whether he's still trying to get the trip postponed till next year!! God! How I pray that it will be . . . Of course I needn't say how secret my views of the matter must be and <u>please burn</u> all these as it would never do for India to think I didn't want to go there!! And I do want to go but not this year.'[78]

The Prime Minister, who also had great affection for the Prince, raised the matter with King George, and on 22 July Philip cabled Edward in Hobart to tell him that he thought they were going to be able to fix things for the India tour to be postponed. Edward wrote to Freda with the good news, and also said that he was 'so intrigued to know how he's done it and how the PM is tackling His Majesty'. Within a week the Prince received the confirmation, telling Freda, 'Good old Philip; I bet I owe more to him than to anyone else for this postponement and how grateful I am to him.'[79] He also wrote to Philip on 3 August from Brisbane, exclaiming, 'Christ! What a relief the King's cable was to me and it's now all blue sky . . . what a great big debt I owe you my dear Philip.'[80]

Upon Edward's return the *Weekly Dispatch* newspaper reported that he and 'Sir Philip Sassoon, the amiable young baronet . . . have been constantly together since the Prince's homecoming.' It noted that 'they have a common interest in their love of sport and dancing'.[81] However, Philip's attention and indulgence could at times become too much for the Prince. He told Freda, 'We must try to somewhat loosen the ropes with which he has bound himself so tightly to us . . . I like a little of Philip very much but not too much.'[82] Yet on Boxing Day the Prince wrote to Philip from Sandringham, 'What a nice quiet Xmas you must have spent at Lympne with Hannah and David [Gubbay]; it's quiet here but oh! how boring and even irksome at times. Thank you again ever so much for all your lovely Xmas presents . . . I don't deserve this spoiling <u>at all</u>.' He also arranged that they should speak over the telephone at seven o'clock the following evening.[83]

In February 1921 Philip resumed his role as an intermediary between his political circle and the Prince, with a dinner for Edward at Park Lane with Lloyd George and Churchill among the guests. A few weeks later a number from this party would be together again with Philip at Trent Park, for what Frances Stevenson called a 'perfect Sunday. The Prince of Wales came with Mrs Dudley Ward. We spoke of [Lytton] Strachey's life of Queen Victoria, which had just been published and the Prince said, "That must be the book the King was talking about this morning. He was very angry and got quite vehement over it." The Prince of Wales had not seen the book so we showed it to him and he presently was discovered in roars of laughter over the description of the Queen and John Brown.'[84]

4

• CENTRE STAGE •

Sir Philip Sassoon is a member for Hythe
He is opulent, generous, swarthy, and lithe,
Obsequious, modest, informal and jejune . . .
The houses he inhabits are costly but chaste
But Sir Philip Sassoon is unerring in taste . . .
Sir Philip Sassoon and his sires, it appears,
Have settled in England for several years
Where their friendly invasion impartially brings
To our Cabinet credit, and cash to our Kings . . .
Sir Philip was always a double event,
A Baghdadi banker, a yeoman of Kent
But now in four parts he's appearing at once,
As a lackey, a landlord, diplomatist, dunce.

C. K. Scott-Moncrieff,
'A Servile Statesman'[1]

Philip Sassoon's New Year party to see in 1921 was a great gathering
of the Port Lympne set. Lloyd George was there, along with Winston
Churchill and Lord Riddell. There was singing around the piano

of popular songs. Lord Riddell recalled that 'LG sang cockles and mussels and one or two other songs with great effect. He would have made a fortune on the music hall stage. Winston sat watching him with the keenest admiration and the eye of an artist.' Churchill, an enthusiastic fan of music hall himself and particularly of the comic star Dan Leno, was not to be outdone, and Riddell noted that he 'regaled us by reciting numerous music hall songs and other verses which he had remembered with little effort, although he had not heard many of them for years'.[2]

Despite the gaiety of the party, the talk was all about the impending government reshuffle that Lloyd George was planning. The Chancellor of the Exchequer, Austen Chamberlain, was vulnerable. He had lost prestige with his failed attempt to bring in a tax on wartime profiteers. Philip had previously warned Lloyd George that disgruntlement with Chamberlain was 'the only subject discussed in the [voting] lobbies'.[3] Coalition MPs, he went on, complained that Austen 'never sees any of the big people in the city and . . . he is solely influenced by the Fabian Oxford undergraduates who are in the Treasury'.[4] Winston Churchill wanted the job, to emulate the highest office achieved by his father, Lord Randolph Churchill, and over a picnic lunch on the Lympne escarpment on New Year's Day he pressed his case on Lloyd George. The Prime Minister had other ideas and asked him to become Secretary of State for the Colonies. Churchill agreed to think about it, and returned to see the Prime Minister at Lympne on 7 January to accept.*

Philip Sassoon also had hopes for ministerial office, and when he left Lloyd George at Lympne for a winter holiday in Switzerland he gave him a letter setting out his case:

---

* Churchill would have to wait a further six weeks before taking up the position.

> You know that my interest in politics is much more than a passing
> fancy or the desire to enjoy such privileges as a seat in the House
> may give. My interest indeed is very deep and it is for this reason
> alone that I am presuming to write to ask that when changes are
> made in the government you will give me a friendly thought and
> if possible obtain for me the chance to show in some minor office
> that in course of time I may become worthy of bigger things . . .
> I have for many months been in close relation with you and these
> months in themselves I feel are an experience of quite inestimable
> value. I shall always be at your service at all times and you know
> how grateful I am to you for everything you have done for me.[5]

Philip had also asked Winston to put in a favourable word, and he
duly wrote to Lloyd George: 'I promised to mention Philip Sassoon
to you. You can judge better than anyone else. Personally I should
like to see him given an opportunity and I think he would do well.'[6]
The call from the Prime Minister did not come; for Lloyd George
such a resourceful parliamentary private secretary would have been
of far more use to him than letting Philip toil away as a junior
minister in a government department. Lloyd George had a high
regard for Philip's abilities, and Frances Stevenson would also recom-
mend him for promotion, but he would remain as the Prime
Minister's PPS for the remainder of the Parliament. This proximity
to Lloyd George had made him a political figure, but his rapid rise
to prominence had received a mixed reception from Westminster
insiders. The press baron Lord Beaverbrook thought Philip was a
'brilliant gossip and a habitual flatterer, indifferent to the status of
his subjects'. He recalled that once at a party at his house, 'in the
midst of a large company I was asked, "Where is Philip?" I replied:
"Flattering somebody somewhere." From behind a pillar nearby
Sassoon cried: "Not you, Max."'[7] The young MP Oswald Mosley*

---

* Mosley sat as a Conservative from 1918 to 1924, before joining the Labour
  Party and later founding the British Union of Fascists.

considered that Sassoon at the time was 'rather a joke among the younger generation for serving Lloyd George as private secretary in peace directly after he had served during the war in the same capacity to General Haig at G.H.Q. in France. [He] was in many ways a most engaging and obliging fellow whose amiable idiosyncrasy was to entertain the great, the bright and the fashionable.'[8] Given Philip's Jewish faith there was also some anti-Semitic rhetoric aimed in his direction as a result of his position in the government. In an anonymous article penned for *Blackwood's Edinburgh Magazine* following Lord Reading's appointment as Viceroy of India it was poisonously written, 'The real danger [of Reading's appointment] is that another Jew is added to the many Jews who are taking part in the government of our empire. Behind all of Mr [Lloyd] George's actions is the hidden hand of Sir Philip Sassoon.'[9] The casual deployment of what might be regarded as derogatory anti-Semitic language was not uncommon in English society. For instance, Virginia Woolf once referred to Philip Sassoon in a letter to her sister Vanessa Bell as an 'underbred Whitechapel Jew.'*[10] Anti-Jewish feeling was also a sentiment that Oswald Mosley would seek to exploit when he launched his British Union of Fascists in the 1930s.

Although Philip missed out on a ministerial appointment from Lloyd George, the Prime Minister did have another gift for him. During an Easter party Philip hosted at Port Lympne, he accompanied Lloyd George to the Sunday service at the Folkestone Baptist Church,† and in the car on the way back the Prime Minister asked him to become a trustee of the National Gallery. The newspapers remarked that, at thirty-two, Philip was 'probably the youngest man' ever to have been appointed,[11] but it suited him perfectly and it was a position he would retain for the rest of his life.

---

* The comment was made in a letter written by Woolf after meeting Philip at a lunch hosted by Sybil Colefax.
† The Folkestone Baptist Church was then located in Rendezvous Street; the building is currently a bar.

On the Easter Monday, Lloyd George completed a reshuffle he had started planning at New Year, but which had taken on greater significance following the resignation from the government of the Conservative leader Andrew Bonar Law eleven days previously. Bonar Law gave ill health as the reason and immediately left the country to recuperate in France. Austen Chamberlain replaced him as leader of the party, and moved from being Chancellor of the Exchequer to Leader of the House of Commons. Sir Robert Horne, the President of the Board of Trade, was invited down to Lympne where Lloyd George asked him to become Chancellor of the Exchequer. Lord Riddell, another guest at Lympne, remembered that Horne 'gave evident signs of elation – not surprising perhaps. Few men have had such a rapid rise.'*[12]

Bonar Law's departure was a heavy blow to the coalition. Philip Sassoon had been warned just before Christmas by Lord Derby that the support of Conservative MPs for the coalition was based on their 'extreme loyalty' to Bonar Law; Derby added that he could not foresee a problem 'as long as Lloyd George and Bonar Law stick together'.[13] From Lloyd George's perspective, the timing of Bonar Law's resignation was also bad. The government was facing growing pressure at home and in its international affairs. The immediate post-war economic boom had turned to bust. The unemployment rate went from 2.7 per cent in May 1920 to 23.4 per cent a year later.[14] There had been serious industrial disputes with the coal and railway trade unions which had threatened to bring the country to a standstill, and the still-rising national debt was creating mounting political pressure to cut government spending. In Ireland, the war of independence against British rule had worsened through 1920 and then reached a crisis point, following the shooting on 21 November 1920 of innocent spectators at Croke Park in Dublin by the Royal Irish Constabulary, in reprisal for the murder of British intelligence agents by the IRA earlier that day. Internationally,

---

* Horne had been elected to Parliament only in 1918.

Germany's refusal or inability to comply with the payments schedule for the reparations demanded by the Allies at the Spa conference raised the prospect of military intervention by the French to seize the assets they believed they were owed.

In April 1921, Philip Sassoon would host a further conference for Lloyd George at Port Lympne to discuss the reparations crisis with the new French Prime Minister, Aristide Briand. The leaders had previously met in February to discuss the same issue at a weekend party hosted by Lloyd George at Chequers.* Philip met Briand upon his arrival at the Dover Admiralty Pier after a 'not bad but very wet' crossing on the steamship *Invicta*.[15] As he had with Millerand the previous year, Philip personally drove Briand to Lympne where Lloyd George was waiting to receive him. Poor weather persisted throughout the conference, with the leaders occasionally making it out on to the terrace wrapped up in their hats and raincoats, to continue their discussions in huddled groups. Fortunately, Lloyd George and Briand got on well, and it was the perfect combination for positive talks. The Prime Minister thought his French counterpart 'genial, humorous, tolerant, broad-minded and warm-hearted', and as a Welshman he considered that, as a Breton, Briand had 'the imagination and suppleness of mind of a purely Celtic race'.[16]

As with the other conferences at Port Lympne, Lord Riddell remembered that 'the entertainment provided by Sassoon for his guests was magnificent – French cooking of the highest order, and plenty of it. A breakfast of several courses, succeeded by a lunch with more courses then a gorgeous tea and in the evening a wonderful dinner.' As they gathered for dinner in the lapis-lazuli dining room with its gold-winged chairs, Riddell asked the French Prime Minister whether he enjoyed being in office for the second time even more than the first. Briand replied, 'The first. I am blasé

---

* Lord Lee of Fareham had presented Chequers to the nation for the use of the Prime Minister of the day in January that year.

now. And then, look at the state of affairs.'[17] Over dinner Lloyd George and Briand discussed the merits of speaking to an open-air audience rather than an invited one in a closed hall. Briand had a preference for open-air speaking, something which Lloyd George said he had never practised, stating, 'It is easier to address 50,000 citizens than 200 trained men.' After dinner, Philip organized a screening of Charlie Chaplin's war film *Shoulder Arms*, which was received with raucous laughter as they watched Chaplin's tramp escape from the trenches disguised as a tree to capture the Kaiser in Berlin.

The serious business of the conference fell down once again on the question of just how tough the Allies were prepared to be towards Germany. The French were anxious to enter the Ruhr at all costs and seize the reparations they were owed. Lloyd George thought invading the Ruhr would be a breach of the peace treaties and something the British could not support. The Reparations Commission recommended at the end of the month that the German government's total payment to the Allies should be 12.5 billion US dollars, the equivalent of 750 billion German marks at 1921 prices, with an immediate deposit of $250 million. The total repayment was one that would be impossible for the Germans to meet. They appealed to the Americans for mediation, but to no avail. The German Chancellor, Konstantin Fehrenbach, decided that his only course was to accept the Allied demands and then resign. To meet the immediate payment, the German government borrowed money from domestic banks and sold large quantities of paper marks on the international currency markets. The result was a collapse in the value of the mark and the arrival of the great German hyperinflation.

The hope of Lloyd George and Philip Sassoon that in the congenial atmosphere of Lympne the French might be persuaded to take a more conciliatory approach to reparations had ultimately come to nothing. In their walks in the gardens of Port Lympne, the leaders of Britain and France had instead sown the seed of future unrest. As A. J. P. Taylor noted in his famous work *The Origins of the Second World War*, 'Reparations counted as a symbol.

They created resentment, suspicion, and international hostility. More than anything else, they cleared the way for the second world war.'[18]

Ireland had also been much on the Prime Minister's mind during the Lympne conference. The one advantage for Lloyd George of Bonar Law's resignation from the government on 17 March was that it gave him greater freedom to explore the possibility of ending the conflict in Ireland, by means of a negotiated settlement with the nationalist leaders. Beaverbrook would later recall that Bonar Law 'was against the whole Irish negotiations – no good in his opinion would come of them'.[19] On 22 April, the day before Lloyd George had welcomed Briand to Port Lympne, Lord Derby,* acting as a special emissary of the government, arrived in Dublin incognito as a 'Mr Edwards' to meet secretly with Éamon de Valera, the President of the Dáil Éireann. The purpose of Derby's mission was to assess the terms by which de Valera and the members of the Dáil would be prepared to enter into peace talks with the British government. Lord Derby returned to England the following morning and came straight down to Port Lympne, where, according to Riddell, 'he had a long talk with LG privately – both very mysterious. LG said he wondered what D wanted to see him about. Of course he knew very well that Derby was going to tell him about what had happened in connection with D's visit to Ireland.'[20] Word had got out about Derby's undercover mission, which was reported by the Dublin correspondent of *The Times* the next day, 24 April. It was also alleged to general amusement that this large and well-known political personality had tried to disguise himself by wearing a pair of horn-rimmed spectacles.[21]

On 12 May, after a lengthy afternoon cabinet discussion, the government rejected the proposal that they should offer a truce and talks to the Irish republican leadership. Yet without talks they

---

* Lord Derby had completed his mission as British Ambassador to France and returned to political life in the UK on 21 November 1920.

faced the prospect of having to enforce martial law across the whole of southern Ireland; and Lloyd George had warned the cabinet that martial law 'practically means no law',[22] in terms of the rights of the citizens who lived there.

Ireland had been a massively contentious issue in the House of Commons before the war. The Liberals, and particularly Lloyd George and Churchill, had been pushing for a home rule settlement, against fierce resistance from the Unionist Conservatives. As a Unionist MP, Philip Sassoon had been no different. He had used his maiden speech in the House of Commons in 1912 to speak against financial powers being given to a new nationalist-dominated assembly in southern Ireland. In March 1914, with Irish home rule imminent, and in response to the Curragh Mutiny,* Philip had reportedly offered 'in the event of hostilities breaking out in Ulster, to provide at his own expense a vessel to take the [Folkestone] battalion [of the national reserve] over to Ireland',[23] to support the Unionists. Yet, after the slaughter of the First World War, he now supported Irish home rule so long as it was not forced on Unionists in the north of Ireland. Philip also had friends with rebel sympathies, notably William Orpen, a Dubliner who had allowed plates of his work to be published in the nationalist *Irish Review*.[24]

Early in 1921 Philip had given a dinner at Park Lane which was attended by another Irish painter, John Lavery, and his wife Hazel. Hazel, whose portrait by her husband as the female personification of Ireland would for many years adorn the banknotes of the independent Irish state, saw the invitation as an opportunity to speak for Ireland. Later, in 1922, she would drive the Irish leader Michael Collins to Port Lympne for a secret meeting with Winston Churchill.[25]

---

* On 20 March 1914, British officers at the Curragh camp in County Kildare, the main British army base in Ireland, threatened to resign rather than be forced to take action against a rebellion by the Ulster Volunteer Force (UVF) against Irish home rule.

Philip Sassoon suggested to Lloyd George that he should host a dinner for the cabinet at his Park Lane mansion where the Prime Minister could try to bring them all closer together on Ireland, as well as on the other difficulties the government was facing. Max Beaverbrook remembered that the Prime Minister used such gatherings at Philip's house to exert 'his charms. That was the object of the Sassoon parties.'[26] Number 25 Park Lane was one of the finest private houses in London, and this informal and luxurious setting provided an excellent opportunity for Lloyd George to persuade his colleagues. It had already proved its value to the Prime Minister as the venue for a successful and 'surreptitious'[27] meeting with the leaders of the miners' unions, Robert Smillie and Frank Hodges, the previous autumn. The readiness of labour leaders to meet with Lloyd George at Park Lane did not go unnoticed. Sassoon's old friend Lord Esher told the Prince of Wales that 'they just revel in luxury and lap up Philip's port and old brandy like puppies'.[28]

As with Port Lympne, there was a touch of mystery and fantasy in Philip's presentation of the house. Paintings by his friend John Singer Sargent, including his portraits of Philip's mother and sister, lined the great marble staircase up to a series of reception rooms. There the late-Victorian mansion enclosed an interior of eighteenth-century French furniture and imported wood panelling of the same period. Many of the paintings, especially those by Reynolds, Zoffany and Gainsborough, showed intimate scenes of life in Georgian England, and there were also Flemish tapestries on the walls in the large drawing room, including one depicting Winston Churchill's ancestor John Churchill, the first Duke of Marlborough. If this collection celebrated a time prior to the creation of the house and the arrival of the Sassoons in England, it was infused with touches of oriental flair representing their eastern heritage, such as Chinese porcelain and ancient Persian carpets from Isfahan.

Josep Sert had been called on by Philip to work at Park Lane, where he decorated a ballroom large enough for four hundred guests, with the walls covered by a 20-foot-high mural called

Caravans of the East. This showed a fantastic scene of camels, elephants and exotic figures including turbaned rajahs winding their way through palm trees, oases and deserts to an ideal city on a distant hill. The mural was painted in Sert's preferred monochrome style, using blue and silver, and the ceiling was transformed into a vortex of dense cloud using mirrors to heighten the sense of infinity.[29] Philip Tilden also made his mark on the mansion by creating a recessed gallery that overlooked the great staircase. He recalled that oyster-coloured glass had been used on its walls, 'darkening shade by shade to brilliant black'. In front of this glass stood porphyry vases containing deep-red roses, creating 'an effect which is not without uniqueness'.[30]

On 30 May the cabinet gathered for a pivotal meeting at Philip Sassoon's temple of eighteenth-century elegance and oriental fantasy. Six days before, elections had been held for the new parliaments for northern and southern Ireland, created by the 1920 Government of Ireland Act. These parliaments had been given home rule powers within the United Kingdom, with certain matters like defence, foreign affairs, international trade and currency reserved for Westminster. In the north, forty of the fifty-two seats were won by Unionists; and in the south, 124 Sinn Féin candidates were returned unopposed, with just four Unionists elected to represent the university seats held by Trinity College Dublin. As Sinn Féin refused to recognize the new southern Ireland parliament, it was effectively defunct as an institution. The day after the elections, the IRA seized the Customs House in Dublin and set it on fire, in the process fighting a pitched battle with the British armed forces. The attack ended in failure for the IRA, but was reminiscent of the occupation of the General Post Office building during the Easter Rising of 1916. The events of these two days made all the more pressing the British cabinet's consideration of the vital question of negotiation or martial law in southern Ireland.

Over dinner Lloyd George set out his case for a negotiated

settlement on Ireland, and the evening may well have been pivotal in changing the attitudes of the cabinet. Shortly afterwards there occurred what Churchill described as the most 'complete and sudden . . . reversal of policy' in the modern history of the British government. 'In May the whole power of the State and the influence of the Coalition were used to "hunt down the murder gang": in June the goal was a lasting reconciliation with the Irish people.'[31]

So whereas it was at Port Lympne a year before that Lloyd George had given his support for the military crackdown in Ireland against the nationalists, it was around Philip Sassoon's dining table in Park Lane that he sought to persuade his colleagues that now was the time for peace. Lloyd George called on the South African leader, Jan Smuts, to act as an unofficial mediator with the Irish. Smuts had the distinction of having been a rebel leader against the British in the Boer War, and then a member of the imperial war cabinet during the First World War. He told the cabinet bluntly that the situation in Ireland was 'an unmeasured calamity; it is in negation of all the principles of Government which we have professed as the basis of Empire, and it must more and more tend to poison both our Empire relations and our foreign relations'.[32] Lloyd George also sought the intervention of King George, and in his speech on 23 June to open the new parliament for northern Ireland in Belfast, His Majesty appealed to 'all Irishmen to pause, to stretch out the hand of forbearance and conciliation, to forgive and forget'.[33]

The following day Lloyd George told the cabinet that de Valera was prepared to discuss a settlement even if that did not guarantee independence. They invited de Valera and the new Prime Minister of Northern Ireland, John Craig,* to come to London for talks. A ceasefire in southern Ireland was agreed as a precursor to their

---

* Craig had been appointed the first Prime Minister of Northern Ireland on 7 June 1921, following the victory of the Ulster Unionists in the elections to the new Northern Ireland parliament on 24 May 1921.

discussions, which started at noon on 11 July. De Valera met with Lloyd George on 13 July; the Prime Minister had fortified himself at dinner with Philip Sassoon and Frances Stevenson at Park Lane the evening before. He had told the cabinet the previous week that he was 'not looking forward to meeting [the Irish leaders] with any satisfaction'. Smuts suggested to him that the thing to do was to let them 'talk themselves to death'. At this suggestion Lloyd George, his memory refreshed by the recent conference with the French at Lympne, remarked, 'Like we used to do with Briand until he was faint and prostrate.'[34] The talks over the shape and agenda for a conference on the future of Ireland continued over the summer, with de Valera announcing on 14 September the names of the Sinn Féin representatives who would take part, and the conference would begin in Downing Street on 11 October.

Philip Sassoon spent August at Lympne, where Lloyd George came to stay for a week. The Prime Minister invited Bonar Law to join them, and made an unsuccessful attempt to seduce him into returning to the government. In September Philip went to stay in Paris and was there when Charlie Chaplin arrived to promote his new film, *The Kid*. Chaplin had just been to London, the first time he had returned to the city of his childhood since he established his worldwide fame as a movie star. The writer and social chronicler of the inter-war years Beverley Nichols remembered that Chaplin was 'received in England like a conquering hero . . . wherever he went he was accompanied by vast crowds and troops of police'.[35]

Philip was desperate to meet Chaplin in Paris, and called on his friend the boxer Georges Carpentier, who knew Chaplin, having met him in New York that July, when Carpentier had fought Jack Dempsey for the heavyweight championship of the world at Jersey City. According to Beverley Nichols, this clash had 'roused the populations of England and America to frenzies of hysteria. People who would normally never have glanced at the result of a boxing match found themselves suddenly caught up in the general excitement, largely, one suspects, because of the considerable physical attractions of the young Frenchman.'[36] The fight was the first ever to take a million dollars at the gate, and although Dempsey won in the fourth round, Carpentier made a big impression on the American audience.

Carpentier knew that Chaplin was staying at the Hôtel Claridge in Paris and agreed to arrange an introduction for Philip there. Chaplin was taking a bath in his suite when Carpentier was announced and, after a warm greeting, he whispered that he had a friend waiting in the sitting room whom he wanted the actor to meet, an Englishman who was 'très important en Angleterre'. So Chaplin, dressed in a bathrobe, met Philip, and thought him 'a picturesque personality, handsome and exotic looking'. That evening they dined together with Sybil, and they invited Chaplin to come and stay at Port Lympne before his return to America; he duly accepted.

Philip was just a few months older than Chaplin, and their childhood homes in London had been less than 3 miles apart. Yet the chasm between the privilege of Sassoon's world and the extreme poverty of Charlie's early life in Kennington could not have been greater. When Philip entered Parliament in 1912, Chaplin was a young touring actor with Fred Karno's company, but became within a few years one of the highest-paid and most celebrated movie actors in the world. Cinema was generally seen as the popular entertainment of the masses, yet Philip was enough of an admirer of Charlie's work to show his films at parties at Port Lympne. Chaplin's championing of the underdog, cocking a snook at the rich and powerful, had also won the spontaneous admiration of men like David Lloyd George; in comparison the Conservative politician Neville Chamberlain did not watch a Chaplin film until 1936.

Philip arranged an appropriate welcome for Chaplin for his stay at Port Lympne. A garden party was in full swing at the mansion when the guests were directed to look to the east to see the approach of the Compagnie des Messageries Aériennes flight from Paris. A Rolls-Royce whisked Chaplin the short distance from the airfield to the house, which he recalled was 'quite thrilling and I felt that I made a very effective entrance to the party'.[37] Chaplin thought Lympne was like 'something out of the Arabian nights', and that the house was furnished with 'flamboyant daring'.[38] Philip had taken the same care in preparing for Chaplin's visit to Lympne as he had for the prime ministers of France. In Paris, Chaplin had mentioned to Philip that he didn't like the dull colours in his hotel room and would have preferred something 'yellow and gold'. When he was shown his room at Lympne, he found that Philip had had it decorated with pastel curtains in those colours. There was also a 'lighted chafing dish to keep soup warm in case I was hungry during the night and in the morning two stalwart butlers wheeled into the room a veritable cafeteria with a choice of American cereals, fish cutlets, and bacon and eggs'. The chefs at Port Lympne were also instructed to make some of Chaplin's favourite food, including treacle pudding and American wheat cakes. The treacle pudding became something of a running theme of Chaplin's tour of England when promoting *The Kid*. He had remarked to a journalist that he was coming back to the land of his childhood and to savour again stewed eels and treacle pudding. As a result he was given the pudding at the Ritz, at a special dinner in his honour at the Garrick Club and at a dinner hosted for him by H. G. Wells. They presumably all thought he wasn't serious about the stewed eels.

Chaplin thought Philip was the 'perfect host. I get English food and treatment. I have a perfect rest, with no duties, and entertainment as I desire it. A day and a half that are most pleasant.'[39] Sybil remembered that Chaplin was 'so funny at the table that the servants couldn't go on serving, because they were laughing so much'.[40]

The visit was the start of a lifelong friendship, and Chaplin also regarded their encounter as the moment that marked his entry into the upper echelons of English society – recognition that, like Sassoon, he craved even though he didn't need it. Chaplin later recalled that 'an introduction to the social set usually comes about by one incident . . . My entrée into the English set came unexpectedly, while I was taking a bath.'[41] For good measure Philip also personally introduced Chaplin to his Savile Row tailors, Anderson & Sheppard.

There was one public duty that Chaplin performed during his stay at Port Lympne, and that was to accompany Philip and Sybil to the schoolhouse in Sandgate for the unveiling of a war memorial. He then joined Philip on a visit to the Star and Garter Hospital, which cared for disabled soldiers, at Enbrook House in the same village. 'Sheer tragedy was here,' Chaplin recalled,

> young men suffering from spinal wounds, some of them with legs withered, some suffering from shell shock. No hope for them, yet they smiled. There was one whose hands were all twisted and he was painting signs with a brush held between his teeth. I looked at the signs. They were mottoes: 'Never say die,' 'Are we downhearted?' A superman . . . We are received politely and with smiles from the crippled lads who are crippled in flesh only. Their spirit is boisterous. I feel a puny atom as they shout 'Good luck to you, Charlie.' I can't talk. There is nothing for me to say.[42]

This confrontation with the brutality and bravery of warfare made a strong impression on both men. Philip was conscious of the criticism that as a senior staff officer he had never seen action during the war. Chaplin had been working in America, and while his films had done much to boost the morale of the soldiers at the front, there were people at the time who thought he should have volunteered for military service.

Chaplin's visit had added to Sassoon's reputation as the

pre-eminent host in England. Who else could bring the Prince of Wales, the Prime Minister and Charlie Chaplin to their table? Philip had arranged a lunch at the Ritz for Chaplin and Lloyd George, but Charlie was delayed and the Prime Minister unable to wait for him, so the opportunity was missed. On 11 October, though, at the prompting of the socialite actress Diana Cooper, Philip hosted a dinner at Park Lane for Lloyd George to meet the great Russian opera singer Feodor Chaliapin, with the writer Maurice Baring acting as interpreter. It was a 'successful party', according to Duff Cooper,[43] who was also among the guests, and an amusing distraction from the great political drama that had started in Downing Street that morning.

After months of negotiations, the formal talks between the British government and the leaders of Sinn Féin, for a peace settlement for Ireland, had begun. At 11 a.m. Philip was in the Cabinet Room at Number 10 with Lloyd George and the Prince of Wales when the Irish delegates for the peace talks arrived, led by Arthur Griffith and Michael Collins. They were asked to wait in Philip's office until the Prince had left. As Edward walked out into Downing Street, he was cheered by the large crowd outside that had assembled to offer the same welcome to the representatives of Sinn Féin.

The British government was represented at the talks by probably the greatest line-up of negotiators it had ever assembled, including Lloyd George, Churchill and Lord Birkenhead. Their goal was to bring a lasting peace to the island of Ireland by establishing a political settlement that would be acceptable to all sides. While the formal talks would take place around the cabinet table, it was in the margins that Lloyd George, with Sassoon's help, would seek to charm and persuade both the Irish nationalists who wanted home rule, and the Unionists like Andrew Bonar Law and John Craig who were against any settlement that would force the people of Ulster to accept the jurisdiction of a Dublin government.

After a month of talks Lloyd George was facing the prospect of the collapse both of the negotiations and of his own coalition government. His offer was that Ireland should be given dominion status, within the Empire and under the King, but still be effectively a free nation, like Canada. Sinn Féin wanted an agreement to cover the whole of the island of Ireland, and the Unionists wanted the six counties of Ulster, which were covered by the Northern Ireland parliament, to stay within the United Kingdom. Lloyd George feared that the impending Conservative Party conference in Liverpool would pass a hostile motion critical of the negotiations and the position taken by the coalition government, and forceful in its defence of the Unionist communities in Ulster. The Prime Minister was not the only person concerned about the Conservative conference. The party leader Austen Chamberlain, who was also a member of the British negotiating team, wrote to his sister Hilda on 13 November in tones reminiscent of Tennyson's 'Charge of the Light Brigade':

> Sinn Fein and Ulster in front, the Diehards on my back and the National Union* meeting on Thursday in Liverpool, the stronghold of Orange Toryism ... And I might add to my catalogue of troubles Bonar Law, an Ulsterman by descent and in spirit, a very ambitious man now astonished at ... his own complete recovery and itching to be back in politics where he is disposed to think that the first place might and ought to be his. I am fighting for my political life.[44]

Lloyd George was never one to let a good crisis go to waste and he knew that the Irish negotiators would rather deal with him

---

* The National Union of Conservative and Unionist Associations represented the grassroots Conservative Party members and local organizations. The National Union organized the annual conference, which was the forerunner of modern party conferences.

than with a Conservative prime minister like Bonar Law. He wanted to use the looming Liverpool conference to work out what the Irish negotiators would be prepared to accept. Philip suggested that Lloyd George should use 25 Park Lane for a crucial private meeting with Arthur Griffith on 12 November, to sound him out on a deal for Irish home rule, excluding Ulster.

Once again, Lloyd George was entrusting the hosting of one of the most important meetings of his premiership to Philip Sassoon. Park Lane had proven to be a successful venue earlier in the year, when Lloyd George persuaded the cabinet over dinner to back a negotiated peace for Ireland. Now, over lunch, he pressed his case to Arthur Griffith. The Ulster Unionist leader John Craig was refusing to discuss the idea of the six counties in the north coming under an all-Ireland parliament, and the Conservatives would never support it. Griffith agreed to Lloyd George's proposal that if at the Conservative conference mention was made of a boundary commission to prepare a border of separation between the north and south, Sinn Féin would not publicly criticize this. Lloyd George saw this as an important concession and a hint that an agreement covering only the southern counties might be acceptable to Sinn Féin. The Deputy Cabinet Secretary Tom Jones made a note of this agreement, which was later used to devastating effect by Lloyd George in the final hours of negotiations for the Irish Treaty. When Griffith tried to dispute separate terms for Ulster, Lloyd George waved Jones's meeting note in the air, the existence of which had been unknown to Collins and the other Irish delegates, and asserted that it was a principle he had already agreed to.

Following his meeting with Griffith, Lloyd George left London with Frances Stevenson to join Philip Sassoon at Trent Park for the weekend, and also to execute the second part of the Prime Minister's plan. Over Sunday lunch Lloyd George sounded out Sir Robert Horne, the Unionist MP and Chancellor of the Exchequer, on the nature of his agreement with Griffith at Park Lane. In the evening, they were joined by Andrew Bonar Law and the press baron Lord Beaverbrook. In sending for Bonar Law, even though he was not a member of the government, Lloyd George was underlining his singular importance on this issue of Ulster: Bonar Law's support, rather than that of Austen Chamberlain, the party leader, would be vital in getting the Conservatives to back any deal. Frances Stevenson recorded their meeting in her diary, based on the Prime Minister's recollection of it:

> D told me, that he had a talk with BL before dinner privately, and D told him quite plainly that he was not playing the game. Bonar flared up and said that if that was the case he would refuse to discuss the matter any further and for a short time there was real unpleasantness. However D eventually talked him round and they sat up discussing till nearly one o'clock. D thinks that Bonar has agreed not to oppose his new proposals for the All Ireland settlement.[45]

Bonar Law was sufficiently reassured that he did not even attend the Liverpool conference. There would be one motion tabled to be debated at the conference by the 'Diehard' Conservative MP, Colonel Gretton, which was critical of the Irish talks. The Prime Minister wanted Philip to go to Liverpool and keep him up to date at Downing Street on the progress of this debate. At lunchtime on 17 November Philip telephoned Thomas Jones at Number 10 to report that things were not going well: 'no one had spoken for the Government; the chairman, Shirley Benn,* had been deplorably weak and . . . one hour had been taken up by Lord Farnham,† an Irish peer and strong opponent of the treaty, and a deputation of loyalists from Ireland'. Lloyd George received the news as he paced

---

* Sir Arthur Shirley Benn, MP for Plymouth Drake and chairman of the National Unionist Association.
† Arthur Maxwell, eleventh Baron Farnham, a leading Unionist.

up and down in the Cabinet Room, but he was not fearful that a change of heart from Bonar Law could lead to a substantial Conservative rebellion, saying, 'If you are going to lead a revolt you must go all out for it.'[46]

The Conservative delegates at the conference didn't like the coalition, and they were concerned that the rights of the Unionists in Ulster should be protected. But they equally didn't want to see civil war in Ireland, or for the Conservative Party to split on the issue. After senior figures like Derby, Birkenhead and Austen Chamberlain urged the conference to support the continuation of the negotiations with the Irish, Gretton's motion was overwhelmingly defeated by 1,730 votes to 70. Philip arrived back at Downing Street with news of the successful outcome of the debate. As he entered the Cabinet Room Lloyd George grabbed him by the shoulder and marched him up and down the length of the room, pretending to play 'See the Conquering Hero Comes' on a cornet. Philip relished passing on his anecdotes of some of the more chaotic proceedings of the conference, which were lapped up by Lloyd George. These included Lord Chaplin making his speech from a seated position on doctor's orders, but unfortunately sitting on his notes and having to dig out a quotation from them, and Lord Derby telling the conference that he was 'not going to be stampeded by anyone until he had made up his mind what was right or wrong'.[47]

The negotiations over the future of Ireland would continue until 6 December, but it was at those crucial private meetings at Park Lane and Trent Park that the settlement started to take shape. The final treaty, which was signed in the Cabinet Room at 10 Downing Street, created an independent Irish Free State within the Commonwealth, but, as the Unionists had demanded, excluded the six counties of Northern Ireland from the agreement. It was proposed, though, that a commission should look to redraw the boundaries of Ulster along sectarian lines. There was no concession, however, to the creation of a Republic of Ireland, an issue which would cause a massive rift amongst the nationalist politicians in Dublin, and lead to civil war. The significance of this was well understood by Michael Collins, who prophetically told Lord Birkenhead that evening that he believed he may have signed his own death warrant.

The day after the treaty signing, Philip Sassoon hosted a dinner at Park Lane for the Prime Minister to mark the fifth anniversary of his period in office. The mood was triumphant because at last there was the chance of peace in Ireland, and a settlement on home rule that had eluded even William Gladstone. The dinner was attended by a good number of the cabinet and faithful friends, but the former Unionist leader from Ulster, Sir Edward Carson, refused to join them in protest at the treaty, which in his view ended for ever the union between Great Britain and Ireland. Carson also believed that Lloyd George had 'betrayed Ulster' and he would have 'nothing to do with him'.[48] Before the First World War Philip Sassoon, then a new MP, had hosted a great Unionist luncheon at Park Lane, which Carson attended, to mark the Hyde Park rally for Ulster. Times had changed, and for Philip, as for many other Conservative MPs, an agreement that would avoid further warfare and preserve the independence of Unionist Ulster was a deal worth fighting for.

Philip's position within Westminster politics had changed as well; although still a Conservative, he was now firmly in Lloyd George's camp and saw him, rather than Austen Chamberlain, as his political chief. He also wanted the Prime Minister to seek a new mandate from the people to continue the Liberal–Conservative coalition for a further five years. In his role as PPS to the Prime Minister, he prepared a memorandum for Lloyd George on 'the advisability of an early election' for him to 'cast [his] eye over' during the Christmas recess.[49] Philip also sent a copy to Winston Churchill. The note is full of sharp political insight that shows how closely Philip monitored events and opinion at Westminster on Lloyd George's behalf. It also underlines how he saw his own personal political position as totally bound to the Prime Minister, even though they were technically in different political parties.

Philip warned Lloyd George that although the government had 'acquired great prestige at home and abroad' from the Irish settlement, the 'business community and the tax payer generally are looking forward to the Geddes committee* to point the way to substantial national economies. While these hopes are at present an advantage it is improbable that they can be fully realised in the current year, and their disappointment will tell heavily against the Government if the general election be put off until after the budget.'

Philip told the Prime Minister, in terms that any political strategist would recognize today, that 'In both industrial and agricultural areas the ordinary household is in receipt of very much smaller wages than a year ago and this is the crux of the whole position. They are disgruntled, worried and going without things they enjoyed quite recently. They are glad to see the Irish question settled, but they are more acutely aware to the needs of their daily life and the comfort of their own homes.'

He also called on Lloyd George to ignore the factionalism of coalition politics at Westminster and to reach out to the people in asking for their support to form a new government:

In a real sense our Party system has not readjusted itself to the after war conditions of the people or the country. The ordinary voter who had no political intrusions during the war (other than from Labour and Socialists) is bewildered by our forensic battles between Liberals of different brands and now between Unionists of different opinions. While these matters interest intensely the few (relatively)

---

* In August 1921 Sir Eric Geddes had been appointed chairman of the Committee on National Expenditure. The purpose of the committee was to make recommendations to the Chancellor of the Exchequer on savings that could be made to public spending. The committee's reports were submitted to the cabinet in December 1921 and January 1922, before publication the following month.

old time caucus men in the towns and villages they convey little to
the great mass (men and women) of the new electorate.

Philip's message to Lloyd George was clear: there had to be an early
election with the coalition standing again as a united force, under
his leadership, and focused on the economy. The first chance to
discuss this would come in the South of France early in the new
year, in the margins of the Cannes conference. The conference had
been called by Lloyd George and the French Premier, Briand, to
discuss the continuing problem of German reparations and the
agenda for a meeting of all the European powers at Genoa in the
spring. The Genoa conference was Lloyd George's great initiative
and he wanted it to be the first summit since Versailles to bring
together Britain, France and Italy with Germany and Soviet Russia.

Philip travelled out to join Lloyd George in Cannes, where the
Prime Minister was staying at the Villa Valetta, which had been put
at his disposal by the financier Sir Albert Stern. They assembled at
the villa to discuss the prospects for an early election with the
Chancellor Robert Horne, Winston Churchill, the War Secretary
Sir Laming Worthington-Evans and Max Beaverbrook.

As with all elections, consideration was given to both the timing
and the resources needed to fight the campaign. The Lloyd George
fund had been swollen from the selling of political honours, and
the Conservatives had been aggrieved to learn that their treasurer,
Horace Farquhar, had transferred large sums of money from the
party's account into the Prime Minister's campaign pot. As the
group discussed this issue, Sir Albert Stern's parrot, perched in a
cage near by, suddenly called out – 'so plainly that it was difficult
to believe the voice was that of a bird'[50] – 'Stop it, Horace!' Then,
in response to Sir Laming's impassioned speech in favour of an
early election, the parrot again interjected, 'You bloody fool! You
bloody fool!'[51]

Like the parrot, Churchill was not convinced by Philip's proposal
for an early election, but Beaverbrook was and organized a further

meeting for Lloyd George with Bonar Law, at the Carlton Hotel in Cannes. The Prime Minister offered him the Foreign Office in return for his support for an early election, but Bonar Law declined. The Conservative leader Austen Chamberlain was also concerned about an early election and rightly gauged that it would be unpopular with his party. He wrote to his sister Hilda in January 1922:

> Of politics I know nothing except what you may read in the papers – that the P.M. and Lord Chancellor want a dissolution and that I am opposed to it on many grounds, amongst which two stand out. 1st we have no right to go till we have carried through our Irish policy (not merely started it) and secondly I think that it will find my party in a very bad temper and a very difficult position.[52]

The prospect of an early election was dealt a further blow by a rebellion of the grassroots Conservative Party. The party chairman, Sir George Younger, without consulting his leader, sent an open letter to all of the local Conservative Associations warning that an early election would split the party between those who supported the Lloyd George coalition and those who were against it. Younger also produced research suggesting that more Conservatives would be elected if they stood on their own and separate from the coalition Liberals – as always the real concern for MPs and candidates. This episode demonstrated Lloyd George's political weakness. He was the head of the government, but did not lead the largest party in the House of Commons. He required the support of the Conservative Party, both to be in government and to seek re-election for the coalition.

The Cannes conference itself was equally full of disappointment for Lloyd George. He recalled years later that it was 'remarkable for the able, impressive and tenacious fight put up by Herr Rathenau [the German representative] to save his country from being driven into insolvency by exactions beyond her capacity to bear. A few months later he was shot down like a wolf in the streets of Berlin by one of his own fellow countrymen.'[53] Briand would also be a victim of the Cannes conference, from where he was recalled to Paris and forced to resign following a motion moved against him by the opposition parties in the National Assembly, as a result, in Lloyd George's words, of distrust at 'the concessions he was rumoured to be making to the Germans'. The pretext for his sacking was an ill-fated photo-opportunity playing golf with Lloyd George at Cannes, which made Briand, who had never played the game before, look both ridiculous and subservient to the British Premier. Their match at the Cannes Golf Club had followed an informal lunch between the two leaders where A. J. Sylvester, Lloyd George's political secretary, remembered, 'As usual, L.G. wanted to create the "right atmosphere" to ensure success . . . So after lunch that day, the fun commenced.'[54]

The loss of Briand and his replacement by Raymond Poincaré was a disaster for Lloyd George's foreign policy and everything he had been working to achieve with the French since the Treaty of Versailles. Writing in 1932, looking back at this moment, he recalled that, compared to Briand, Poincaré was

> cold, reserved, rigid, with a mind of unimaginative and ungovern-able legalism. He has neither humour nor good humour. In confer-ence he was dour and morose . . . he is the most un-French Frenchman I ever met . . . He wanted to cripple Germany, and render her impotent for future aggression . . . The fall of M. Briand sent the world rolling towards the catastrophe which culminated in 1931.* Had he remained in office, European appeasement from the Urals to the Rhine might have been reached in 1922 and the troubles of the last ten years . . . averted.[55]

---

* Lloyd George was referring to the world economic crisis of 1931, and the massive political instability that this had caused in countries like Germany. He also blamed Poincaré's hostility to Germany and Russia for the failure of the 1922 Genoa conference to create closer relations between the European powers.

Lloyd George held an unsuccessful meeting with Poincaré at Boulogne on 26 February 1922, before returning to Port Lympne in low spirits, weighed down by political pressures at home and abroad. The following morning he summoned A. J. Sylvester and told him, 'I've given serious and earnest thought to the matter of retaining the Premiership, and have decided that I should give the Tories a chance. Chamberlain should have the opportunity.'[56]

Sylvester remembered:

Having dictated the letter to Chamberlain he entered his waiting car and told me to get it typed out and follow him to London in another car. Sir Philip had several cars which were at the disposal of the Premier, and so, leaving me at Lympne to type out the letter offering to resign in favour of Austen Chamberlain, LG drove away. It did not take me long to complete the typing, and as I finished it, a fast open car was driven round to the front door. Without any regard to speed limits, the chauffeur drove after the car conveying the Prime Minister, and soon we had overtaken it. The two cars stopped and I handed LG the letter.[57]

Chamberlain declined Lloyd George's offer, knowing that it would not be easy for him to lead a government and a divided Conservative Party: sixty Diehard Conservatives had voted against the Irish Treaty in the House of Commons, there was still Bonar Law agitating in the wings, and among party members there was growing resentment towards the coalition. Even Philip Sassoon's local association would raise concerns, with the *Dover Express* reporting, 'Some of the Folkestone Conservatives are agitating for opposition to the Coalition Government.'[58]

Austen Chamberlain had little sympathy for grassroots opinion and confided to his sister Hilda, 'Our local Associations are full of old prewar Tories who have learned nothing and forgotten nothing and who are I am quite convinced unrepresentative of the bulk of the electorate. They are a positive danger to us and may easily be our ruin.'[59]

Philip was increasingly concerned about the future of Lloyd George's premiership, telling his old friend and mentor of the war years, Lord Esher, on 6 March:

> I feel in my bones that LG ought for his own sake to go at once. No patch up will avert the coming smash & he has a chance of jumping clear. But Winston (whose views are always personal) advised him to hang on because Winston does not want to give up his job and I am sure he means to join the Tories at the earliest possible moment. I hope LG will do something for me in any event, but I am not counting on it too much – for I know his nature. It is thrilling & heart breaking at the same time. How right I was when I urged the January election.[60]

Three days later, Edwin Montagu, the Secretary of State for India and one of the Liberal members of the cabinet, was compelled to resign by Lloyd George for authorizing the publication of a sensitive diplomatic telegram from the Viceroy of India without the approval of the cabinet. This telegram implied support from the government in India for Turkey in its war with Greece, in order to appease Muslim opinion on the sub-continent. This was contrary to the policy of Lloyd George and the Foreign Secretary Lord Curzon: to support the Greek forces and the international boundaries created by the peace settlement that Turkey had been required to accept at the end of the First World War.

Montagu's resignation, followed by a bitter speech in Cambridge on 11 March in which he criticized the government and the Prime Minister's dictatorial style, caused a political storm in Westminster. On the same day, Lloyd George retreated to take a two-week holiday at his home in Criccieth in Wales.

Philip wrote to Lloyd George on 13 March with a heartfelt plea to his 'political chief' to return to the fray. This was based on more than just personal loyalty or opportunism; he was greatly concerned by what the collapse of the Lloyd George coalition might mean. For Philip, it was the chance to create a new political force out of the pre-war party system; this new Liberal–Conservative party would steal the centre ground, combining economic dynamism and social reform. Philip wanted the radical socialists in the Labour Party and the diehard Conservatives, who so hated upwardly mobile young men like him, to be pushed to the margins. Also, if this opportunity for the best talents to work together in the interests of the nation and the world was lost, would that not be a betrayal of the legacy of the war, and a greater failure if it led to a return to pre-war tribal politics?

In his letter Philip wrote:

I feel sure that lately you must have been strongly tempted to resign. My own belief is that the time to have done so has now gone by . . . the prestige of the government in particular and of the coalition in general has been badly shaken . . . every day that matters are allowed to drift the situation worsens and I see no hope of improvement failing strong and definite action by you. A few weeks or even days ago I think it would have been possible for you to have given a lead to Liberalism, as against extreme Labour and Conservatism alike, and to have carried an important section of the younger generation of Conservatives with you. That opportunity seems to have gone.

There remains therefore, as I see it, only one course that can keep you at the head of affairs where you ought to be and that is to declare boldly for fusion and to go to the country on a national platform. There would have to be further concessions to the Conservative element, but these would unite behind you the strongest single party not only in parliament but in the country and your personal prestige, together with the knowledge that the principles of true Liberalism were not being sacrificed, would carry with you a number of Liberals fully sufficient to give you a clear majority. There is no other way by which a clear majority could be obtained by any party.

If Lloyd George did not follow this course, Philip went on,

> I regard it as a thing inevitable that the difficulties of the current administration will increase from week to week. It is enough in politics for the rumour to get about that the ship is sinking not only for the rats to leave it but for someone or other to lend the elements a helping hand by scuttling the vessel.
>
> If you do not now make sure of the moderate Conservatives and moderate Liberals, guiding both along the path of a really national policy, I fear that you may inevitably be led to resign by events. In that case, I am convinced that Winston will find a way to form an alliance with the Conservatives himself.
>
> I feel more strongly than I can express in words that definite action by you should not be postponed longer than the period necessary to see the Irish Bill through parliament . . . it cannot be easy for you at Criccieth to keep in proper touch . . . Need I say that Lympne is open to you. The sea breezes of Kent are from the point of view of health no bad substitute for the winds and mountains of Wales.[61]

Lloyd George wrote to Frances Stevenson after receiving Sassoon's letter and urged her to 'Tell Philip I am very pleased with this letter. Ask him to keep writing to me. Tell him I won't even try to make up my mind about anything until I feel quite fit. A tired judgement is no judgement at all. I agree with him in his estimate of Winston. Max [Beaverbrook] has written to me on the same lines.'[62]

A debate on a motion of confidence in the government, which if lost would mean an immediate election, was set for 3 April, and its successful passage would help to dampen any concern about the imminent collapse of the government. Yet the underlying problems remained, and with them a growing concern that Philip shared with Lloyd George: that Winston Churchill was looking for a pretext to resign from the cabinet on an issue that would secure him a good deal of support from Conservative MPs, thereby burnishing his own credentials as a future coalition leader. The issue Philip thought Churchill had chosen was the question of formal recognition of the Soviet government, which was a necessary precondition for its inclusion at the forthcoming Genoa conference. Philip wrote to Lloyd George on 24 March:

> I saw this morning Beaverbrook and Bonar Law. The former thinks that Winston is determined to resign over the recognition question and join the Die Hards. He thinks you can rely on Austen and most of the Conservatives following you. Bonar on the other hand thinks that Winston will only go if he can rely on a very serious revolt in the Conservative Party – that this would not arise unless you were absolutely 'intransigent' on the question and that in that case the whole Conservative Party would go in a body. He had a talk with Austen the day before yesterday and he says that Austen is not at all aware of the general disgruntlement that exists – Bonar can never be accused of using rose coloured spectacles!
>
> Horne thinks Winston will burn his boats tomorrow at Northampton [where he was due to give a big speech]. But I should not imagine he will do more than stage the pyre.

Demonstrating his usefulness as the Prime Minister's eyes and ears, Philip had more to say:

> Personally I have not been able in the House to discover (except of course in the smouldering Die Hard bosoms) any intense feeling on the subject of Recognition. I expect you will find more difficulty in the Cabinet than in the House of Commons. I don't think FE [Smith] knows where he is at all. It is becoming increasingly difficult to find any sequence in his acts or words, on the other hand his movements are easy to follow. He and Freddie Guest

[Secretary of State for Air], along with Mona Dunn [Smith's mistress], and Scatters [Sir Matthew Wilson, a socialite MP] were supping and dancing on the roof garden of the Criterion restaurant till past 1 o'clock this morning.

Will you let me know if I can look forward to your dining with me on Monday. If so who would you like to have. I have got Trent ready for you if you find that Danehurst [a house on the Port Lympne estate that Lloyd George often used] is too far off.[63]

Yet the moment passed. Philip was right in guessing that Churchill would 'stage the pyre' at Northampton but not actually set it alight. The confidence motion in the government was won on 3 April, and Philip joined Lloyd George at Genoa for the start of the conference on 10 April, which was held in the Palazzo San Giorgio, overlooked by a statue of Columbus sitting on a pale marble throne. The arrival of Lloyd George, with Philip's influence clearly evident, impressed a young Ernest Hemingway, who was in the press gallery covering the conference for the *Toronto Star*. He wrote, 'The hall is nearly full when the British delegation enters. They have come in motorcars through the troop-lined streets and enter with élan. They are the best-dressed delegation.'[64]

There was little more to be said for the Genoa conference, however, because it was scuppered from the start by the French Premier, Poincaré, who refused to attend. The conference had been Lloyd George's initiative and had attracted the representatives of thirty-four nations to discuss how they could get the European economy moving again, settle the issue of German reparations and open up trade with Russia. 'Its results', though, according to the Deputy Cabinet Secretary Thomas Jones, 'were inconclusive, and confessed failure was avoided by the expedient of adjourning to a gathering of experts at The Hague . . . This postponement provided a face-saving truce of a few months, and when it failed left each power free to take its own line.'[65]

Philip, who had returned early to Westminster, kept Lloyd George up to date in Genoa with regular letters, but then found himself in hot water when he was caught out sharing some of the secrets of the budget with businessmen at a meeting of the Folkestone Chamber of Commerce, of which he was president. As PPS to the Prime Minister he would have sat in on discussions of the budget, and he had made his remarks in Folkestone only an hour or so before the Chancellor delivered his statement to the House of Commons. Nevertheless, someone had tipped off the Anti-Waste League MP James Erskine, who raised it on the floor of the House; this led to a fulsome apology from a mortified Sassoon.[66]

Philip's main interest in the budget that year was to press for a cause in which he had considerable personal interest as a patron of the arts and a trustee of the National Gallery. In the debate on the budget in the House he called for more financial assistance to be given by the government to museums and galleries. Raising the problem of 'the dispersal of our national art treasures', he told Parliament: 'I now invite the House to give it most sympathetic consideration and attention, because I do not think it is sufficiently realised how largely our national galleries and museums in London and in the provinces that are now open to the public exist for the benefit of the poorer sections of the population, or how largely they are frequented by people who have no other means of gratifying their love for rare and beautiful things.'[67]

The Chancellor Robert Horne rewarded Philip's persistence by announcing to Parliament on 3 August that the government would support the creation of a list of works of paramount importance that should be purchased for the nation if and when they became available. Philip's successful initiative received the grateful thanks of the board of the National Gallery, with its director Sir Charles Holmes writing to thank him for 'the very great service you have rendered to this gallery and the Arts', and stating that the announcement was 'a real landmark in the artistic policy of the country'.[68] Sir Charles's letter was gratefully received by Philip, who replied that 'nothing could have given me greater pleasure. I was so afraid when I joined the Board that I should not be able to justify my existence on it, that your kind words are more gratifying that I can possibly tell you.'[69]

In July 1922, Philip hosted a summer party at Park Lane with a number of leading politicians among the guests. Churchill, who stayed until 2 a.m., noted one particular incident in a letter to Clementine: 'The old boy [Asquith] turned up at Philip's party vy heavily loaded. The PM accompanied him up the stairs and was chivalrous enough to cede him the banister. It was a wounding sight. He kissed a great many people affectionately. I presume they were all relations. Really this letter consists in telling "sad stories of the death of Kings".'[70]

Yet this display of political chivalry could not mask the increasingly febrile atmosphere in Westminster. A few days later Austen Chamberlain and Lord Birkenhead held a very bad-tempered meeting with the Conservative junior ministers in the government, where they insisted that if they formed the largest party after the election the Prime Minister should not be Lloyd George but a Conservative. Chamberlain recalled that 'F. E. scolded and browbeat them with an intellectual arrogance which nearly produced a row there and then and did infinite harm . . . Balfour spoke persuasively but it is astonishing how little weight he now carries with the Party.'[71]

On 5 August, the first weekend of the parliamentary summer recess, Philip Sassoon held a party at Port Lympne for old friends, including Arthur Balfour, Lady Desborough, Evan Charteris and Hugh Cecil. Philip had also collected Churchill from his house in Sussex Square in Bayswater and drove him to Lympne for dinner. Winston told Clementine that he should 'have liked to linger here longer',[72] but he was travelling to meet Max Beaverbrook at Boulogne the following morning. Winston and Max then motored on to Deauville and stayed at the Royal Hotel, where the Aga Khan was also a guest. The Aga Khan encouraged Beaverbrook to travel to Constantinople to get a better understanding of the growing tensions between Greece and Turkey. It was good advice, as it was this conflict that would provide the pretext for the collapse of Lloyd George's government.

Later in August Turkey launched an offensive which drove the Greeks out of the territories in Asia Minor they had occupied since the peace treaties and back across the straits to Europe. Thomas Jones remembered that 'For a moment it seemed that Kemal* might follow them and set the Balkans ablaze.'[73] Lloyd George asked for support from Italy, France and the Dominions, but there was no enthusiasm for a new war. British troops stood alone in defence of the neutral zones along the straits in Asia Minor, and at Chanak, just across the water from Gallipoli, they faced attack from Turkish forces. On 16 September the cabinet issued a statement threatening war with Turkey if it attacked Chanak. The Turks backed down, but this was not seen as a victory for Lloyd George. As Jones recalled, 'The outcry in war-weary Britain was immediate and widespread.'[74]

On 17 September the cabinet met at Chequers and secretly agreed that as soon as the crisis in Turkey allowed they would fight the next general election on a united, national platform. On 25 September, Austen Chamberlain briefed all of the Conservative ministers on this plan and believed them to be in agreement, with the exception of Stanley Baldwin. Three days later Philip Sassoon lunched with Sam Hoare MP and Winston Churchill. There Philip let slip Lloyd George's plan to call a general election for 28 October – in other words, before the Conservative conference in November. The reason for this, Philip explained, was that 'there was no particular point in giving the Prime Minister an unnecessary kick', which is what he would get from the party conference. Hoare replied that he didn't think it would make much difference 'as the majority

---

* Mustafa Kemal Pasha, later known as Atatürk, was the leader of the Turkish National Movement in the Turkish War of Independence (1919–22). A former army officer, who had been a front-line commander at Gallipoli during the First World War, he would become the first President of Turkey, and is credited with creating the modern Turkish state.

of Conservatives were anyhow going to stand and be returned as independents at the election'.[75]

However, in sharing this information with Sam Hoare, Philip had unwittingly helped to set in train the series of events that led to the famous meeting at the Carlton Club on Pall Mall on 19 October which brought down Lloyd George. Hoare contacted Bonar Law the day after his lunch with Philip and urged swift action to upset the Prime Minister's plan.

On 15 October, a dinner was held at Churchill's house in Sussex Square with Lloyd George, Austen Chamberlain and Lord Birkenhead to try to find a way to head off the growing political crisis and the determination of a growing number of Conservative MPs to end the coalition. It was here that Chamberlain decided on organizing the meeting of MPs at the Carlton Club.

The following day Sam Hoare had a letter published in *The Times* with the support of Stanley Baldwin, calling for the return of the party system, rather than the creation of a new centre party to oppose Labour. He claimed that it was 'useless' for the Conservative leadership to 'attempt to impose from above the continuance of an arrangement which nine out of ten of the party desire to see ended'. He added:

> When Mr Chamberlain says that the Conservative Party cannot hope for a clear majority after the general election, he may be right or he may be wrong. No one has ever been able to foretell correctly the result of any general election, least of all a general election with an electorate that has been hugely increased. But Conservatives who, like myself, believe that the vital need is not so much to form a Government as to keep the party united are not convinced by this argument.[76]

On the day before the Carlton Club meeting, nearly sixty Conservative MPs had met at Hoare's house, and the tone there was very anti-coalition. Later that evening Hoare met with Bonar

Law at his home in Onslow Gardens, and after intense lobbying from Beaverbrook, Bonar Law told him that he had 'decided to go to the [Carlton Club] meeting and I intend to make a speech at it'.[77] Hoare wrote the motion that was put to the Carlton Club meeting in the name of the MP Ernest Pretyman: 'that this meeting of Conservative Members of the House of Commons declares its opinion that the Conservative Party whilst willing to co-operate with the Coalition Liberals should fight the election as an independent party with its own leader and its own programme'. The motion was carried by 185 votes to 88, leading to Austen Chamberlain's resignation as leader of the party.[78]

Philip Sassoon telephoned the result through to Downing Street, speaking to Thomas Jones, who gave the news to the Prime Minister. Philip then left the Carlton Club to drive to Number 10 and as he walked to his car in Carlton Gardens was spotted by Stanley Baldwin's wife Lucy and Mimi Davidson, the wife of J. C. C. Davidson, Baldwin's PPS. As Davidson recalled, 'a pale, sallow and obviously greatly worried Philip Sassoon emerged and ran past them to where his car was parked higher up the road . . . Mimi turned to Mrs Baldwin and said, "Look at Philip – we must have won."'[79]

The Cabinet Secretary, Maurice Hankey, wrote in his diary, 'I heard the result at 1.15pm and went straight to 10 Downing Street . . . I met the PM in the lavatory. "Hankey," he said, "you have written your last minutes for me. I have asked the King to come to town and this afternoon I shall resign and you will have another Prime Minister."'[80] The King wrote in his diary after Lloyd George's resignation, 'I am sorry he is going, but some day he will be Prime Minister again.'[81]

Lloyd George would of course never hold office again, but he rewarded many of his closest allies and advisers in the list of honours on the dissolution of parliament. Philip Sassoon was not forgotten by his chief and was awarded the Knight Grand Cross of the Order of the British Empire (GBE). The King had thought that the GBE for Philip was 'too much' and that a KBE, which ranked below, would be 'quite enough';[82] nevertheless, Lloyd George's recommendation prevailed. Philip had been since his father's death in 1912 the holder of the baronetcy first awarded to his grandfather, but like Sir Albert Sassoon he had now also received a knighthood in his own right, in recognition of his service to his country.

Bonar Law was appointed Prime Minister and the general election was set for 15 November. There would be no coalition candidates, so for Conservatives like Philip Sassoon who had been loyal to Lloyd George, the question naturally arose as to how they should seek to present themselves in the campaign.

Philip was clear on this point, writing to the *Folkestone Express* on 28 October that he would 'stand at the coming election as a Conservative, as I have done in past elections. While the alliance between Conservatives and Liberals was in being, I supported to the best of my ability and opportunities the Coalition government under the leadership of Mr Lloyd George and Mr Austen Chamberlain; believing as I did, and still do, that such a form of government was for the best interests of the country in most anxious and difficult days.'[83]

Although Philip was standing as a Conservative, he had by no means broken his links with the Lloyd George Liberals and on 2 November attended an election strategy meeting at Churchill's house in Sussex Square, along with another Liberal minister, H. A. L. Fisher; four days later he saw Churchill again for lunch. Between these dates, on 4 November, he was adopted unanimously as the Conservative candidate in his constituency at a rally at Folkestone town hall. Addressing the meeting, he was critical of the Carlton Club meeting that had brought about the fall of Lloyd George. 'Frankly I regret it,' he said.

I voted with Mr Austen Chamberlain and Lord Balfour at the Carlton club. I share their opinion that the nation is not as yet sufficiently out of the wood of post-war dangers to be able to dispense safely with the power and authority which the coalition government drew, from the fact that it represented the two historic parties in the state and the united talent and statesmanship of the leaders of those two great parties. I remember the debt which my party as a party owes to the assistance Lloyd George gave us at the last election. It is common knowledge that in many a contest at that election it was the personal weight and the prestige of Mr Lloyd George's name that carried the Conservative candidate to the head of the poll.

He continued his praise for his 'political chief' and held open the prospect of his returning to office:

no one can deny the greatness of the service Mr Lloyd George has rendered to his country as Prime Minister . . . (cries of hear hear from the audience) . . . Are those services so spent today that they can be of no further use to his country? Is the position of our country, and wise and ordered government within it, so assured today that we can afford to discard and throw aside the ablest statesman of his age? . . .

It was therefore with real sorrow and regret that I heard the result announced of the voting at the Carlton club meeting . . . I look back with what I feel is pardonable pride to the period of my association with our great Prime Minister as his political secretary. I am proud and grateful for the friendship he and other Liberal members of his cabinet have given me.[84]

Philip Sassoon was returned unopposed as the Member for the Hythe constituency, but his years of working for Lloyd George were at an end.

• FLYING MINISTER •

Gee it was late – that raw black night
And we were almost all quite tight
'Mid beauty' and the flowing wine
With clouds of nicotine divine
We sat
And watched
And waited
Till lo! The small machine began
To 'tic, tic.' Then the little band
Ran smoothly out in Philip's hand
Curling, curling like a snake
Till Philip's hand began to shake
Impossible!
'Twas like the writing on the wall
That told of old King Nib's sad fall
When in the dawn we learnt it all
Old England's choice, we clearly saw
Was Max!
I beg pardon! Mister B Law

William Orpen, 'November 1922'[1]

The ticker tape bearing the general election results poured through Philip Sassoon's fingers and on to the floor of the ballroom of 25 Park Lane. Although he had been re-elected unopposed as a Conservative, he hoped the old coalition that had been brought down at the Carlton Club a few weeks before would be restored by the electorate. Yet as the constituency results were announced to the guests, including the former Prime Minister David Lloyd George, it was clear that Andrew Bonar Law and the Conservatives, with the strong support of the press baron Max Beaverbrook, were heading for a clear overall majority. Lloyd George's National Liberals were relegated to fourth place, behind Labour and the Asquith Liberals; even Winston Churchill had lost his seat in Dundee. It was a humiliating reversal and vindicated Conservatives like Stanley Baldwin and Sam Hoare, who had believed that their party could win without Lloyd George.

On 17 November 1922, just two days after the election, the leading members of the old Lloyd George coalition gathered for dinner at Sassoon's house in Park Lane to 'consider the results'.[2] The key question for them was whether the coalitionists should form a new centre party or return to their traditional Liberal and Conservative groups. Austen Chamberlain recalled that at the dinner he said although he 'would not now join the Government . . . [he] was going to remain a Unionist and would not join a Centre Party and did not intend to attack or criticize the Govt unless obliged to do so . . . L. G. said that was his idea also. He did not mean to act like an ordinary chief of Opposition and to seek grounds of criticism.'[3]

However, the following day Lord Riddell visited Lloyd George at his home at Churt* in Surrey and found that he had far from given up on the idea of creating a new political grouping. 'The

---

* Lloyd George's house, Bron-y-de (Welsh for 'south facing'), was designed and constructed with the help of Philip Tilden between 1920 and 1922.

change in the atmosphere since he had been out of office is amazing. Now he is working like a little dynamo to break up the Conservative Party by bringing the more advanced section to his flag, to join up with the "Wee Frees" [independent Liberals] and to detach the more moderate members of the Labour Party – this with the object of forming a Centre Party of which he will be the leader.'[4]

The big beasts of the old coalition hoped that the burdens of office might prove too much for this new 'second eleven' govern-ment, as Churchill had dismissively referred to them. Austen Chamberlain told his sister Ida, 'I give them four years. I can do a lot of reading and gardening in that time.'[5] Robert Blake observed in his history of the Conservative Party that 'The Coalition Conservatives muttered crossly in the wilderness. But they accounted for most of the talent in the party, and Bonar Law regarded it as one of his main objectives to secure their return.'[6] For the time being, though, they were on the outside of govern-ment and would have to wait for an opportunity to return to power.

Philip Sassoon enjoyed a quiet and contemplative Christmas at Port Lympne, along with Sybil and her children. For most of the previous eight years the routine of his working life had been dictated by the demands of his chiefs, first Douglas Haig then Lloyd George. Now free from the ties of office, and indifferent to the early busi-ness of the new government, he took his usual winter sports holiday in Switzerland, followed by a trip to Italy and Egypt, where he was joined by his friends Sir Louis Mallet and Lady Juliet Duff. He nevertheless kept an eye on political events from afar, and on 1 February 1923 sent a bulletin to Lloyd George from the Grand Hotel in Rome, addressing him out of habit and preference as 'My dear P.M.':

What an awful mess everything is in at home and abroad . . . we have got failure to agree all round – in America, France and

Lausanne [where the peace treaty between the Allies and Turkey was to be agreed] . . . I am told that [the Turks] came quite determined to come to a settlement and that now they are equally determined never to settle anything with Curzon [the Foreign Secretary]. And yet I hear he fully expects to be Prime Minister in May!

I am just arrived here from St Moritz which I enjoyed as much as usual. Except that it is always too cold out of doors and too hot indoors . . . all the ugly women were so amorous. I am going to Egypt tomorrow to muck about among the tombs and see the latest Pharaoh. I shall be back on 12th March – so please, Sir, don't forget all about me before then. What a marvellous press the new Government have got and even so they can't go straight anywhere. Mussolini seems popular here and if the House attempts to show any lip he brings up his army and they soon shut up![7]

Philip's tour through Italy and Egypt would be his first substantial holiday since he had been demobilized from the army in 1919. While politics was Philip's chosen career, his preferred escape and relaxation was found in art. From Italy he wrote to Sybil, exclaiming, 'Rome is like a cocktail to the soul, and I have been throbbing with thrills all day.'[8] Two days later he added,

There is no doubt that here Ancient Rome quite outshines the Renaissance. It is not only finer work, but a far more potent influence . . . The Pantheon is the most beautiful temple I have ever seen, and the only complete ancient Roman building in Rome . . . The Sistine Chapel is quite perfect, and the Stanza quite good for Raphael – but then I don't care for Raphael. There is a long corridor panelled up in painted fresco maps – sapphire sea and emerald land – quite lovely, and just the thing for Sert to copy for me.[9]

In November 1922, the archaeologist and Egyptologist Howard Carter, along with his patron Lord Carnarvon, had thrilled the world with the uncovering of the tomb of Tutankhamun in the Valley of the Kings, still the finest of its kind ever discovered. Philip arrived in Egypt from Italy in order to 'see the latest Pharaoh' in the midst of the excitement and general clamour generated by visitors eager to glimpse the treasures of the King's resting place. He wrote to Sybil from Luxor:

> We went down to the tomb today, and I must say that it does give one rather a thrill. They have taken out nearly all the things now, and the only things left are a couch, slung between two elongated lions – all brilliantly gilt – rather pantomime but rather Lympne-ish . . . [There are] two really magnificent statues of the King guarding the sealed door. These are life size – black and gold eyes of precious stones and sandals of real gold. You can see through a hole in the wall into the next chamber, which is stacked with things one on top of the other.
>
> The Tomb is much smaller than I expected and quite undecor-ated; they are opening the third chamber on Sunday, and I think we will try to stop off here on our way back for a night if we can get a permit to see the new discoveries – i.e., the third room. Carnarvon tells me the things are really wonderful.[10]

Howard Carter's discovery had made him and Tutankhamun world-wide celebrities, and therefore Philip Sassoon's early arrival at the tomb might seem as natural as his first impromptu meeting with Charlie Chaplin in his suite in Paris. Yet Philip was captivated by this window into the undisturbed world of ancient Egypt, to a time seven hundred years before his Sassoon ancestors were taken captive from Jerusalem to Babylon by Nebuchadnezzar. Perhaps Philip's family had also been in Egypt in the time of Tutankhamun, before their exodus to Israel.

After a trip on the Nile, Philip returned to Luxor and was given a tour of the newly opened rooms in the tomb by Lord Carnarvon, who, he told Sybil, showed us everything. I must say it gave me one of the biggest thrills of my life.

The first room is almost entirely filled by the sarcophagus – which is about nine feet high and about twenty-four long – an immense affair, all gilt with a very jolly pattern of blue glass. The passage round it is only a very few inches wide and you have to squeeze your way around with considerable difficulty . . . Opening from this room there is a smaller one literally heaped with marvels. Facing one at the end is a large gold shrine about five feet high – with a double frieze of blue and gold cobras, and certainly containing the canopic vases . . . I again examined the two life-sized statues of the King that guard the inner chamber. They are magnificent – marvellous in expression and repose . . .

You cannot imagine what one feels looking at that sarcophagus that has lain here hidden for three thousand years – brilliant – glittering as if it had been completed only yesterday, and when one thinks that inside lies the Belle aux Bois Dormants – this Rip Van Winkle wrapt in his age-long sleep, defying the process of time – immutable – serene. How he must be placing his finger to his nose at us poor prying creatures of a minute who to-morrow will vanish into dust. He has conquered the infinite and made it everlasting – this King who lived four hundred years before Homer. Here he lies with infinite chic and cachet and surrounded by his household gods and treasures; next to these exquisite refined things how vulgar seem the glories of Versailles.[11]

Two days later, still on a high from his visit to the tomb, Philip wrote again to Sybil from Cairo, 'I am still gloating over all Carnarvon showed us in the Valley of Kings. We were very lucky as hardly anyone has seen the new room in the tomb and the storeroom.'[12]

Philip returned home and to the House of Commons in late March, and the *Folkestone Herald* reported that he looked 'bronzed and happy' after this trip to Egypt.[13] The timeless qualities of the pharaohs provided an extreme contrast to the constantly shifting sands of Westminster politics, where the Prime Minister Andrew Bonar Law was on the way out, after only a few months in power. Although just over four years older that Lloyd George, he was physically frail and in poor health. He was in pain and suffering from a bad throat which no medication seemed able to improve. In April, Stanley Baldwin had been required to intervene on his behalf in a debate as his voice was so weak he couldn't be heard in the chamber of the House of Commons, and even in cabinet meetings he was unable to make any meaningful contribution to the discussions. On 26 April, Bonar Law informed his senior ministers that he intended to go abroad for a few weeks for a complete rest, and if that did no good he would have to seriously consider resigning. Yet his condition grew worse and on 17 May, at Lord Beaverbrook's insistence, he was seen in his suite in the Hôtel de Crillon in Paris by the King's doctor, Sir Thomas Horder. Horder didn't disclose his diagnosis to Bonar Law, but instead told Beaverbrook that the Prime Minister was suffering from inoperable throat cancer, and should stand down from office; he had, as it transpired, less than six months to live. That evening Beaverbrook duly convinced his old friend to retire, although the announcement would be held back for a few days. The press baron was also well aware of the manoeuvres in Westminster already under way over the succession.

The Foreign Secretary, Lord Curzon, thought the premiership should be his by right, but his haughty manner had made him a lot of enemies. The coalition Conservatives had also questioned his decision to remain in office after the Carlton Club meeting and serve under Bonar Law. The Chancellor, Stanley Baldwin, had the support of the rank-and-file members of the Conservative Party in the House of Commons, but he was inexperienced and, for Philip Sassoon and his friends, singled out for his disloyalty to the former leader Austen Chamberlain.

On 15 May, two days before Bonar Law's cancer was diagnosed,

Philip met in London with leading members of the old coalition government, including Lord Birkenhead and Sir Robert Horne; they agreed to press for Lord Derby, who was War Secretary once again, as a compromise candidate to become the leader of a reunited Conservative Party. Philip was deputized by the group to head straight out to Paris to seek the support of Beaverbrook, who reacted warmly to the approach. Bonar Law's resignation was formally announced on 20 May, and back in London Philip met with Lord Derby that same day, to try to persuade him that he should take up the premiership, and to let him know that he would have the support of both Beaverbrook and Lord Rothermere, as well as the coalition Conservatives.

Philip wrote to Beaverbrook straight after the meeting:

I have been down to see Derby this morning. He says that (1) he will never serve under Curzon (2) that he never told Baldwin he would serve under him. But he began by saying that if Baldwin asked him to serve under him he would accept – he ended by saying that he would tell Baldwin that he would only serve under him on condition that he (Baldwin) could persuade Horne and Austen to serve under him too.

I think that is good enough as neither Horne nor Austen will serve under anyone except Derby. Derby is quite ready to take it on if pressed, for a short time. Horne said that Bonar should be told that 'the only hope of unity lies with Derby, and that under anyone else the party will remain disrupted, increasingly and beyond hope' . . .

I know how worried you are by the illness of your old friend and feel so much for you. I am so sad about it myself. Lympne is at his disposal whenever he wants it. It should do him good to go down there and he would be away from everything and everybody.[14]

Beaverbrook played a pivotal role throughout this crisis, because of his personal friendship with Bonar Law, and his status, following the death of Lord Northcliffe the previous year, as Britain's leading press baron. Philip wanted Max to persuade Bonar Law to name Derby as his successor, but the outgoing Prime Minister declined. It was in any case too late. J. C. C. Davidson, who had been parliamentary private secretary to Bonar Law, was working behind the scenes to ensure that Baldwin was preferred, and the King duly asked him to become Prime Minister on 22 May. Philip met with Beaverbrook for lunch that day to press again for his support for inclusion of senior coalition Conservatives in the new government. He reiterated his case in a letter sent later that afternoon:

I am most grateful for the confidence you always show towards me. You know you can always rely on my not failing you. I do beg that you will do all you can to press for the inclusion of Austen, after all the Daily Express has never attacked him until a few weeks ago.

And apart from that one cannot level against him any single of the accusations that people do against FE. He has been extremely dignified and has shown no bitterness although he had a bitter pill to swallow at the Carlton Club meeting – bitterer than anyone else.

However buoyant the government may feel now their position is going to be very different minus Bonar and all he stood for and with LG and his followers in active opposition and they cannot and should not neglect any opportunity of closing their ranks and I don't like the idea of the Amerys* and Boyd Carpenters† being the people solely to crack the whip. So please do what you can

---

* Rt Hon. Leo Amery MP, First Lord of the Admiralty (October 1922 to January 1924), Secretary of State for the Colonies (November 1924 to June 1929).

† Archibald Boyd-Carpenter MP, parliamentary secretary at the Ministry of Labour (November 1922 to March 1923), Paymaster General (March 1923 to January 1924).

Max. I am sure it is for you with your immense influence to come out strongly now.[15]

The new Prime Minister offered the chancellorship to Sir Robert Horne, but he declined, and that was the end of the rapprochement with the coalition Conservatives, who remained in the wilderness, licking their wounds from another emphatic defeat. J. C. C. Davidson recalled in his memoirs that 'when the vital moment came . . . they displayed the same lack of knowledge of the House of Commons and public sentiment as they had done at the Carlton Club six months before. Their judgement was clouded by their opposition to the man who had belled the Coalition Cat on 22 October 1922.'[16]

Yet it was not that Philip and his friends were blinded by prejudice against Baldwin, just that they embraced a more colourful and dynamic form of politics. Philip was attracted not just to success but to brilliance in others, qualities that he couldn't find in men like Baldwin. It would also be hard to imagine that the new Prime Minister would take any great interest, as Lloyd George had done, in gossiping over cocktails with the artists, sportsmen and movie stars who mingled with the politicians at Philip's parties.

Baldwin would be a very infrequent guest at Park Lane and Trent Park over the next decade and a half, whereas friends like Winston Churchill, Duff Cooper and later Anthony Eden would be mainstays of Philip's dinners and house parties. In an interview with Beverley Nichols, Duff Cooper sought to define that spirit of Toryism to which Philip Sassoon most certainly conformed. He said, 'I think Bagehot summed it up best when he said "Toryism means enjoyment." If you agree to that, then the great political parties of England fall back, quite naturally, into two main divisions. You get the spirit of the Ironsides – a very valuable spirit in some ways, but one which was never gay, even in the height of triumph. On the other side you get the spirit of the Cavaliers, gay even in defeat.'[17]

Philip was certainly a 'Cavalier' and was determined to be gay in defeat in the summer of 1923, putting aside his setbacks around the succession of the Conservative Party leadership. His friend Lytton Strachey described a party given by Philip that June at Park Lane: 'You never saw the like. Winston was there and I talked to him a good deal. Do you know in spite of everything I couldn't help liking him. H. G. [Wells] says very much the same thing in "Men like gods"; one somehow can't dislike the poor creature. He was delighted when I said I thought his book [*The World Crisis*] very well done, and hardly seemed to mind when I added that I also thought it very wicked.'[18] Strachey had applied to be recognized as a conscientious objector during the war and had been very critical at the time of the leadership of politicians like Lloyd George and Churchill. About Churchill in particular he had written:

> Though Time from History's pages much may blot,
> Some things there are can never be forgot;
> And in Gallipoli's delicious name,
> Wxxxxxx, your own shall find eternal fame.[19]

In July Philip gave a great dinner at Park Lane for the Prince of Wales and leading members of the old coalition, and the following spring he held a ball where 'The Prince of Wales and [his younger brother] Prince George and the gay young set which includes the pretty Australian Countess of Loughborough* . . . were all dancing indefatigably . . . Flowers were in almost pre-war luxuriance and the whole hall was ablaze with blue and mauve hyacinth.'[20]

It was at one of Philip's Park Lane balls in the 1920s that Oswald Mosley first caught sight of his future wife, Diana Mitford: 'she looked wonderful among the rose-entwined pillars of the "voluptous Orient" as the music of the best of orchestras was wafted

---

* Sheila Chisholm was an Australian society beauty who married Lord Loughborough. She was a friend of the Prince of Wales and Freda Dudley Ward, and would often be a guest at Philip Sassoon's parties.

together with the best of scents through air heavy laden with all Sassoon's most hospitable artifices'.[21]

Stanley Baldwin spent the summer of 1923 as usual at Aix-les-Bains where he contemplated a deteriorating political situation in Europe and the ongoing problems with the weak economy and high unemployment at home. In January, the French Premier Raymond Poincaré had shattered all that Lloyd George had been working for when he sent his troops to occupy the Ruhr Valley and seize the Germans' coal and steel in place of the war reparations France was owed. It was a move that Philip Sassoon, whose Lympne conferences had sought to avoid such a confrontation, thought had 'indefinitely postponed' the recovery of Europe. 'The hope of natural and steady renewal of our own commercial prosperity has vanished. Nothing is now more sure than the tragic spectre of unemployment.'[22]

In response to the rising tensions in Europe and unemployment at home, Baldwin considered returning to the old Conservative policy of trade tariffs and preference for goods from the Empire in order to protect home industries and jobs. The debate of free trade versus tariff reform shattered the Conservative Party before the war, and had contributed to its election defeats in 1906 and 1910. Tariff reform had been seen as a policy for business and the producers, as it protected them from cheaper imported goods. However, free trade benefited the consumer as it was perceived to bring lower prices in the shops. Baldwin now believed that as the pressing demand was for saving and creating new jobs, the case for tariff reform had to be made. When Bonar Law had won his general election victory the previous year, he promised that he would not consider such reform without consulting the electorate, and the new Prime Minister also felt bound to honour this pledge. Against the advice of his colleagues, who had urged him to wait, that autumn Baldwin announced that he would be calling a general election on the question of tariff reform. The campaign would bring together the broader family of the

Conservative Party; the coalitionists' leader Austen Chamberlain had been born into the reform movement started by his father, and men like Philip Sassoon had always stood for election supporting it. The election also had the potentially disastrous impact for the Conservatives of reuniting the Liberal Party in defence of free trade.

Philip Sassoon, in once again accepting the nomination of the Folkestone and Hythe Conservatives, 'announced himself to be a supporter of Stanley Baldwin and said the Conservative Party were out to find work for the workless. That would be accomplished by the imposition of tariffs.'[23] Philip further paid tribute to Bonar Law, who had died on 30 October, calling him 'one of the kindliest, most loyal and high principled of men who ever played a distinguished part in British politics'.[24]

Philip's personal election would be another walk-over, as once again no other candidate stood against him, but when the nation went to the polls on 6 December 1923 the result was a calamity for Baldwin and the Conservative Party. They were returned with the largest number of seats, 258, but no overall majority. In second place were Labour with 191, with the rejuvenated Liberals on 158. If there was an opportunity for the old coalitionists to strike and try to form a new national government, it was now, but the moment escaped them. As the election campaign had focused on tariff reform, it made a new coalition with Lloyd George and the Liberals all but impossible. There was much criticism of Baldwin, but even though it was only six months after his appointment, there was now no clear alternative as leader; Balfour was considered too old, Austen Chamberlain could not unite the party, and following the steady growth in support for the Labour Party, the idea of a prime minister coming from the House of Lords was unthinkable.

As the Conservatives were unable to form a new government, all Stanley Baldwin could do was advise the King to send for Ramsay MacDonald, who in January 1924 became the first Labour Prime Minister. This radical concept, which would have been impossible before the war, was now considered to be a safe experiment. Without a majority, and not even the largest party in the House of Commons, the Labour government had to rely on support from the Liberals, and its life would be chaotic and short. This Liberal support was the final straw for Winston Churchill, who was still out of Parliament, having lost to the Labour candidate in Leicester West in the 1923 election. Philip Sassoon believed that Churchill had been looking for an excuse to rejoin the Conservatives since the dying days of the Lloyd George coalition, and the opportunity presented itself in March 1924 with a parliamentary by-election in the Westminster Abbey constituency. Philip told Churchill, 'I am so glad you are standing. You are BOUND to get in. Let me know how I can help you. I should like to help in every way possible.'[25] Churchill stood as an independent 'Constitutionalist', but Philip felt that Baldwin should have contrived to allow him to stand for, or unopposed by, their party. Sassoon complained over lunch to Austen Chamberlain that Baldwin should have done more to support Churchill's candidacy, and he was co-signatory of a letter sent to Baldwin which stated, in terms reviving the spirit of the old coalition, 'We feel that it would be an advantage to our party in the present and impending conflict with Socialism if we could gain the adherence of a body of Liberals in the House and in the country who while preserving their own identity would work loyally and effectively with us on main issues. We feel that Mr Churchill's candidature . . . is a long step further towards this result.'[26] Churchill narrowly lost out to the official Conservative candidate, but was shortly afterwards selected by the party to stand in the safe seat of Epping at the next general election.

In opposition the Conservatives decided to abandon all their talk of tariff reform and instead launched a vigorous anti-socialist campaign, based on the assumption that Labour were the front for a planned Bolshevik take-over of Britain. The Labour government was defeated in the House of Commons in the autumn, and an election was called for 29 October. Four days before the poll, the British papers published a letter, purporting to have been sent by the senior Soviet politician Grigory Zinoviev to the Communist Party of Britain, calling for increased agitation. While there is little evidence that this letter, accepted as valid at the time but since believed to be a forgery, affected the Labour vote, it may have helped bring a swift end to the Liberal revival of the previous year. The Conservatives were able to present themselves as the only real opponents of socialism, as the Liberals had supported Labour for much of their brief time in government.

The Conservatives were swept back into power with 412 seats and a majority of over 100; the Liberals were reduced to just 40 seats. Philip Sassoon also easily defeated his Labour opponent, Constantine Gallop. The former champions of coalition, such as Philip, had been steadfast in their support of Baldwin during the election campaign. The large Conservative majority and the commanding personal position that it gave the Prime Minister now provided him with the opportunity to reunite the party in government. On the night after the election, Philip hosted a dinner at Park Lane for some of the senior figures from the coalition era like Winston Churchill and Lord Birkenhead, along with Max Beaverbrook, and Baldwin supporters including Sam Hoare and Philip Lloyd-Graeme. There was considerable speculation that Churchill would be offered a cabinet post, with Birkenhead exclaiming to him across the table, 'I suppose you expect to get office?' Churchill replied, 'That will depend very much on what I'm offered.' 'No,' said Birkenhead, 'you have been hungering and thirsting for office for two years and you will take anything they offer you.'[27] A report of the dinner made its way back to Baldwin, but he had already decided to bring Churchill back. He offered him the position of Chancellor of the Exchequer, which left many of his senior colleagues aghast. Churchill gladly accepted, telling the Prime Minister, 'You have done more for me than Lloyd George ever did.'[28] There was reward also for Austen Chamberlain, who returned to government as Foreign Secretary.

Philip Sassoon's unanswered request to Lloyd George for ministerial office would likewise now be granted by Baldwin. Philip remembered, 'On Tuesday evening, 11th November, I was rung up at Lympne by the PM offering me the post of Under-secretary of State for Air. I was delighted . . . (1) It is the one live and expanding service (2) Because I prefer to work under Sam Hoare [the new Secretary of State] to anyone else (3) Because I know all the chiefs in the Ministry so well from the war . . . The Prince [of Wales] rang me up to say he'd drink a cocktail on the strength of it.'[29]

Philip received a congratulatory letter from his former chief, Douglas Haig, who wrote, 'I was delighted to see that you are now one of "H.M. Ministers". My very hearty congratulations to you and may you rise to the highest position in that line.'[30]

It was the perfect appointment for Philip. He had a genuine passion for aviation, having maintained his own private planes since the war at the aerodrome at Lympne. Mastery of the air would be the key to defence at home and across the Empire, and Britain had developed a world-leading advantage in this new and important industry. Although Philip's promotion may have felt to him like it had been a long time coming, he was still a few weeks short of his thirty-sixth birthday, with the prospect of a long ministerial career ahead of him.

Winston Churchill wrote to congratulate Philip: 'You will be well placed at Lympne to watch developments and inspect various [air] stations. In fact I think you must have built your home there upon a prophetic inspiration. I am glad that we are all together.'[31] Philip replied, still gushing with excitement at his new post:

Thank you ten thousand times for your most charming letter which has given me enormous pleasure. Thank you for all you did on my behalf. It was very kind of you and I am certain I owe my job a great deal to your efforts on my behalf. You know that I am grateful. Nothing could suit me better than being here as I love the work and consider myself extremely lucky to be working under such a nice fellow as Sam. It is marvellous that you should be at the Exchequer, that we should all be together. It is a jolly troupe and I hope will prove a successful one. I am looking forward to having Clemmie to stay with me this week. À bientôt Winston and again thank you for everything. What a good friend you have been to me all my life. I am so happy.[32]

Philip was certainly a good friend to Winston as well. Churchill was temporarily without a home in London, and stayed with Philip in Park Lane until moving to 11 Downing Street in January 1925. Philip recorded one evening that he 'Drove Winston home and sat in his room 'til one o'clock while he rehearsed his speech for next Wednesday on the Imperial conference . . . he was rather nervous about it.'[33] He also noted that Winston enjoyed riding on the mechanical horse simulator that Philip had installed in his bathroom.* Philip arranged for John Singer Sargent to draw Churchill in his robes as Chancellor of the Exchequer, a portrait that hangs in the hall at Chartwell. He also made a Christmas gift to Winston of a painting by John Lewis Brown of two cavalry officers on horseback which Churchill had 'admired' at Trent Park. 'I am sending it to you with my best [underlined four times] wishes,' Philip told him, 'in the hope that you may find a corner for it at Chartwell';[34] the painting still hangs in Churchill's study at his beloved Kent home, and Chartwell contains a number of other paintings executed by Churchill on his many visits to Port Lympne. Philip's parties also provided Winston with regular contact with stimulating artists and writers outside the world of pure politics – men like Orpen, Lavery, George Bernard Shaw and H. G. Wells.

---

* Mechanical horse simulators were used by polo players to practise their swings.

From the mid-1920s, some of Philip's greatest social gatherings were held at Trent Park, his estate near Barnet in north London. His father had taken the lease on Trent from the Duchy of Lancaster a few years before he died, and Philip managed to acquire the freehold in 1922. Situated just 12 miles from central London, it was the perfect location to entertain his friends, an idyllic country retreat that by 1933 would also be within a short walking distance of the end of the Piccadilly Line.*

Country Life magazine declared,

> It would be difficult to find a more perfect setting for a country house than that afforded by this site on the south edge of Enfield Chase. A broad, gentle valley is watered by a stream which expands into a lake dividing the park in two. The park is a typical example of Humphrey Repton, who at the end of the eighteenth century was employed to 'landscape' this wild bit of the Royal Forest which George III had given to Dr Sir Richard Jebb and commanded him to name Trent Park.'[35]

Yet while the estate sat on this ancient royal hunting ground, the mansion house had been rebuilt in the mid-nineteenth century, and Philip would transform it beyond recognition. At Trent, he would give full expression to his love of eighteenth-century art and design. His style, as was fashionable in the 1920s and '30s, embraced the pre-industrial world. After the horrors of the First World War this marked a return to a gentler and more refined age.

There would be substantial building works on the exterior of the house, creating proportions and lines more in keeping with Georgian architecture and design. Philip purchased bricks and stonework for Trent from Devonshire House, the Palladian mansion

---

* Cockfosters Station on Cockfosters Road opened on 31 July 1933, completing the extension of London Underground's Piccadilly Line from Finsbury Park. 'Trent Park' had been suggested as an alternative name for the station.

on the edge of Green Park, designed by William Kent for the dukes of Devonshire and demolished in 1924. It really was a sign of the times that while the old English families were struggling with death duties and inherited debts, it was the Sassoons with their new money from trade and investment who were expanding. The weathered brick and stonework made Trent appear much older and more established than it was. *Country Life* exclaimed, 'An ugly Victorian building has been transformed into a stately yet simple country house in the pure English tradition.'[36]

Philip's friend the writer Osbert Sitwell had attended a prep school close to Trent and thirty years later, while staying there, he recalled the transformation of the building he had known in his youth:

> I used to walk by it every Sunday; before that is to say, Philip had started to make a kind of paradise of it, touching it with magic, so that, where formerly had glowed a mid-Victorian mansion of mauve brick, with designs in black brick covering its face and a roof of mauve slate, turreted and slightly frenchified, now stood an old house of rose red brick and stone cornering, long settled and stained by time; before too, statues and lead sphinxes, smiling from their pedestals, and shepherds fluting under ilex groves, and orangeries and foundations and pyramids, seeming to have been rooted in the bracken for centuries, had made their appearance, and tall old trees, magnolias, and the rarest shrubs that sprung from the ground with something of the same pride with which the swans and multi-coloured water birds displayed their plumage on the lake below.[37]

Just as with the mansion in Park Lane, Philip auctioned off most of the contents of Trent that he had inherited from his father, replacing the Edwardian excess of gold and highly polished mahogany with old English silver and characterful walnut. Like any great collector, he was governed not by sentimentality but rather by the desire to acquire the best possible examples of the styles and designs that pleased him. *Country Life* noted of Philip's new presentation of the interior of Trent, 'The furniture is very much of the kind that accumulates in a country house through centuries of use, though of rather finer quality than is usual, and arranged with distinctly more taste.' Eighteenth-century furniture predominated, with paintings from the same period by great artists like Gainsborough and Zoffany, which focused on the details of family life in the period. As at Park Lane there were also Chinese cabinets, Flemish tapestries and Persian carpets. Philip was interested in the character of these furnishings; the natural patina that colours old silver and bronze, the highly refined finish and detail of Chinese lacquerwork, the rich pattern of the wood on a walnut table or cabinet, and the textures of tapestries and fine carpets. These all emphasized the unique craft and quality of materials that had gone into creating an exceptional piece.

Whereas Port Lympne was a bold statement in modern design with everything commissioned from contemporary artists, Trent was a home that the Sassoon family might have lived in had they arrived in England with the same wealth and status a hundred years previously. The grounds of Trent Park contained plenty of modern conveniences, though, including a heated swimming pool and tennis courts, which could be covered to allow play during the winter months. Philip also created a private golf course and an airstrip to land his planes. The fashionable garden designer Norah Lindsay was commissioned to work on the grounds. Norah was an old family friend from Philip's mother's circle; in 1895, when she married Sir Harry Lindsay, the brother of the Duchess of Rutland, Lady Desborough's son Julian Grenfell was one of the pageboys. However, the marriage failed and in 1924, facing financial ruin, Norah decided to make a living from her passion for garden design, drawing on the patronage of her wealthy friends, including Nancy Astor, Frances Horner, another of Philip's mother's friends, and Consuelo Balsan, the former Duchess of Marlborough. Philip was her greatest patron; they became close friends and confidants, and she was a frequent social and working guest on his estates.

Norah created a water garden around part of the lake at Trent, as well as a scented garden of soft blues, whites and yellows around the swimming pool. Writing in *Country Life* in 1929, she described the secret of her great borders at Trent: 'wide borders lie in pairs, on a gentle slope, with broad grass paths surrounding them on every side so that the untrammelled eye can rove easily up this glade of brilliance, noting the incandescent orange and scarlet of the distant beds, the rich purples and blues of the middle ones, and the soft assuaging creams, and pastel shades of the two at the end'.[38]

Winston Churchill would come to paint in the gardens at Trent and the Prince of Wales to play golf. Every July, Philip would host a series of weekend garden parties where politicians, sportsmen, artists and writers would mix with the younger royals and Sassoon's other celebrity friends. Philip's friend the novelist Alice Dudeney remembered that when attending the big garden parties there were 'nearing Trent whole strings of cars, the road lined with people and on every tree and at every corner placards: "to Trent"'.[39]

Once you had crossed the threshold you might find the Duke of York playing tennis with the Wimbledon champion Jean Borotra, and Winston Churchill arguing about socialism with George Bernard Shaw. Victor Cazalet* recalled an occasion when 'Shaw got very much the worst of the argument, but it seemed to make very little difference to him'.[40] For one party Philip managed to entice Fred Astaire and his sister Adele to Trent; they had been performing at the Empire Theatre, Leicester Square, in the hit musical *Lady, Be Good*.[41]

Just as during Lloyd George's post-war premiership, Philip Sassoon's wealth and social status gave him a position in politics

---

* MP for Chippenham (1924–43). Cazalet was wealthy and aged only twenty-eight when first elected to Parliament. He had served with distinction in the First World War, being awarded the Military Cross in 1917.

that far exceeded his official rank as a junior member of the government. Philip regularly hosted, and was a frequent guest at, dinners and lunches attended by the most senior members of the government. A few months after being made a minister, he joined a dinner given for Queen Mary by Walter Guinness,* with Winston Churchill, Sam Hoare, Arthur Balfour and Lord Derby. In February 1926, Philip was also among Churchill's guests for a dinner at Chartwell, where again Guinness and Hoare were in attendance, along with Max Beaverbrook, Professor Lindemann† and Hugh Cecil.‡

Philip also started hosting a remarkable series of weekly lunches for senior politicians, known as the 'cabinet lunches', which were held in grand style in the dining room at Park Lane. These gatherings were held after a morning meeting of the cabinet, with ministers and other guests of suitable and senior political standing. For Philip, they were the next best thing to being at the cabinet meetings themselves, and they established Park Lane as a meeting place for all senior Conservatives, not just the old coalitionists. Neville Chamberlain, who would never be a frequent guest around Sassoon's table, reported that before a lunch party at Park Lane Philip 'had been to the [Royal Horticultural Society] show and knowing apparently nothing about Cymbidiums had been greatly struck by them. So he had bought about half of Alexander's exhibit and there they were all

---

* An Anglo-Irish businessman and politician, Guinness would later serve in Churchill's wartime government. He was a Conservative Party MP for Bury St Edmonds from 1907 until 1931, and was ennobled as Lord Moyne in 1932.

† Frederick Lindemann was Professor of Experimental Philosophy at the University of Oxford, as well as an expert pilot. Known as 'The Prof', he became part of Churchill's inner circle in his campaign for Britain to rearm in the 1930s.

‡ Lord Hugh Cecil was MP for the University of Oxford (1910–37). He was the youngest son of the third Marquis of Salisbury, and in 1908 had been best man at Winston and Clementine Churchill's wedding.

through the house though they had just come up from Lympne. Just like Monte Cristo.'*[41]

Chamberlain's comparison between Philip and the wealthy yet mysterious Count of Monte Cristo is telling. In Alexandre Dumas's famous novel, the Count's house at Auteuil had been 'scented with its master's favourite perfumes' by 'loading the ante-chambers, staircases, and chimneys with flowers'. When giving a dinner, Monte Cristo 'endeavoured completely to overturn the Parisian ideas, and to free the curiosity as much as the appetite of his guests. It was an Oriental feast that he offered them, but of such a kind as the Arabian fairies might be supposed to prepare. Every delicious fruit that the four quarters of the globe could provide was heaped in vases from China and jars from Japan.'[43]

Like Monte Cristo, Philip sought not just to entertain, but to transport his guests at occasions that were touched with fantasy. His sister Sybil was more prosaic than Neville Chamberlain in her recollection of the Park Lane cabinet lunches: 'It was a nice house and good food. I suppose they liked to be there rather than at somebody else's house which would have given them boiled mutton . . . They stayed in the dining room until three or half past when they were having arguments.'[44]

The Colonial Secretary, Leo Amery, remembered an occasion after cabinet when 'Winston, Sam [Hoare], Philip [Cunliffe-]Lister† and myself then met again at Philip Sassoon's plus FE [Smith], who had not turned up at the Cabinet pretending that he had not known it was fixed for that morning. Winston is in very good form and rather

---

*   H. G. Alexander owned the famous Westonbirt orchid collection. He was regarded as the foremost orchid hybridist of the first half of the twentieth century, and was a gold medal winner for orchids at the Royal Horticultural Society's annual show at Chelsea. When he retired in 1960 he endowed the Westonbirt Orchid Medal which is presented annually by the RHS.

†   Cunliffe-Lister was the MP for Hendon (1918–35) and President of the Board of Trade prior to his elevation to the House of Lords as Lord Swinton.

amusing on the subject of Austen's triumphs,* which have been
mainly forced upon him.' Amery also recalled another lunch where
'Winston, Philip [Cunliffe-Lister] and I had a great triangular debate
on safeguarding,† Winston very excited and trotting out all the worst
old Free Trade stuff of the campaign of twenty years ago.'[45]

Philip settled quickly into ministerial life at the Air Ministry,
working under Sam Hoare; his appointment as Under-Secretary of
State had actually been at Hoare's request. Although they had been
completely divided in their views on the Lloyd George coalition,
Hoare had appreciated what a useful ally Philip could be. Hoare
was an ambitious man, and placement within Philip's social circle
would do his political standing and profile no harm, and as a keen
sportsman himself, weekends of tennis at Trent were a further
attraction. Hoare was married to Maud, the sister of Earl Beauchamp,
who (as already noted) would be forced to leave the country in
1931 in order to escape prosecution for his homosexuality. The
Hoares had no children, and throughout his life there was private
speculation that Sam was gay in sympathy, if not actively homosexual.[46] Philip and Sam shared a genuine passion for and interest
in the development of the air force and of air communications
routes across the Empire. Philip had established his credentials as a
future Air Minister earlier in 1924, with a speech in the House of
Commons on the issue of air force administration. In it, he set out
his personal manifesto for the Air Ministry, showing great foresight
on the growing importance of air defence:

---

* Austen Chamberlain had signed the Locarno Treaties in October 1925 with
France, Germany, Belgium and Italy, which were supposed to guarantee
peace in western Europe.
† The Safeguarding of Industries Act of 1925 extended the provisions of a
1921 Act of Parliament to protect British industry from unfair overseas
competition. The Conservatives had supported tariff reform for many years,
whereas for Churchill, who had been an out-and-out free-trader, this was a
compromise on his previous position.

The ordinary citizen is beginning to realise very acutely that his position in the next war, if there is one, is going to be very different from the position of his kind in all past wars, not excluding the last war. Before the development of flying, when the question of defence was under discussion, he had inevitably at the back of his mind the thought that, after all, it was primarily the job of the fighting Services, that the Army and Navy were there to bear the brunt of the first attack, and that if the affair became serious there would always be time to raise the necessary forces and take the necessary precautions. But to-day the whole situation is reversed. The first people to bear the brunt of an attack upon the security of these islands will be the man and woman in the street, going about their round of daily business. It will be the ordinary peaceful citizen whose lungs will be the first to be affected by poison gas, whose body will be rent, and whose home will be destroyed by the bombs of the invader. I think the ordinary elector is beginning to realise with acute anxiety this new fact of war, and there is, after all, something perhaps to be said for the paradox that in the next war the safest place for a man will be in the fighting Services. There, at least, he will have a gas mask issued to him, and he will be taught how to use it and how to defend himself, so far as defence is possible . . . the country would like to have an air defence of a sufficient standard to make it unsafe for another country to attack us, and they will not grudge the cost of such a standard, nor do I think they will be content with less . . .

'A strong, active, civil air industry is vital,' Philip continued,

not only to act as a reinforcement of the military arm in case of need, but also for the usages and for the general purposes of such an Empire as ours. We have been told that in Iraq the aeroplanes have been able to take the place of 24 battalions of infantry. That shows what vast economies can be effected when aeroplanes discharge the military burdens of Empire, and still vaster economies could be effected by a properly established civil air service taking on the commercial development of our immense Imperial resources, and also acting as a reservoir, certainly for men, and perhaps for machines. I hope the Government will push on with the scheme which the Under-Secretary mentioned when he referred to the Auxiliary Territorial Air Force Bill, which would train pilots as well as ground men, and I am sure that with that it would form a valuable source for getting recruits of the best kind. The best pilots are necessarily young, and if something could be done for boys in our public schools and young men in our universities on the lines of the Officers' Training Corps, which might enable them to qualify as pilots, I am sure that many would come along, and the recruiting difficulty would be overcome.[47]

One of Philip's first conferences as a minister would be with Sam Hoare and the Colonial Secretary, Leo Amery, in Baghdad, considering the role of the air force in helping to keep the peace in Iraq. They would also push Winston Churchill for more money from the Treasury for the air force, though with only moderate success. Hoare remembered that Churchill as Chancellor of the Exchequer 'maintained the most rigid doctrine of economy, and applied it with a relentless hand to all military expenditure ... The programme of fifty-two squadrons for Home Defence that had been regarded in 1923 as the barest minimum was pushed into the distant future, with the inevitable result that a crushing handicap was placed on us in the race for air parity in later years.'[48]

The development of the auxiliary air force, where part-time pilots were trained for flying in fighter squadrons and for bombing raids, was a particular passion for Philip Sassoon. The auxiliary air squadrons typically attracted wealthy young men who had the time and the means to learn to fly and even maintain their own aircraft. One of the most celebrated of these units was the 601 (County of London) Auxiliary Air Squadron, which was founded in 1925 at White's club by Lord Edward 'Ned' Grosvenor. Its home

David Sassoon (seated) and his eldest sons, left to right, Elias, Abdullah Albert and S. D. Sassoon, c. 1857

Young Philip Sassoon

Philip Sassoon by Glyn Philpot, 1914

Lady Aline Sassoon by John Singer
Sargent, 1907

Sybil, Countess of Rocksavage,
in the ballroom at 25 Park Lane,
by Charles Sims, c. 1923

Philip Sassoon in Strange Company by Max Beerbohm, 1913

The unveiling of the foundation stone for Philip Sassoon's housing scheme at The Durlocks, in Folkestone, 1919

Field Marshal Sir Douglas Haig, with Philip Sassoon, on board the Commander in Chief's train during the First World War

Philip Sassoon, flanked by Sir Louis Mallet and Lady Juliet Duff, visiting the tomb of Tutankhamun, 1923

Philip Sassoon and David Lloyd George at Port Lympne, 1920

Philip Sassoon and the Prince of Wales at Port Lympne, 1920

1921 Anglo-French conference at Port Lympne. From the left: Ralph Wigram, Lord Riddell, Philip Kerr, Philip Sassoon and Maurice Hankey. Lloyd George is holding a walking stick with Sybil to his left and Robert Vansittart behind him. The French Prime Minister, Aristide Briand, is third from the right

Philip Sassoon, the Prince of Wales and Winston Churchill dressed for polo at Roehampton, 1921

Winston Churchill painting the view of Romney Marsh from the terrace at Port Lympne, 1926

Tennis at Port Lympne, 1920, and skiing in San Moritz, c. 1930

Lytton Strachey and Baba Curzon at Port Lympne with Philip Sassoon, 1922

Charlie Chaplin at Port Lympne, 1921, with, left to right, Hannah Gubbay, Sybil Rocksavage and Philip Sassoon

Charlie Chaplin at Trent Park, 1931

The Port Lympne estate, 1926, with Philip Sassoon on the Trojan Stairs, 1929

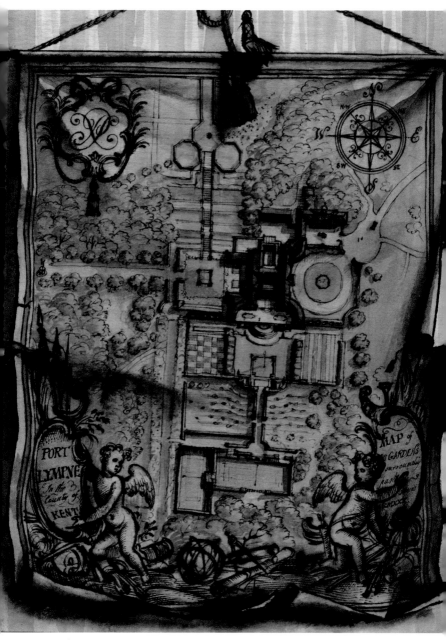

Plan of Port Lympne by Rex Whistler, 1929

The Trent Park estate

Philip Sassoon at Trent Park with the future King George VI (far right, partially obscured by Duff Cooper in the foreground) and Queen Elizabeth (seated, second row, second from left)

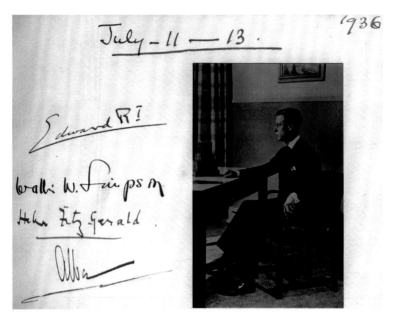

Snapshots from the Trent Park visitors' books, recording the visits of King Edward VIII and Wallis Simpson, just months before Edward's abdication in December 1936, and of Princesses Margaret and Elizabeth

Philip Sassoon on his Third Route air tour, 1928

Philip at the wheel of his 1930 model Humber Snipe, with his distinctive cobra on top of the radiator

Members of the RAF and other guests relaxing at Port Lympne, 1933

At Port Lympne, 1935: left to right, Bob Boothby, Noël Coward, Sybil, Philip Sassoon, Drogo Montagu, Loel Guinness and Rupert Belleville

Philip Sassoon in RAF uniform as commanding officer of the 601 Auxiliary Air Squadron, known as the 'Millionaire's Mob'

Philip Sassoon standing behind President and Madame Lebrun of France, Westminster Hall, 23 March 1939, less than three months before his death

base was at Northolt in west London, but from 1926 the squadron held its August summer camps at Lympne, with the young flying officers in frequent attendance at Philip's garden parties, and spending afternoons sunbathing and swimming in the pool. Some of Philip's friends may have exchanged knowing smiles at the sight of these athletic young men draped around his estate, but there was an official purpose to his hospitality as well. He wanted to make the air force 'smart' to encourage able young men seeking adventure into the RAF, and invitations to parties at Trent or Lympne helped further the social cachet of the auxiliary air squadrons, many of whose members would later fly with great distinction in the Battle of Britain.

Members of the 601 Squadron, such as James Hawtrey, Rupert Belleville, Drogo Montagu and Loel Guinness, became firm friends of Philip's and were often guests at his parties. Belleville had something of a reputation as a tearaway; he would later befriend Ernest Hemingway in Spain during the Civil War, and formed a close personal relationship with Venetia Montagu.* Loel Guinness joined Philip in Parliament in 1931 and served as his parliamentary private secretary at the Air Ministry. In the same year Philip became godfather to Loel's son Patrick.

The airmen enjoyed plenty of hijinks during the summer camps at Lympne. On one occasion, Pilot Officer Roger Bushell 'borrowed' a plane belonging to Lord Beaverbrook's son Max Aitken, who was also a member of the squadron, and flew it down to the Botolph's Bridge pub on Romney Marsh. Unfortunately he crash-landed into a hedge, escaping injury but destroying the plane and knocking over a road sign reading 'To Dymchurch', which Bushell kept and presented as a trophy to the squadron.

As Air Minister, Philip was also a great supporter of air racing,

---

* The widow of Edwin Montagu, the former Secretary of State for India. Before their marriage, as Venetia Stanley, she had a romantic friendship with the then Prime Minister Herbert Asquith.

and encouraged the international Schneider Trophy races for sea-
planes, which challenged the principal aircraft manufacturers to
compete against each other with innovations in aerodynamics. The
leading entrants typically came from France, Italy, Great Britain and
the USA, and the trophy was competed for like the Americas Cup
in sailing, with the winning nation having the right to host the
competition the following year. Crowds of fashionable air-race watch-
ers would gather in the 1920s at venues like Cowes and Monaco,
and in 1927 Philip travelled to Venice to support the government-
backed teams. British success that year was delivered by Supermarine,
a Southampton-based company which would later develop the
Spitfire fighter plane. The secrets of success in the Schneider Trophy
were speed and manoeuvrability, and both attributes were fine-tuned
by Supermarine in their manufacture of the Spitfire.

It was at the Schneider Trophy races in Venice that Philip
befriended Mussolini's Aviation Minister, Italo Balbo, a leading
fascist who in 1922, aged just twenty-six, had been one of the
principal architects of the March on Rome that helped bring
Mussolini to power. Philip's sister Sybil, who had accompanied him
to Venice, thought that Balbo was 'a very delightful person, a real
character from the XVIth century'.[49] The following spring, through
Balbo, Philip returned to Italy for audiences in Rome with both
Mussolini and Pope Pius XI. He concluded that 'the Pope's is much
the best show and he really is the great swell in Rome. He never
enjoyed himself more than when I was with him. I think he was
so thankful to be with a heathen and not to have to talk shop. He
was exquisitely dressed in white moire and sapphires and kept me
over an hour – with 50,000 Easter pilgrims waiting to see him pass
in front of them.'[50]

Philip's main aim at the Air Ministry had been to develop the
potency of the RAF, with an emphasis on attracting more talented
young men to sign up, championing advances in aircraft design
and if possible getting more investment from the Treasury. These
were all initiatives that would serve the air force well in the future.

The ministry also had a strategic interest in the development of civilian air travel across the Empire, and in particular on the route to India. It was by then possible to make the journey by air from London to Bombay in five days, as opposed to fifteen by ship. Philip believed that the air route to the east would soon 'become an ordinary commonplace thing, like so many other of the wonders of our day'.[51] Imperial Airways, whose chairman was Philip's friend Eric Geddes, was going to start a regular service to India in 1929 and the Air Ministry decided that before civilian aircraft made the journey the RAF should fly the course. Philip was asked to lead the expedition in September 1928, which he described and published in his book *The Third Route*, in order 'to make the possibilities of air travel more widely known and better understood'.[52] The title of Philip's book reflected his confidence that the new air route would mark a breakthrough in travel to India as significant as Vasco da Gama's navigation around the Cape of Good Hope in 1497, and the opening of the Suez Canal in 1869 (the first and second routes). Philip's journey was expanded to include a series of inspections of RAF stations across Egypt and the Sudan, the Middle East and India, which lasted for six weeks. The survey of this network of bases supporting the use of air power in policing the Empire was the real reason for the tour.

At 6.45 a.m. on 29 September, Philip set off from the Cattewater RAF seaplane base in Plymouth Sound on board a Blackburn Iris II flying boat, accompanied by Air Commodore Arthur Longmore and two pilots from the flying boat development flight at Felixstowe. They stopped to refuel at the French seaplane base at Etang d'Hourtin, near Biarritz, and ended their first day at Marseille, where Philip was joined for dinner by his old friend Sir Louis Mallet. The following afternoon they reached Naples, where they were met and given dinner by Balbo, who presented Philip with a 'silver flying trophy, executed with the art for which Italy is famous and on so magnificent a scale that I dared not add it to my luggage. It travelled home independently.' Philip wrote of Balbo: 'Under Mussolini, no man in Italy has done more than he to develop Italy's air-mindedness, or to bring the Italian air force to the high degree of excellence it has attained.'

The Italian air force gave Philip an escort from Naples as they flew across Italy towards the Ionian Sea and the Greek islands beyond. 'Our position,' he recalled,

> when we had left the last faint outline of Italy behind and sea and sky met in an unbroken horizon all around us, became quite wonderful. We found ourselves suspended in utter isolation between an unflecked sky and an unflecked sea, blue reflecting and intensifying blue. We spun along as though cupped between two azure cymbals, resonant with sound which seemed of deeper meaning than the roaring of man-made engines. I shall never forget the first sight of Cephalonia and Zante, etched in ivory upon the horizon.

From Greece they headed to Egypt, where Philip exchanged his seaplane for a Fairey IIIF day bomber, to make an inspection of RAF stations along the Nile, as far south as Khartoum. There was still time for sightseeing, with Philip directing the planes to fly over the pyramids at Giza, and in Cairo he went to the museum to examine the artefacts from the tomb of Tutankhamun, some of which he had seen in situ when they were excavated in 1923. He recalled, 'even that experience had scarcely prepared me for the richness, the massed magnificence and the exquisite workmanship of the complete collection ... The prodigal use of gold is most impressive, and when one thinks that all these splendid objects are but the funeral trappings of one of the lesser Pharaohs who died in his early youth, one can begin to understand the old saying that the sands of Egypt were of gold.'

His onward passage from Cairo to India almost retraced the history of his Sassoon family, and their journey after leaving the

Holy Land centuries before the birth of Christ to travel on to Iraq, Persia and then Bombay. Yet in his published account of the journey he gives readers no insight into his personal connection with the ancient cities he passes. Despite being the heir of two of the greatest Jewish families of the nineteenth century, he simply notes that Jerusalem from the air is 'a pale city scattered over pale hills, with the Mosque of Omar standing out in very noticeable prominence'. Philip's first impressions of Baghdad, the city where his ancestors had traded for centuries and where they had been leading members of the Jewish community, were mixed. 'Romance must have departed Baghdad with the Caliphs,' he wrote. 'To-day it is a disappointing place, and is more like a great overgrown village than the capital of the land where civilisation had its birth.' However, after a day spent in the city of his forefathers, and a swim in the warm waters of the River Tigris, before dinner with King Faisal at the British High Commissioner's residence, he had changed his opinion about Baghdad. 'Parts of it are certainly rather dirty and, with the exception of the mosques, there are few buildings which repay a second glance; but it still preserves the atmosphere of days long past.' He thought that King Faisal was 'very charming and [he] is an excellent French scholar, in spite of his modest disclaimers. I drank coffee with him in his unpretentious audience room, outside of which the Tigris idly flows, and while we talked watched the black melon boats (guffas I discovered they were called) waddling slowly by.'

Leaving Baghdad on 13 October for the 300-mile journey to the port of Basra, Philip followed by air the line of the River Euphrates, and the escape from persecution of his great-grandfather David Sassoon a hundred years before. This was the event that changed the fate and fortunes of his family, but Philip doesn't mention it at all. Perhaps he didn't want to disturb his travel journal with personal anecdotes, although he was happy to do so when talking about the tomb of Tutankhamun or his friendship with General Balbo. It is more likely that he simply wanted to present himself as an urbane English traveller and minister of the Crown, and not to dwell on the Sassoon family's eastern heritage. Basra itself made a positive impression: Philip thought it an 'Arab Venice, full of creeks and canals along which pale blue gondolas thread the universal date farms. These are everywhere, the fertile soil and abundant moisture making for wonderful growth, and in the spring peach trees blossom beneath the palms.'

David Sassoon had fled Iraq from Basra to the coastal town of Bushire, which in 1928 was the home to the British naval squadron in the Persian Gulf. Philip's family connection with this town, the place where his grandfather's bar mitzvah had been held, was again left out of his account. Philip makes a rather dismissive reference to Bushire: 'With its white stone buildings it looks from the air a very tidy town, and there are a number of nice houses on its outskirts. I am told that its appearance belies it, and that closer inspection would reveal the usual smells and dirt in an unusually concentrated form.'

When David Sassoon fled to Bushire, he carried with him pearls sewn into the hem of his cloak, and it was the plight of the pearl divers working in the Persian Gulf that moved Philip more:

the divers work in pairs, ten or a dozen forming the crew of small sailing boats which go out in great fleets of sixty or seventy vessels. Armed with an iron-wood spike as a protection against sharks and further insured by the incantations of a shark-charmer, naked except for a girdle to which to attach his basket the diver descends to the bottom with the aid of a great stone tied to the line to which he clings. A clip on the nose does duty for a diving dress, and so equipped a good diver may remain down for as long as eighty seconds, filling his basket with oysters. It is a most exhausting profession, and most divers die young; for they are to all intents and purposes slaves, and have to pay for their wretched winter keep by diving all the summer.

Today this lack of personal narrative in Philip's travel journal seems odd, as if he wanted to downplay his eastern heritage, and the Sassoons' more modest circumstances before they made their fortune in Bombay. One fellow MP, Bob Boothby, remembered an occasion when he visited Philip at Port Lympne and found him reading a book in the library and wearing a fez. Philip told him that he had never forgotten his eastern heritage.[53] That may have been true, but nor did he seek to draw any particular public attention to it. There remained within Philip Sassoon's character, despite his status and creative mindset, an awareness of the importance of external conformity in the English society of his time.

On 16 October Philip landed in the British Raj, at Karachi, where he was greeted by Air Vice-Marshal Sir Geoffrey Salmond, commander of the RAF in India, and a telegram of welcome from the Viceroy, Lord Irwin, who would later inherit the title Lord Halifax and attain the office of Foreign Secretary. Philip's return to the land of his father's birth would not include visiting the family estate at Poona or the Sassoon Dock in Bombay. From Karachi, he flew to Jodhpur, and then to the government centre of New Delhi, with a few days' rest with the Viceroy at his residence in Simla. Otherwise Philip's principal objective in India was to inspect the RAF stations in the North West Frontier, the front line of the Empire against the rebellious tribes in Afghanistan.

Jodhpur provided the most magnificent welcome of Philip's tour. From the air he thought it 'A beautiful city, gay with palaces and lakes, with a magnificent old fort of red stone and age-long City walls set with seventy gates. Above the fort completing the perfect outline of the city, a superb palace built into the living rock.' A 'huge crowd' had assembled to see Philip's plane land, and a fleet of pale-blue Rolls-Royce cars escorted him and his party through the city. The Maharajah of Jodhpur was away in England, so Philip was instead hosted by his uncle, who arranged for a state dinner party to honour the visit. 'It proved to be a most admirably arranged and imposing function,' Philip recorded, 'though somewhat to my regret, the dishes were chiefly European. Indian guests and servants alike were splendidly clothed, yet alike in perfect taste; the Princes wearing long white coats with jewelled buttons and pale tartan turbans; the servants all dressed in green and gold with green and gold turbans.'

Another great crowd gathered the following morning to see Philip and three accompanying escort planes depart for lunch in New Delhi. There, under the direction of the architects Edwin Lutyens and Herbert Baker, who had also built Philip's Port Lympne mansion, a great new administrative centre for India was being constructed. Sassoon noted that 'The new capital is not yet finished,* but enough has been done to enable one to obtain a very clear conception of what the whole will one day be. It is undoubtedly well worthy to be a seat of Empire and the centre of the Government of India . . . The peoples of India are admirers of fine architecture, and pomp and pageant have always meant much to them. They will undoubtedly find all three at Delhi.' Little did Philip appreciate that this new citadel, perhaps the greatest architectural monument to the global power of the British Empire, would be completed in the dying decades of the Raj.

They flew from Delhi to Ambala at the foot of the Himalayas, to take the mountain train to Simla. The Viceroy moved to the crisp clean air of Simla in April each year when the heat of the plain became too oppressive in New Delhi. There the seat of British government would remain until December, when the Viceroy departed by tradition to spend the Christmas season in Calcutta. September and October were the best times to be at Simla, when the summer monsoons gave way, in Lord Irwin's words, to a 'clean atmosphere in which every line and shadow stood out sharp and unmistakable; the smell of vegetation reviving and refreshed; a sun perpetually shining out of a cloudless sky; and in the great distances

---

* Lord Irwin would not move into the immense new Vice-Regal Lodge until December 1929.

the ridges of snow mountains catching all the changing lights until these faded into darkness with the last rose-coloured rays of the setting sun'.[54]

Philip noted the transformation of the environment as the train took him up into the mountains towards Simla:

> every moment as we climbed into a cooler and moister climate the vegetation became more luxuriant. I made my first close acquaintance with mango trees, and marvelled at the forests of deodars and the variety of conifers and rhododendrons. All the little stations which we passed were gay with cosmos, zinnias and dahlias, and looped up with jasmine. Every moment we got glorious views across deep, verdant valleys with snow-capped mountains towering in the distance. Then suddenly we would be plunged into the darkness of a tunnel, to emerge in a few moments into dazzling sunlight and to be enchanted with a still more wonderful example of the beauty and majesty of the hills.

The final journey from the rail station at Simla to the Vice-Regal Lodge, the highest point in the town, had to be made by rickshaw as the roads were so narrow that the use of cars was strictly reserved for the Viceroy, the Commander in Chief of the armed forces and the Governor of the province. Philip declared, 'if I had to choose between the life of a rickshaw man at Simla and that of a Pearl Diver in the Persian gulf I should be hard put to it to decide which was the less undesirable. I confess that I felt rather uncomfortable at being dragged up those steep hillsides by man power; but it is the custom of the country, and I believe that those who live there soon get used to the idea.' He 'was delighted to find the Viceroy looking so fit and well, notwithstanding that his term of office has so far been no easy one', as a result of the growing political tensions in India arising from the campaign of Mahatma Gandhi and the Congress Party for self-government. Philip also recalled that 'during the afternoon Lord Irwin and I had the most delightful talk together on all manner of subjects, not omitting the many strange flowers and trees with which the garden was filled and the troops of wild monkeys which appeared to swarm everywhere. No place seems sacred to the monkeys, but I understand that the monkeys themselves are sacred.'

The following evening, Sassoon departed for Lahore and the inspection of the RAF stations of the North West Frontier, and he recalled in his journal that 'the sight of Simla by night as we rushed away from it towards the plains, was inexpressibly beautiful – a Valhalla of lights that quite eclipsed the Milky Way'.

At the air stations in Peshawar, Miramshah and Quetta, the 'guardians of the frontier' (as Philip called them) were engaged in a ceaseless campaign of tactical strikes against the rebellious Afghan tribes of a nature that would be familiar to all who have engaged in similar actions over the succeeding decades of warfare in that troubled land.

'Though punitive expeditions carried out by the air force do not last as long as did the old ground expeditions,' Philip wrote,

they may yet take some considerable time before a really obstinate tribe is brought to acknowledge defeat. In such cases a very large amount of flying has to be done over extraordinarily wild and difficult country, with a corresponding risk of forced landings. Among the great mountains are many caves, which have been known to, and from time to time used by, the native population since the memory of man. When their villages are bombed the tribes retreat with their goods and chattels to these caves, where there is safe shelter for man and beast. All the aeroplanes can do is harass the tribesmen and their flocks and herds when they come out. The work is arduous and unremitting, and the contest resolves itself into a question whether the airmen or the tribesmen can hold out the longer. The tribesmen waste a good deal of ammunition by shooting at the machines. The aeroplanes drop a certain number of bombs, which impress the tribesmen with the necessity of keeping under cover; but very few casualties are incurred on either side. Obviously such a state of things may on occasions continue for quite a long time. Indeed, it has been suggested that in many cases the deadlock would probably have gone on much longer than in fact it did, had it not been that the caves were so full of fleas that ultimately even the case-hardened villagers came to consider surrender the lesser evil of the two.

Philip had championed the efficiency and effectiveness of the RAF in undertaking this kind of work. A couple of months after his visit to the territory, in December 1928, and faced with rising tensions and the threat of civil war in Afghanistan, the RAF also executed the first ever large-scale airlift, when nearly six hundred European diplomatic staff and their families were carried out of Kabul to safety.

It would be hard to imagine a more isolated corner of the British Empire than Miramshah. The air base was set on a small mountain plateau, hemmed in on all sides by great mountains. When Philip arrived on Trafalgar Day, 21 October, it would have been no less surprising to meet Lord Nelson than the war hero who was there to greet him.

Aircraftman Shaw, better known as Lawrence of Arabia, had sought a life of relative obscurity in the RAF following his heroics when leading the desert revolt against the Ottoman Empire in the Great War. Miramshah greatly appealed to Lawrence. As he wrote to a friend:

I've moved from Karachi, and come up to the most remote RAF station in India – and the smallest. We are only 26, all told, with 5 officers, and we sit with 700 Indian Scouts in a brick and earth fort behind barbed wire complete with searchlights and machine guns. Round us, a few miles off, in a ring are low bare porcelain coloured hills, with chipped edges and a broken-bottle skyline. Afghanistan is 10 miles off. The quietness of the place is uncanny

– ominous, I was nearly saying: for the scouts and ourselves live in different compartments of the fort, and never meet: and so there's no noise of men: and no birds or beasts – except a jackal concert for five minutes about 10pm each night, when the search-lights start. The Indian sentries flicker the beams across the plain, hoping to make them flash in the animals' eyes . . . We are not allowed beyond the barbed wire by day, or outside the fort walls by night . . . the only temptations of Miramshah are boredom and idleness.[55]

Philip thought Lawrence 'seemed thoroughly happy in his self-chosen exile', yet it was not to last for long. The rebellion in Afghanistan would lead to Lawrence's return to England, not on grounds of his personal safety, but because many regarded him as Britain's master spy and if he was known to be in the North West Frontier it would arouse suspicion. Philip noted, 'I feel myself impelled to the belief that Lawrence's decision to hide himself from the public eye was due in part to an instinctive feeling that his life's work was done. There have been men like that in England's history before. Men who seem to have been created for one end and, having achieved it, have passed comet-like from the eyes of their fellow men.'[56]

Yet Lawrence fell under Sassoon's spell, and their meeting was the start of a lasting friendship. They had in common a love of ancient civilizations and a passion for aviation; Lawrence would attach himself to the British racing team for the 1929 Schneider Trophy. An invitation from Philip Sassoon also offered his friends, many of them, like Lawrence, among the greatest celebrities of their day, the chance to relax in an environment of perfect luxury and discretion. There is no doubt that Philip was attracted by success, but he only required his friends to be themselves. The boxer Georges Carpentier, who also starred in several films after retiring from the sport, remembered that Philip never once asked him about his profession. He understood, as well as they did, that there was the mask of public expectation that had to be worn, but also a private self that required the opportunity for expression in the company of friends.

Philip's flight from Miramshah to Quetta marked the start of the journey home. At Karachi, they picked up Sir Denys Bray, the Foreign Secretary of India, who was on his way to a conference in London but wanted a lift as far as Basra. Their otherwise smooth journey was interrupted by a forced landing at Jask on the Persian Gulf coast, owing to engine trouble. Here they were held for thirty-six hours, staying at the residence of a Mr Thomson of the Indo-European Telegraph Department, while they awaited the parts required by the plane, and clearance from the local officials to depart. Back at Basra, Philip deposited Sir Denys and took a detour from his official programme to visit the archaeologist Leonard Woolley and see his excavation works at the ruined Sumerian city of Ur, approximately halfway between the Persian Gulf and the modern city of Baghdad. Woolley's discovery of this ancient civilization had led to the theory that the story of Noah and the flood in Genesis was based on a localized event in that region, and Philip acknowledged as a result of their conversations 'the cultural debt which the Western civilisations of our own day have inherited, through the channel of Jewish writings and Greek learning, from those strange early peoples of Sumer who, until some thirty years ago, were forgotten as though they had never been'.

The remainder of Philip's visit to Iraq was focused firmly on the problems of the twentieth century, many of which endure to this day. He returned to Baghdad during the week of the great horse show, with racing and polo matches, for which 'all the big sheikhs come in from the desert'. Then it was on to Mosul to review the RAF's operations in the north of the country. The possession of Mosul had been a matter of some dispute. Turkey had argued against the proposal to include the city within Iraq as part of the dissolution of the Ottoman Empire after the war. Mosul was originally to have been incorporated into the new Syrian state inspired by the Sykes–Picot agreement,* but when large quantities of oil were discovered in its surrounds British interest in Mosul increased. Lloyd George successfully argued at the 1920 San Remo conference, where Philip had been part of the delegation supporting the Prime Minister, that it should be included in the new Iraq under a British mandate. Philip's first impression of Mosul was that the mixed races and religions of the town were brought together simply by a mutual interest in trade and commerce: 'the good feeling in the town is native and is not the recent creation of the Pax Britannica'.

He also noted that:

Iraq was the first country in which was tried the experiment of maintaining peace and order by air power. It was an experiment forced upon Great Britain by the immense cost of maintaining adequate control by ground forces. It has succeeded to the utmost of our expectations . . . the despatch of a column of all arms into a little known and hostile country is always a costly business, both in men and money. Though the enemy's villages be burned and his stock, it may be, destroyed or driven off, it is usually a matter of great difficulty to bring the actual offenders to book. The expedition withdraws, losing many men to snipers on the way, and the enemy returns to his burnt out homesteads filled with a consuming desire to get his own back.

Philip added a telling insight into the troubles of Iraq in 1928, which still bedevil the region today: 'Almost the whole of the peasant classes of Iraq are Shi'ites and one of the chief problems of Iraq, which must somehow be solved if Iraq is to reap the full benefit of its new found

---

* The 1916 Sykes–Picot agreement, named after its creators Sir Mark Sykes MP and the French diplomat François Georges-Picot, was made secretly between the British and French government, with the assent of the Russian Empire. It proposed how the Allies should divide between them the Arab territories of the Ottoman Empire after the war.

independence, is to reconcile the Shi'ites with the Sunni upper class, so that all can co-operate as a united people for the common welfare.'

Philip's return journey to Europe followed the North African coast towards Malta, flying over Egypt and the Italian colony of Libya. Observing from the air, he noted, 'Benghazi is going ahead fast. It is a mixture of Venetian and Arab style; pink palaces and palm trees. It is a romantic looking place. There are a number of fine new houses, masses of soldiers, an aerodrome at which six squadrons are stationed. It affords a good example of the progressive policy of Mussolini.' Flying north from Malta along the coast of Sicily, he also experienced the spectacle of Mount Etna in full eruption, its most significant since 1669: 'a great cloud of steam and smoke shot with the glow of fires round its middle and burning villages at its foot; but the top showing fairly clear and covered with snow'. His final stop was on the west coast of France with Baron Rothschild at Château Lafite, and Sassoon typically makes no mention in his book that he was a relation.

Philip returned home, landing at Calshot on Southampton Water on 13 November, after covering 17,000 miles and visiting twenty-five RAF stations. He told the journalists awaiting his return that 'From every point of view the flight was a great success and the machine behaved splendidly.'[57] King George V sent a telegram: 'I heartily congratulate you on your safe return from your long flight and I feel sure that your visit to the numerous stations of the Royal Air Force between this country and India will prove of great benefit to the service.'[58] Philip's constituency newspaper, the *Folkestone Herald*, also congratulated him with the warm words, 'His trip . . . cannot fail to be handed down in our history as a brilliant example of service to the Empire and devotion to duty.'[59]

Throughout his air tour, people at home had been kept abreast of his progress with regular bulletins in the newspapers. On his return he gave lectures about it and in May 1929 published his chronicle of the tour in *The Third Route*. T. E. Lawrence, who received in his view a mercifully brief mention, wrote to congratulate Philip on the book:

Yesterday I re-read your Third Route (in my usual fashion, which is to toss through a new book in an hour, first time and if it seems to ask for more, to go through it again slowly, after a fortnight). Yours did definitely ask for it . . . The strongest impression The Third Route conveyed to me was freshness . . . seeing everything with a pair of new eyes and you have written it down exactly as you saw it, in your own words. Like having eyes talk . . . Your book feels easy, as if you had written it easily. Curious since fortune made you complicated! Natural ease is not very admirable, but ease of this kind, which comes only with very hard work, is well worth its difficulty.[60]

Philip's friend the Romanian princess and Parisian socialite Marthe Bibesco prepared the French translation of *The Third Route* and as a present he gave her an emerald and sapphire brooch which Napoleon had given to Marie Walewska when he learnt she was expecting his child. The artist and illustrator Rex Whistler designed the endpapers for the book, and his reward would be further lucrative Sassoon commissions.

Philip was welcomed back to Westminster with a private dinner at the end of November 1928, jointly celebrating his return and Winston Churchill's birthday. Gossip in Parliament was increasingly focused on the impending general election, expected in the summer. Conservative Party confidence was high, and after their large parliamentary majority in 1924, the Tories expected to retain office. There was more speculation about which politicians would be the personal winners in the post-election ministerial reshuffle. Churchill was expected to leave the Treasury, making way for Neville Chamberlain, and move to either the Foreign Office or the India Office. Before one of the cabinet lunches at Park Lane, Thomas Jones, the Deputy Cabinet Secretary who had also been part of Lloyd George's private office, asked Philip who he thought deserved promotion in the new government. He recorded Philip as replying that his favourite was Anthony Eden [who was at the time PPS to the Foreign Secretary]. Duff Cooper could speak but could he work with others? He was egocentric to a colossal degree, but this confidence could take him some distance. Sam Hoare ought to go to the India Office where someone was badly needed who would work at the job. As you entered the place you were now overpowered with miasma. Our talk was interrupted by the arrival of Ministers from this morning's Cabinet meeting.'[61]

Philip's preference for Cooper and Hoare was understandable. Duff was an old friend, and Sam his colleague at the Air Ministry, and both had a soft spot for Sassoon's lavish entertaining. Anthony Eden was a new star in the political firmament. Then just thirty-one, he had been in the House of Commons for nearly six years. During the war he had served with distinction, winning the Military Cross, and at twenty-one became the youngest brigade major in the British army. Eden cut a glamorous figure, but was also vain. His political rival R. A. 'Rab' Butler described him as 'half mad baronet, half beautiful woman'.[62] Like Philip, Eden had been educated at Eton, and after the war took his place at Christ Church, Oxford. There he was part of the 'aesthete' set and founded the Uffizi Society, whose purpose was to discuss painters and paintings past and present.[63] Its members included the future MPs and society hosts Henry 'Chips' Channon and Victor Cazalet, and Eddy Sackville-West, with whom Eden also had a sexual relationship.*[64] In 1923, the year Eden entered Parliament, he married Beatrice Beckett, and his romantic life thereafter remained focused on women. Both Anthony and Beatrice Eden would become frequent guests of Philip's at Trent and Lympne.

Thomas Jones made a note of the general discussion at the Park Lane cabinet lunch in his diary:

---

* Eden also had an affair at Oxford with the Bloomsbury Group artist Eardley Knollys.

We sat at the round table, our host having on his right Hailsham,* Cunliffe-Lister, and Winston; on his left Neville Chamberlain, Sam Hoare, Walter Guinness and Thomas Jones (who was opposite PS). They began with cabinet gossip where they had been discussing the East Africa report and sending Sammy Wilson† to Kenya. 'Why will Leo [Amery] insist on answering every speaker at cabinet? Why does someone not pull his coat and stop him?' Then some ridicule of Jix‡ followed. The Home Secretary gets himself into the papers daily. At the moment he is posing as a Puritan [over his objections to D. H. Lawrence's *Lady Chatterley's Lover*, which had recently been banned from sale in Britain] . . . Nobody had heard of his books except Winston . . .

Much speculation about the Election, and general agreement that 'We must get our people properly frightened at the prospect of a Socialist government.' Winston (more voluble as the luncheon proceeded) inclined on the whole to wish Labour could be in for a short spell to allow him to display his powers in Opposition. He had never had the experience except during the war. What was the Labour Government like? he asked his colleagues. 'Awful,' replied Cunliffe-Lister. 'It was like hammering a pillow.' They also congratulated Hailsham for his son becoming President of the Oxford Union.§ 65

Sam Hoare recalled that in the run-up to the election everyone was 'confident of a Conservative victory. At Philip Sassoon's weekly luncheons we found everyone, except perhaps Winston, in a happy mood. Davidson [the Conservative Party chairman] was sure of a clear majority and according to such impartial advisers as Tom

---

* Douglas Hogg, first Viscount Hailsham, who was Lord Chancellor at that time.
† Sir Samuel Wilson, Permanent Under-Secretary of State for the Colonies.
‡ Sir William Joynson-Hicks, Home Secretary.
§ Hailsham's son was Quentin Hogg, who would also later serve as Lord Chancellor (1970–4 and 1979–87).

Jones ... the Socialists had no real hope of becoming the largest party in the House of Commons.'[66]

At a further Park Lane lunch, on 24 April 1929, Churchill placed a bet that the Conservatives would win just 278 seats, a prediction that turned out to be far more accurate than those of Jones and Davidson. At the election on 30 May the Conservatives held just 260 seats, a net loss of 152 constituencies, including those of some of the leading younger MPs like Duff Cooper and Harold Macmillan. Labour were the largest party on 278 but, as in 1923, had no majority. Lloyd George's united and reinvigorated Liberals had thrown everything they had into the election to try to break back into a leading position in national politics. Although they had won just under a quarter of the votes cast across the country, they held only fifty-nine constituencies. Even so, the result still meant they controlled the balance of power.

The Conservatives were surprised, but their campaign had been lacklustre, focused on the uninspiring message of 'Safety First'. In the wake of the general strike of 1926, the greatest industrial action the country had ever seen, and with high and rising unemployment, this message did little to reassure the electorate that it was best to stick with Baldwin. Nevertheless, Philip Sassoon was safely returned in Folkestone and Hythe, where the *Herald* reported that he had warned the electorate about the dangers of a socialist government and adopted the campaign slogan of 'straight and together' in his public address to the voters.[67]

Baldwin's reaction to defeat shows that politicians are often creatures of habit. He had become Prime Minister as a result of the leading part he played in bringing down Lloyd George's Liberal–Conservative coalition. The general election of 1929 left Lloyd George holding the balance of power with the opportunity to influence the formation of the new government. There was even the risk that Churchill, who had already been talking to Lloyd George, would press for some kind of pact with the Liberals. Baldwin was determined not to let this happen, so he resigned immediately, which obliged the King to send for the Labour leader Ramsay MacDonald to be the next Prime Minister. As Labour didn't have a majority, there was always the prospect of an early election.

The Conservatives' election defeat meant Philip Sassoon's departure from the Air Ministry. He wrote to Sam Hoare, 'You know how happy I have been working with you and how much I appreciate all the unfailing kindness you have always shown me. These last four and a half years have been among the happiest in my life and I owe it all to you. I hope that before long we shall be working together again. Please use Trent as if it were your own.'[68] Generous offers of accommodation were also extended to other senior refugees from government. Churchill stayed once again in rooms at Park Lane, and Trent Park was put at the disposal of Stanley Baldwin and his wife Lucy, who remarked that it was 'like we are in the Island of the Blessed. This is such a beautiful place.'[69]

Philip's friend the art historian and director of the National Gallery Kenneth Clark wrote in his memoirs that 'The politicians who accepted Philip's hospitality might be described as the unorthodox Tory fringe . . . I doubt if Mr Baldwin ever crossed one of Philip's thresholds.'[70] Yet Baldwin did, if not often. He typically returned during the Easter holiday to use Trent privately for a couple of days, and the great carpet of spring flowers in front of the house was planted at Philip's request for the enjoyment of the Baldwins. It was a display that Thomas Jones delighted in when visiting them at Trent: it was a 'most wonderful show of daffodils and narcissus, thousands upon thousands, literally'.[71]

Philip's kindness to Baldwin reflected his gratitude for having been included in the government rather than any personal political alignment. It was also an acknowledgement of Baldwin's skill in party management in bringing the former coalition Conservatives firmly back into the fold. Unlike in 1923, there was no plotting around Philip's table to promote an alternative to Baldwin as leader. In any case, the Lords Derby and Birkenhead were now out of mainstream politics, and Austen Chamberlain was long past the point where he could be seen as a credible prime minister. If Baldwin had been forced out in the wake of the election defeat, it would have been to Neville Chamberlain rather than Winston Churchill that the leadership of the party would have fallen, a result that would have done nothing to give any cheer to the old coalition Conservatives.

• CAVALCADE •

In the strange illusion,
Chaos and confusion
People seem to lose their way.
What is there to strive for,
Love or keep alive for,
Say, 'Hey, hey!'
Call it a day?

Noël Coward,
'Twentieth Century Blues',
from *Cavalcade* (1931)

In the summer of 1929, free from his ministerial responsibilities, Philip Sassoon turned to two of his great private passions, aviation and art. Although he had owned aircraft for ten years, he had never actually learnt to fly. He asked Air Chief Marshal Sir John Salmond to dinner to identify the best instructor in the RAF. Flight Lieutenant Dermot Boyle (like Sir John and his brother Geoffrey Salmond, whom Philip had met in Karachi, a future Chief of the Air Staff) was recommended and Salmond had him posted to the 601 Auxiliary Air Squadron, where Philip had now been appointed the honorary commanding officer. Despite Philip's tens of thousands of air miles as a passenger, he was not a natural student of flight. When Boyle was asked how the flying lessons were progressing, he replied, 'I'm not teaching him to fly, only to land.'[1] Nevertheless, while in training at RAF Cranwell, Philip crash-landed into a hedge and had to telephone the base at Hendon to ask for another Avro plane, telling the young duty officer, Geordie Ward, 'I'm OK but I'm afraid the aircraft is confetti.'[2]

Philip received encouragement from his friend the Prince of Wales, already a qualified pilot, who wrote to ask, 'How is the flying getting on and have you got any sense in the air at all yet? I can assure you it took me a long time to reach that stage and am in doubt even now sometimes as to whether I've reached it or not. There's no doubt but that it's . . . safer than motoring and far more fun.'[3] Philip duly received his wings, after twice the usual number of hours of instruction, and his comrades in the 601 Squadron noted that his first solo landing was at Cranwell, which had the longest runway in the country.

In August Philip gave his now customary summer party at Lympne during the 601 Squadron's summer training camp. Clementine Churchill was among the guests and wrote to tell Winston, who was away on a speaking tour in North America, 'Diana [their daughter] and I have been to Lympne where everything was as luxurious and beautiful as ever – The Auxiliary Airmen . . . were swooping about everywhere (flying rather low I thought) and being hospitably entertained by Philip Sassoon.'[4]

The Schneider Trophy competition (now biannual) returned to England, at Cowes in September, following the victory of the Supermarine team in Venice in 1927. Philip, although no longer a minister, acted as the official host through his position as president of the Royal Aeronautical Society, an honour that had been granted following his Third Route air expedition to India. At Nubia House in Cowes, where Sir Godfrey Baring traditionally hosted royalty during the annual sailing week, Philip entertained the Prince of

Wales, his sister Sybil and other followers of air racing like Gordon
Selfridge Jr, the son of the retail tycoon, and his brother in-law, the
French aviator Jacques de Sibour. Selfridge had survived a plane
crash the previous year flying back from Africa in tandem with his
sister Violette and Jacques. T. E. Lawrence, in his capacity as
'Aircraftman Shaw', had been attached to the British team as clerk
to Wing Commander Sydney Smith. He was spotted talking with
the Italian Air Minister, Balbo, and given strict instructions by Sir
Hugh Trenchard, the Chief of the Air Staff, that he must observe
rank and not speak to any 'great men' or he would be instantly
dismissed. Trenchard specifically listed Philip Sassoon and Winston
Churchill as examples of the 'great men' to whom Lawrence was
forbidden to talk, even though they were both friends.

The Prime Minister, Ramsay MacDonald, along with Sam Hoare,
watched the seaplane races from the deck of the aircraft carrier
HMS *Argus*. Philip Sassoon, however, joined the Prince of Wales
on board Sir Henry Segrave's speedboat, *White Cloud II*. Segrave
was a glamorous young racing champion, who in 1924 had become
the first British driver to win a Grand Prix in a British car, and
would later be the first person to hold simultaneously the water
and land speed records.

It was Philip's 'proud duty' to present the Schneider Trophy at
a dinner for four hundred guests given aboard the ocean liner the
Orford* in Cowes harbour the evening after the racing. Great Britain
had retained the trophy, led by Flight Officer Dick Waghorn in a
Supermarine Rolls-Royce 6. Philip thought that Waghorn's performance had been 'awe-inspiring, when one realised the terrific forces
which were acting upon machine and pilot'.[5] Waghorn would all
too soon fall prey to those 'terrific forces' when he was killed in
1931 test-flying a Hawker Horsley bomber, with a prototype Rolls-
Royce Buzzard engine. Henry Segrave would become another

---

* The *Orford* was a P&O liner, launched in 1928; it would be destroyed by
German forces during the Second World War.

martyr to the pioneering science of seeking higher levels of speed when he was tragically killed in June 1930, just after setting a new water speed record on Lake Windermere. Later that year, in October, the Air Minister in the Labour government, Lord Thomson, would be killed when the *R101* airship crashed near Beauvais on its maiden flight from England to Karachi. The airship had been commissioned by the government and Philip had visited the 'great new airship shed' that had been built to receive it in Karachi during his Third Route expedition. Then he had written, 'Seen here at what must one day take rank as one of the chief air ports of the Empire, it brought home to me a vivid realisation of the fact that the airship is destined to be in the near future a most important factor in the development of the Empire's air communications.'[6]

Forty-eight of the fifty-four passengers lost their lives in the *R101* disaster, including senior officials from the Air Ministry and another friend of Philip's, Sir Sefton Brancker, the chairman of the Royal Aeronautical Club's racing committee, who had been a guest at Port Lympne just a few weeks before. The accident resulted in a greater number of fatalities than the *Hindenburg* disaster in 1937, and led to the cancellation of the government's airship programme. The tragedy of lives cut down in their prime never seemed far from the world of Philip Sassoon.

Philip's passion for the cutting-edge innovation of the aviation industry, with its thrills and manifest personal dangers, contrasted strongly with his love of eighteenth-century art, but both provided a sense of escapism. Riding a speedboat to watch the Schneider Trophy racing and being absorbed in the life of the Gainsborough family in rural Suffolk were both experiences that transported him out of the everyday, into worlds of bravery and beauty.

In 1921, as we have seen, Philip had been appointed by Lloyd George to the board of trustees of the National Gallery, and had persuaded the government to create a fund to support the purchase of important artworks to build up the gallery's collection. He also ran a series of annual exhibitions from his home in Park Lane, mainly focused on eighteenth-century art, furniture and silver, to raise money for the Royal Northern Hospital. The hospital provided free medical care to the poor of north London in an era before the National Health Service. Philip had been the treasurer of the hospital for several years, and the Prince of Wales was its president. In May 1927 Philip had organized, with the help of Lady Loughborough, a fundraising ball at the Royal Albert Hall, where the star guest alongside the Prince was the American aviator Charles Lindbergh, who had just completed the first non-stop transatlantic flight in his aeroplane the *Spirit of St Louis*. Lindbergh was Philip's guest in his box at the Albert Hall, and later, to the delight of the ball-goers, climbed into the royal box next door to greet the Prince of Wales when he arrived.[7]

Philip Sassoon's private-view art shows at Park Lane were a great draw for fashionable London society, and the most celebrated of these was in March 1930 with an exhibition of eighty-one English 'conversation piece' paintings by eighteenth-century artists like Gainsborough, Zoffany and Reynolds. An exception was made for the one contemporary 'conversation piece' in the exhibition, Sir John Lavery's group portrait of the royal family, which was loaned by Queen Mary.*

Unlike formal portraits underlining the status of a single person, these conversation pieces showed the psychological relationships between members of the same family or among close friends in locations that held some great significance in their lives. Philip loved the 'intimacy with the period'[8] that the pictures conveyed, and the incredible detail that captured the subjects' lives; it was this intimacy that led some reviewers to call the exhibition a 'peep show'.

Most of the works had never been seen in public before, except

---

* This painting is now in the permanent collection of the National Portrait Gallery. Gainsborough's painting of himself and his family, which was also shown in the exhibition, was presented to the gallery by the Cholmondeley estate in lieu of tax on Sybil's death, with the agreement of the gallery that it should be held in memory of Philip.

for a few which had emerged in sales at Christie's or Sotheby's to help clear death duties or debts from the post-war financial crises.* The timing of the exhibition may also have contributed to its appeal, falling less than six months after the Wall Street Crash of October 1929. Philip Sassoon's world had not been troubled by the financial crisis in New York, and for a few shillings you could be transported, 'away from the bustle, hurry and fret of the twentieth century to the brink of an existence . . . more seemly, decorous and dignified than our own'.[9] The television dramatization of Evelyn Waugh's *Brideshead Revisited* would have a similar appeal during the economic downturn of the early 1980s. People queuing along Stanhope Gate to pass through the turnstile at 45 Park Lane were given a further reminder of the passing of the old world. Opposite them they would have seen builders constructing a great new hotel on the site of the demolished Dorchester House, which had been one of the great private mansions of Victorian London.

Philip's 'peep show' exhibition not only impressed the art critics, but started a fashion in high society for 'conversation photographs'. Philip's friend Noël Coward would go on to produce a romantic comedy with music, set in the Regency period, called *Conversation Piece*; the art critic Sacherverell Sitwell's 1936 book on conversation pieces is dedicated to Philip.[†] While some of the visitors to Park Lane in March 1930 came to appreciate the art, most had come to exhibit themselves and peep into Philip's fashionable world. There among the Gainsboroughs and Zoffanys you might find the Prince of Wales and Charlie Chaplin, Winston Churchill and T. E. Lawrence. Standing in the ballroom with its mirrored ceiling creating a vortex of dense cloud stretching to infinity, they felt part of that high society to which Philip Sassoon belonged.

---

* The paintings were nearly all held in private collections, including Philip Sassoon's two Gainsboroughs and Zoffanys, and a painting by James Seymour loaned by the Duke of York.

† Sacherverell was the brother of Philip's friend Osbert Sitwell.

But Philip was a serious connoisseur of eighteenth-century art, rather than just a wealthy man buying up the work of fashionable artists. At the end of March 1930, he advised his fellow trustees of the National Gallery against the purchase of a Gainsborough offered for sale by the Earl of Sefton. The painting was of the Earl's ancestor Isabella, Viscountess Molyneux, later the Countess of Sefton, and was given a thorough examination by Philip's critical eye. He told the gallery's board:

Gainsborough was never at his happiest with full length portraits. In general they are not so good as his smaller canvases . . . The work in question was executed in the painter's Bath period, when he was still a young man and his technique still weak . . . The portrait in question is of a very plain woman. It is obvious from the appearance of the work that Gainsborough himself thought so. The painting of the face shows either that the painter took very little trouble with it, or that he went over it again and again in the vain endeavour to get it right. Whichever process he followed, the result is out of tone with the rest of the picture, and is badly painted and flat . . .

There are obvious defects, due probably to inexperience, in the figure and composition of the painting. The right arm is stuck out in an unnatural attitude, the hand gripping a small piece of black scarf which adds nothing to the picture. The arm is badly posed and wooden . . . The best that can be said of the picture is that it is good in spots, that it is an 'artist's' picture. I agree . . . that one of the functions of a Gallery is to provide hints to living painters. But another is to please the general public and guide the public taste. A comparison with the numberless other paintings in the National Gallery shows that it is quite possible to combine both functions in the same picture.

The asking price was £35,000 to £40,000 – a sum, continued Philip, that 'will "empty the till" . . . I would like to add that I am as anxious as any of my colleagues on the Board to see a better representation of the English school. But I do not think that this particular picture is likely to add anything to the Gallery because, although parts of it are superbly painted, it is on the whole inferior in quality and interest to the three full and two smaller canvases (the artist's daughters) that we already possess.'[10] The painting was not purchased by the National Gallery, but was later presented by the government to the Walker Art Gallery in Liverpool.

The Prince of Wales had also been appointed to the board of trustees, with Sassoon's encouragement, and his and Philip's antics during meetings attracted opprobrium from some of the more conservative members, such as the chairman, the Earl of Crawford. Crawford wrote, unhappily, of one trustees' meeting:

> about halfway through our proceedings, which happened to be extremely important, the Prince of Wales got bored and began to smoke ... The cigarette however enlivened the Prince and he began to talk to his neighbours, Sassoon and [Viscount] D'Abernon. The latter grows slow and deaf, but his voice is still resonant. Sassoon on the other hand with his raucous Syrian voice, and his acute desire to 'honour the King', chattered away – and between them the two made business practically impossible ... so far as I could make out, the chatter was chiefly about racing and society.[11]

There remained something of a clash of styles between Crawford and Sassoon. The Earl recorded in his diary a trustees' lunch hosted by Philip at Park Lane: 'What a lunch Sassoon gives! I have always had the pardonable ambition to make the acquaintance of a Grand Cocotte. Sassoon's lunch is precisely the style and manner of lunch I should expect from the G. C. Table napkins are yellow satin. Fruit for the four of us would have fed twenty people. Salad for four filled a large bowl as big as a large washing basin.' Following a similar occasion at Trent Park, Crawford exclaimed: 'the quality of our luncheon, the luxury of the housekeeping, the gardens, cars, tennis court (covered in and with a professional in attendance) – everything points to a most lavish and unchecked expenditure . . . what fantastic sums that young man must spend on his entertainments'.[12]

The board of trustees also included Philip's friend Evan Charteris, and he successfully lobbied along with Lord Lee of Fareham for the inclusion of Sir Joseph Duveen, the great art dealer and benefactor. Duveen had generously supported the building of new exhibition rooms at both the National Gallery and the Tate Gallery, where Philip was also on the board, as well as donating artworks. Like Sassoon, Duveen was also a trustee of the Wallace Collection. Philip's friend the writer Lytton Strachey provided his own unique insight into life at the National Gallery in the summer of 1930:

> I had a curious adventure at the National Gallery where I went yesterday to see the Duveen room – a decidedly twilight effect: but spacing out the Italian pictures produces on the whole a fair effect. There was a black-haired tart marching around in India rubber boots, and longing to be picked up. We both lingered in the strangest manner in front of various master-pieces – wandering from room to room. Then on looking round I perceived a more attractive tart – fair haired this time – bright yellow and thick hair – a pink face – and plenty of vitality. So I transferred my attentions, and began to move in his direction when on looking more closely I observed that it was the Prince of Wales – no doubt at all – a custodian bowing and scraping, and Philip Sassoon also in attendance. I then became terrified that the latter would see me and insist on an introduction, so I fled – perhaps foolishly – perhaps it might have been the beginning of a really entertaining affair. And by that time the poor black haired tart had entirely disappeared. Perhaps he was the ex-King of Portugal.[13]

The summer of 1930 was a carefree time for Philip Sassoon, but looking back it was the start of the end of an era. The autumn of that year brought personal tragedy with the loss of a number of friends in accidents, and 1931 saw political turmoil and economic crisis in Britain. A. J. P. Taylor suggested that 'September 1931 marked the watershed of English history between the wars . . . The "twenties" and the "thirties" were felt to be distinct periods even at the time, and September 1931 drew the line between them.'[14] July and August 1930 were, then, the Indian summer of the Roaring Twenties.

Philip wrote to Lytton Strachey urging him to return to Lympne: 'The object of these lines is to try and tempt you here again this August or September. Will you help me to convert my hope into a reality? The garden is improved and grown up (the reverse of what happens to us).'[15] Strachey resisted Philip's temptations, but Norah Lindsay returned to ensure that the grounds reached their usual heights of perfection, and the RAF officers from 601 Squadron, stationed for their summer camp at Lympne, were again regularly entertained at Philip's parties. One weekend Tom Mitford remembered that Philip instructed the guests, including Winston and Clementine Churchill, Sir Samuel and Lady Hoare, and Lawrence of Arabia, that they were to make a flying visit to Tom's sister Diana Guinness* at her home in Biddesden, on the Hampshire–Wiltshire border. Seven small aircraft flying in close formation transported the party, with Philip and Winston taking the controls, along with pilots from 601 Squadron.

Another frequent guest at both Lympne and Trent at this time was the young MP Bob Boothby. Boothby had entered the House of Commons in 1924, aged just twenty-four, and had served as parliamentary private secretary to Winston Churchill while the latter was Chancellor of the Exchequer. Queen Elizabeth the Queen Mother reflected years later that Boothby was 'a lovely man. He

---

* Diana Mitford was married to Walter Guinness. She would later marry Oswald Mosley.

was a bounder but not a cad. He was very amusing.'[16] He was bisexual, had numerous affairs with men and women throughout his life, and was a great admirer of Philip Sassoon, whom he thought 'the greatest host and the greatest gardener I have ever known, and in the right mood the best company. For ten years he shaped my life.'[17] Philip gave him the use of the French House, an old Tudor farm on the edge of the Port Lympne estate that he had restored with the help of the architect Herbert Baker.

Just a few miles from Lympne was Noël Coward's farmhouse Goldenhurst, at Aldington, which also had a beautiful outlook across Romney Marsh towards the English Channel. It was while living there that Coward enjoyed one of his most productive periods, including writing one of his best-known songs, 'A Room with a View'. Philip and Boothby would often join the guests for one of Coward's theatrical parties at Goldenhurst, and Noël was frequently entertained, along with his manager and sometime partner Jack Wilson, at Lympne and Trent Park.

Philip also invited Noël to become vice president of the Lympne Flying Club, of which he himself was president, and they would both host cocktail parties for their friends and the competitors in the annual air rally. Cole Lesley, Coward's secretary and companion, remembered:

Noël always gave his rout on the Saturday, when the day's flying was over. Dubonnet cocktails were then the order of the day and I made 'the best I have ever tasted, I *must* have another' by putting in only enough Dubonnet to give colour; the rest was gin. So again the affair became a riot; there are photos of Boothby and Godfrey Winn* frolicking on the lawn; I remember . . . Philip Sassoon saying almost continuously to his dog, 'Blazer, Blazer, Blazer – oh – you're – so – SWEET!'[18]

---

* An actor and writer, Winn was also a star columnist for the *Daily Mirror* and the *Sunday Express*.

In August 1930, Philip invited Noël to lunch at Lympne with T. E. Lawrence, which sparked a friendship between the two men that lasted until Lawrence's death in 1935. Lawrence wrote to his friend Charlotte Shaw, the wife of George Bernard Shaw, 'On Wednesday I lunched with Philip Sassoon, with whom came Noël Coward. He is not deep but remarkable. A hasty kind of genius. I wonder what his origin is? His prose is quick, balanced, alive.'[19] Following their lunch Coward invited Lawrence to come and watch the rehearsals in the West End for his latest play, *Private Lives*, which he did and which he greatly enjoyed.

Boothby recalled that 'The decade 1925–1935 was, for me, one of sheer enjoyment – life on the Lympne "Ridge" was one of endless gaiety and entertainment . . . Philip Sassoon epitomized it, and I owe to him far more enjoyment than to anyone else. He had a kind of genius.'[20] Noël Coward also considered that Philip 'and all he stood for was a phenomenon that would never recur'.[21]

Sporting celebrities were always an attraction at Philip's parties. Earlier in the year he had arranged for the American golf champion Bobby Jones to join him and the Prince of Wales for a game on the private course at Trent Park. In 1930, Jones achieved a then unprecedented grand slam of the major golfing tournaments, a feat that confirmed his status as one of the world's leading sportsmen. The previous year Philip and the Prince had played a private round at Swinley Forest Golf Club with another great American champion, Walter Hagen, who had just won the Open Championship. Hagen sent them both some wooden clubs as gifts after the match and congratulated the Prince on being 'determined to make himself a really first class golfer'.[22]

At the end of August 1930, the latest sporting sensation was the Australian cricketer Don Bradman. Bradman was duly invited to Port Lympne along with the England captain, Bob Wyatt, to a party held a week after the completion of the Ashes series, which Australia had won 2–1. Bradman had just turned twenty-two but was the hero of the series, averaging 139, including a world record 334 at

Headingley. The press had hailed him as a 'miracle' and declared that 'No Australian cricketer has received so many plaudits from the London press as Don Bradman.'[23] He had been presented to the Prince of Wales at the Oval Test match, and was now Philip's star guest at Lympne, in a party that also included Winston Churchill and the artist Rex Whistler.

Whistler had been a regular at Lympne that summer and the visitors' book contains some beautiful illustrations made during his stays. Rex had designed the endpapers for *The Third Route* and Sassoon was keen to engage him in further work at Port Lympne and Trent Park. At Trent he completed a series of mural pieces, but at Lympne he was granted a larger commission to create a work to decorate all of the walls and ceilings of the former billiard room. The process of agreeing the design with Sassoon appears to have been somewhat tortuous. Whistler recalled in a letter to a friend, 'His Majesty has commanded my presence down at Lympne. It's a great bore, but I shall be taking further drawings down with me, and I hope that this time the business will be settled – though there will be the agony of saying the price.'[24]

Philip paid him £800 (nearly £50,000 at today's prices) and in his excitement Rex let this slip out over dinner at the Savoy Grill with Cecil Beaton and Tom Driberg.* To Whistler's embarrassment and Philip's annoyance, Driberg included this story in his 'Talk of London' column in the *Daily Express*. Rex sent Philip a letter decorated with a burning sheet of paper at the top and an urn with 'REMORSE' written on it at the bottom. He prostrated himself to Philip, declaring that he was 'miserable about that wretched press notice of the painted room. Everyone thinks me the most loathsome swine, I'm sure; and I can hardly expect them to credit the fact (although it is a fact) that I never for one instant thought that the information might reach the papers . . . do please forgive me

---

* The openly homosexual Driberg had been a school friend of Evelyn Waugh at Lancing. He would later become a Labour Party MP.

for having unintentionally been the cause of this horrid piece of vulgarity.'[25]

The mural, known as the *Tent Room*, was completed in the autumn of 1932, and it is probably one of the finest surviving examples of Whistler's work. The room creates the impression of being beneath an ornate canopy, with exposed sides, through which can be seen a fantasy scene of an eighteenth-century town built in Palladian style. There is an image of Faringdon, the country house belonging to Philip's great friend Gerald Berners. Berners is depicted approaching the house, but as a child, and in the grounds stands a woman dressed in black mourning clothes. Berners' parents had recently died and their loss may, in Whistler's eyes, have brought on feelings of childlike helplessness – emotions that for Philip may have recalled the sudden loss of his own parents in 1909 and 1912. The church of St Martin in the Fields in Trafalgar Square also appears within Whistler's Palladian town, and there is a reference to Philip's Park Lane mansion, but here it has been painted as a London townhouse of the Regency period, rather than the Victorian building it was. On the outer wall of the house in Park Lane is a poster for a loan exhibition: 'The Four Georges, pictures Gainsborough, and furniture etc, of these four Kings at 25 Park Lane'. This is a direct reference to the exhibition Philip held there in March 1931.

Rather as the architect Philip Tilden had during the completion of the Lympne estate after the First World War, Whistler would install himself for several weeks to work on the murals, often painting as a weekend party carried on around him. It is a scene reminiscent of Evelyn Waugh's depiction of the artist Charles Ryder doing the same in *Brideshead Revisited*. Whistler spent most of the summer of 1932 painting at Lympne, where he became something of an attraction for Philip's weekend guests; this pleased Phillip but impeded progress on the work.

On one occasion Rex wrote to his friend the writer Edith Olivier, 'Think of me and the agony I shall be in as I arrive [at Lympne].

I shall put a brave face on it I hope but imagine the torture it is. Having to walk across the garden to a huge round table on the terrace (if it's hot) with lots of horrid people and strangers sitting about and having to eat sticky food with the sun in my eyes and be introduced and asked questions.'[26] There was another letter to Edith from Lympne on 2 October as Rex approached the end of the project:

> the painting's not . . . quite finished yet. I had a slight skirmish with Philip over it, for when he and the household were preparing to leave for good, several weeks ago, he electrified me by saying that he wanted me to come away too, and leave all the painting to be done next summer . . . Of course it is just when the place is empty that I can do any serious work, and can do as much in a day as I do in a week when the house is full of people. I insisted on being allowed to stay . . . He was annoyed plainly but reluctantly agreed . . . I have never before been pressed to leave my work unfinished and found it quite a new sensation to be insisting upon finishing . . . of course, the payment for this work forms an all-important item in my income for this year . . . However it is now nearly finished, and I hope to be free in about 9 or 10 days from now.[27]

Philip commissioned other alterations to the decor at Port Lympne around this time. The heavy black and gold mural by the Catalan artist Sert which dominated the drawing room, and about which Philip had always had doubts, was removed and instead the room, according to Chips Channon, was 'a mixture of fashionable whites, distressed white, off white, cream'.[28] Kenneth Clark remembered that the room 'was hung in white lamé, the furniture was white and gold'.[29] As Beverley Nichols recalled, 'Always remember the importance of white when you are trying to form a mental picture of the Twenties. It did not dominate, but it provided many delightful passages.'[30] At Lympne, with the summer sun pouring through the south-facing windows, it must have produced a most dazzling effect, the room transformed from Sert's dark mural depicting the defeat of Germany in the war to a vision of redemption and the afterlife. Against these white textures Philip hung around the room his collection of John Singer Sargent watercolours.

Christmas 1930 had been spent at Trent Park. There was a political party before the start of the festive season, with Stanley Baldwin, Sam Hoare, Walter Guinness and Bob Boothby, and on Christmas Day Sybil and her family joined Philip. From Boxing Day through to the New Year there was a weekend-party atmosphere, with the guests drawn mainly from Philip's circle of gay and single friends. Marie Belloc Lowndes, who frequently stayed at Trent on New Year's Eve, was there, and Norah Lindsay came before setting off with Philip for a trip to Venice. Gerald Berners, Noël Coward and Jack Wilson, Louis Mallet, Tom Mitford and Rex Whistler were also part of the throng.

The gaiety of Trent Park would soon give way to the grim realities of the growing economic and political pressures facing the country. In April 1931 Philip had to undergo the unpleasant but necessary removal of his tonsils, following persistent difficulties with his throat. The operation, performed at Philip's home in Park Lane, was pronounced to be a success, but it left him feeling rather jaded and lacking his usual zest. Harold Nicolson, a journalist at that time, stayed with Philip for a party at Trent a few weeks later, and captured a snapshot of Philip at what seems like a turning point in his life:

Motored down late to Trent. Philip is alone in the house, a slim, Baghdadi figure, slightly long in the tooth, dressed in a double-breasted, silk-fronted blue smoking-jacket with slippers of zebra hide. He has now finished the decoration of Trent and is a strange, lonely, un-English little figure, flitting among these vast apartments, removed from the ordinary passions, difficulties and necessities of life. He always seems to me the most unreal creature I have known.

People who care over-much for the works of man end by losing all sense of the works of God, and even their friends become for them mere pieces of decoration to be put about the room.[31]

There would be no slowing in Philip's pace of life, and the seemingly endless routine of work, travel and entertainment; his garden parties at Trent that summer would contain the usual mix of princes, statesmen and cultural leaders. His most important work in government was also ahead of him, but the summer of 1931 brought to an end the early optimism of the 1920s, when he was among the 'jolly troupe'[32] of ministers on a mission to reconstruct a society shattered by war. The party would go on for Philip and his friends until the summer of 1939, but as the threats of economic depression and then of war grew, it was a world that was starting to draw towards its close.

In his book *The Truth about Reparations and War-Debts*, David Lloyd George quoted the observation of a leading economist that 1931 was a 'year of unparalleled economic collapse throughout the world. International trade has been utterly disrupted; the international gold monetary standard has been almost completely abandoned; the central banking system, from which so many great things were expected ten years ago, has been severely strained . . . It was the year of great depression. It was the most gloomy of the mournful sequence that has filed past since the hectic hopefulness of 1919 and 1920.'[33]

The Wall Street Crash had depressed the economies of the United States and the European nations like Germany that relied upon American banks for credit. Markets for British exports collapsed, prompting further increases in unemployment at home and a rising budget deficit. The Labour government was forced to look for savings to bring the budget back into balance, and the threat of a collapse in confidence in Britain and the City of London on the international financial markets forced it to act quickly.

The Chancellor of the Exchequer, Philip Snowden, told his

colleagues in August that there would have to be a 10 per cent cut in unemployment benefit as part of the cost-saving measures that were required. Nine members of the cabinet resigned, refusing to accept the proposals, a blow which made it impossible for MacDonald's government, which did not in any case have a majority in the House of Commons, to continue. However, rather than a new Conservative–Liberal coalition taking up the reins, a national government was formed with MacDonald continuing as Prime Minister. The idea had first been proposed by Herbert Samuel, who was standing in for Lloyd George as leader of the Liberals; the former Prime Minister was on leave of absence following a major operation. Stanley Baldwin had been keen to endorse the Liberal proposal, no doubt calculating that a national government would be able to spread the political unpopularity of the decisions that would need to be made across all three parties. Philip Sassoon regarded it as a 'duty' to

> support the National Government in carrying into effect the special task for which it has been constituted . . . We have got to ensure that the existing fabric of the state is not overwhelmed by irreparable financial disaster. The National Government is not a coalition. We are not any of us being asked to coalesce, but to co-operate . . . The National Government has been allotted a definite task. On the completion of that task, it is understood that Parliament should be dissolved as soon as circumstances permit and each of the political parties should be left as free as it has hitherto been to advocate its own policy.[34]

Philip would now return to the government and to his former job as Minister for Aviation, although there would be no role for Winston Churchill, who was disliked by Labour and had broken with Stanley Baldwin over the question of devolving greater powers of self-government to India. Despite repeated offers, Lloyd George also declined the opportunity to join the national government, focusing instead on recovering from his illness and writing his war memoirs. He was also concerned that the national government would advocate protectionist policies that he would be unable to support.

Philip Sassoon's prediction that the national government would come together to sort out the country's finances and then dissolve to allow the parties to put forward their own manifestos was premature. The National Government was in effect a three-party coalition, but without an agreed programme or a mandate to implement it. The cabinet discussed the idea of calling a general election in which the members of the coalition would stand as 'National' candidates under a common manifesto. The final decision to call for a dissolution of Parliament, for an election on 27 October, was taken between Ramsay MacDonald and Stanley Baldwin at a meeting at Philip's Trent Park estate.

Shortly after the dissolution had been announced, Philip made clear his intention to stand in support of the national government, in an impromptu speech at the Hythe Conservative Club. After arriving at 9.30 p.m. and playing darts for half an hour with the members, he was invited by the club chairman Ray Munds to say a few words. Philip told them plainly:

What I can say is this, if you bring us back, a National Government, with a substantial majority we will do all in our power to bring the country back to the measure of prosperity you all desire. I am not making a lot of promises, but we are going to do our best and the issue is a very simple one. It lies between your voting for the return of a government which will do all in its power to bring back national stability and national security to the country, and the other alternative, the return not necessarily of a Socialist government but of a Communist government possibly, which would certainly bring ruin to the country.

He added that while everyone knew that it was hard to make cuts, 'it was better to have those cuts than no wages or pay at all', a comment the members greeted with applause. Philip concluded, warming to his theme in front of a friendly audience, that 'if a Socialist government was returned it meant the downfall and collapse of the country. Credit abroad would cease completely, and the whole structure and fabric on which they had depended for so long would disappear.'[35]

Philip was comfortably re-elected in Folkestone and Hythe, even with the distraction of Charlie Chaplin coming to stay at Trent Park in the last week of the campaign. The national picture was overwhelming, with 470 Conservatives elected. Both the Labour and Liberal parties had split into factions that supported the national government and those who did not. The result was that Lloyd George led a group of just four independent Liberals and Arthur Henderson a group of forty-six independent Labour candidates. Amazingly, Ramsay MacDonald continued as head of the national government, even though his 'National Labour' delegation consisted of just thirteen MPs.

Philip Sassoon was reappointed to the Air Ministry, where he would soon be at the centre of the greatest political debate of the 1930s: the question of air defence and Britain's lack of preparedness for another war in Europe.

• THE GATHERING STORM •

I cannot help prefacing the few remarks I wish to address
to the House by paying the usual deserved tribute to the
Under-Secretary of State [Philip Sassoon]. He puts a
glamour over a sorry story with a regularity which is
almost a danger to the community.

John Moore-Brabazon MP,
air force estimates debate,
House of Commons, 19 March 1935

At the dispatch box of the House of Commons, Philip Sassoon was
smooth, assured and always immaculately presented. He was not
one of the great orators of his day, but he calmly dealt with the
House, speaking without notes, and had the ability to hold a wide
range of facts and figures in his head, ready to be produced upon
demand. The aura of an oriental potentate had remained since the
caricaturist Max Beerbohm depicted him in 1913 sitting on the
green benches of the House of Commons in the lotus position. In
1930, the Labour MP Ellen Wilkinson had written a portrait of
Philip in her book *Peeps at Politicians*, entitled the 'The Lad with
the Delicate Air':

Sir Philip Sassoon seems to have been wafted into the House of Commons on a magic carpet and to look around with a detached air as though wondering at the strange animals the Fates have brought him to see . . . He has a habit of standing on one foot as though just waiting for a breeze to take him to the clouds. An atmosphere of luxury and mystery surrounds him . . . What does he think about behind that ivory mask? . . . Has Sir Philip, in that fascinating lisp of his, ever committed himself positively even to the fairly safe assertion that two and two make four? When he entertains at the House of Commons, whether on the Terrace in the summer or in the Harcourt Room* in the winter, his women guests are always the most beautiful in the room. He is almost too refined, too fastidious, too perfectly conscious of what is the best in life, and with his wealth far too able to secure it.[1]

Back at the Air Ministry in the new government, Philip was now working under Lord Londonderry, as Sam Hoare had been promoted to Secretary of State for India. While he still held the title of Under-Secretary of State for Air, his status was now greater in the Commons as he was the lead government minister for the department, with Londonderry sitting in the House of Lords. This meant that Philip would be responsible for presenting the government estimates for expenditure on the air force through much of the period of Winston Churchill's campaign to get Britain to rearm in the face of the growing threat, as he correctly perceived it, of Nazi Germany. The Conservatives had been out of office for two years, but in that period the political world had been completely transformed as a result of the world economic crisis. In Germany, Adolf Hitler's Nazi Party had held just twelve seats in the Reichstag in 1929, but in the election of the summer of 1932 would become the largest force with 230 representatives. In 1931, Japan had

---

* The Harcourt Room was a large dining room near to the terrace of the House of Commons. It is today known as the Churchill Room.

invaded Manchuria in China, setting up its own puppet government in the region. The threat of political instability leading to war had seemed a remote possibility in 1929, but things were less certain now.

The plan for the air force when Philip was first at the Air Ministry in 1924 had been to provide for a home defence force of fifty-two squadrons, a number which was regarded even then as the 'barest minimum'.[2] Yet in February 1932 there were still only forty-two squadrons in service for this purpose, and the government was spending less on air defence than it had in 1925. There was no chance of an increase, as the economic situation made cuts throughout Whitehall, including the armed forces' budgets, the government's main priority. Philip told the House of Commons on 10 March 1932, when presenting the spending estimates for the air force, that they bore

in every part the imprint of a sincere and, I venture to submit, successful effort to contribute substantially towards the urgent requirements of the financial situation, without permanently impairing the high standard of efficiency of the Air Services. The net Estimates, at £17,400,000, are down by no less a figure than £700,000, a particularly heavy decline on the comparatively small total expenditure of an expanding and developing Service . . . As the House will realise, to effect so large an economy with a minimum of injury to the Service has been a difficult task, and one to which the Air Council have devoted long and anxious thought. That has only been achieved by a variety of expedients, many of them admittedly makeshift measures which it will not be possible to repeat another year.[3]

At the beginning of the year, Philip had also made an air tour covering some eight thousand miles, revisiting many of the air stations he had seen on his Third Route tour in 1928. These included Malta, Egypt, Palestine, Jordan, Iraq, the Persian Gulf and India. He told the House of Commons, following his presentation of the air estimates, that

> The journey brought home to me, even more forcibly than did my former official tour, the far-reaching character of the revolution, for it is no less, which air transport is effecting in the sphere of world communications. For, whereas the stages of my former tour were specifically worked out beforehand and the tour itself was really in the nature of a test or experiment, my last journey was one which might have been carried out by any private individual who was sufficiently interested in the different places to which it took me.[4]

Philip's statement reflected his own deeply held belief in the vital strategic importance of air services to Great Britain.

Sassoon's overall performance in his first major outing in the House of Commons on behalf of the government was well received. One parliamentary lobby correspondent observed that Philip 'showed himself quite competent to discharge the function of the Minister in the Commons instead of the Lords. He spoke from only a few notes, and must have committed his long and carefully thought out speech to memory, for there was no break either in the flow of his words or in the sequence of his thoughts.'[5]

Philip had always lobbied within government for more financial support for the development of the air force, including in the 1920s when Winston Churchill was Chancellor of the Exchequer. Yet he had now to face two great obstacles: the massive pressure for budget savings, and the general pacifism that gripped so many Members in the House of Commons, as well as the majority of the public. Looking back at this period, Sam Hoare recalled that 'A very British characteristic reinforced this semi-pacifist tradition. We are bad haters. Having been reluctantly drawn into a fight, we wish to forgive our enemies as soon as it is finished, and forget their evil deeds ... This tendency to forgive and forget was further strengthened by the wish to be freed from the financial burden of armaments.'[6]

In the weeks that followed Philip's presentation of the air estimates, the government would step up its arguments in favour of a general disarmament through the World Disarmament Conference in Geneva. Here the member states of the League of Nations* tried and failed for two years to reconcile the French demands for security with the Germans' wish for equal recognition in terms of armaments, and Britain's desire for reductions in the size and scope of all armed forces. According to Churchill, this was the start of the wasted 'Locust Years', and in May 1932 he gave his 'first formal warning of approaching war', telling the House of Commons, 'I would say to those who would like to see Germany and France on an equal footing in armaments: "Do you wish for war?"'[7]

In July, Churchill was at Trent Park for Philip's one big garden party of the season, where the Duke and Duchess of York were the guests of honour. Winston would spend the rest of the summer considering war of a different era, visiting southern Germany to research his biography of John Churchill, the first Duke of Marlborough. He was there during the election campaign and was much struck by images of youths marching in Nazi parades, and it was this trip that convinced him of the serious intent of the new regime.

When Parliament returned in the autumn, Churchill drew on this experience for a speech in the House of Commons, in which he warned MPs:

Do not delude yourselves. Do not let His Majesty's Government believe, I am sure they do not believe, that all Germany is asking

---

* The League of Nations was founded in 1920, following the conclusion of the Versailles peace conference at the end of the First World War. A forerunner to the modern United Nations, it was an attempt to create a forum for the great powers to discuss and settle their political differences.

for is equal status . . . by indefinitely deferred stages. That is not what Germany is seeking. All these bands of sturdy Teutonic youths, marching along the streets and roads of Germany, with the light in their eyes of desire to suffer for their Fatherland, are not looking for status. They are looking for weapons, and, when they have weapons, believe me they will then ask for the return, the restoration of lost territories and lost colonies.[8]

Churchill was not the only person in Philip Sassoon's circle to be concerned about Germany's intentions. At a party at Port Lympne in September, Philip's guests included his old friend the Romanian princess Marthe Bibesco and her husband George, who was president of the International Aeronautical Federation and regularly visited Germany. Looking from the terrace at Lympne across the Romney Marsh to the sea, George warned Philip, 'You had better start building air defences along the Channel. It won't be long now before the German air force is equal to that of Britain.'[9]

For his visit to Germany that summer, Churchill was joined by Professor Frederick Lindemann, who had become his 'chief adviser on the scientific aspects of modern war and particularly air defence'.[10] Lindemann had been so moved by what he had seen with Churchill in Germany that in the autumn of 1932 he started approaching Jewish scientists, including Albert Einstein, to encourage them to come and take up posts at Oxford and other English universities.

Churchill's two other main advisers, who provided him with intelligence on German rearmament, were also known to Philip. Desmond Morton, who in 1932 was head of the Industrial Intelligence Centre of the Committee for Imperial Defence, had worked alongside Philip in Douglas Haig's private office during the last year of the First World War. The other, Ralph Wigram, was a high-flying official at the Foreign Office who specialized in Germany and central Europe. He began passing documents on Germany to Churchill in 1934, and started to meet him frequently the following

year. Philip had first met Wigram during the Lympne conferences
with the French in the early 1920s, and he and his wife Ava were
invited back to Philip's Kent estate for summer parties in 1934, 1935
and 1936. Wigram had returned to the Foreign Office and London
in 1933, after nine years working as First Secretary at the British
Embassy in Paris. It is still noteworthy that he entered Philip's social
circle at around the same time that he started supporting Churchill.

In Churchill's account of the pre-war years, *The Gathering Storm*,
he explains that 'From other directions I was able to check and
furnish information in the whole field of our air defence. In this
way I became as well instructed as many Ministers of the Crown
. . . My personal relations with Ministers and also with many of
their high officials were close and easy, and although I was often
their critic we maintained a spirit of comradeship.'[11]

Philip would certainly fall into this category. He and Winston had
been friends since the end of the war, and enjoyed close relations
and frequent social contact throughout the 1930s. Given Churchill's
general dislike of small talk, and Philip's ability to hold great details
from the government's air defence strategy in his head, it would
be impossible to believe that this was something they didn't
frequently discuss. In his memoirs, Churchill was critical of the
failure of ministers to heed his warnings, and Frances Stevenson
recalled in her diary an impromptu meeting between Lloyd George
and Churchill where they railed against the Secretary of State for
Air, 'that half-wit Charlie Londonderry'.[12] However, there was no
direct criticism of Philip from Churchill.

Churchill assembled a parliamentary group to support his
campaign and named Austen Chamberlain, Robert Horne, Edward
Grigg, Lord Winterton, Brendan Bracken and Henry Croft as the
core members of this team, and further noted that 'several others
formed our circle. We met regularly and to a large extent pooled
our information.'[13] Philip Sassoon would have been constrained,
as a minister, from being involved with the tabling of motions or
organizing debates designed to criticize government policy. However,

the senior members of this Churchill group were also close associates of Philip's. In addition to Churchill himself, Brendan Bracken and Robert Horne had been frequent guests of Philip's, and he had extended an open invitation to Austen Chamberlain to attend the cabinet lunches at Park Lane, even after he had left the government. It is noteworthy as well that Churchill's support from Austen Chamberlain and Robert Horne brought together once more three of the heavyweights from the era of the Lloyd George coalition, men who had sat around Philip Sassoon's dining table in Park Lane, plotting without success in 1923 to try to frustrate the ascent of Stanley Baldwin to the premiership.

On 20 November 1932, Philip attended a dinner given by the great society hostess Mrs Greville, where the guests included Horne and Professor Lindemann. Austen Chamberlain wrote to his sister Hilda in December recalling a lunch of Philip's at Park Lane where one of the major topics of conversation had been 'the incredible ineptitude, egotism and idleness of mind of Stanley Baldwin. That subject kept the floor till we parted. Not a soul had a good word to say for him except myself and my praise was strictly confined to his Peace in our Time speech* and to the support (though not the help) which he gave me as Foreign Minister. His reputation in the country is inexplicable to anyone who has worked with or under him in Cabinet and council.'[14]

Philip Sassoon was certainly working hard to defend the air defence budget from further cuts. Anthony Eden, who was at that time the Minister for the League of Nations at the Foreign Office, had suggested to the government that cuts in the military air force, or even its total abolition, might be one of the few areas where it would be possible to reach agreement between Britain and France at the Disarmament

---

* Speech given by Stanley Baldwin in the House of Commons on 6 March 1925 which received wide acclaim in the press. It called for an approach to labour relations that would bring about industrial peace, rather than confrontation between the trades unions, employers and the government.

Conference. Eden relates in his memoirs, 'I had written to Baldwin ... pointing out that since we were so weak in air power, any international limitations were bound to be to our advantage. Baldwin had tried hard in the summer of 1932 to persuade the Government to offer the total abolition of the military and naval air arm, but the objections of the Air Ministry and, more surprisingly, the Admiralty proved too strong.'[15] However, at the beginning of 1933, this proposal came forward for consideration again, something that may have persuaded Philip Sassoon to make a rather audacious move.

On 30 January 1933, Adolf Hitler was appointed Chancellor of Germany, and within days Philip decided to fly to Berlin, with Bob Boothby in support, to see what was going on. Boothby remembered that after they had arrived, 'A German friend of mine told him [Sassoon] that Goering [Hitler's Air Minister] was *au fond* a good apple. This delighted him and, much to the indignation of our ambassador, he himself made an appointment to see Goering the next day.'[16] A. L. Kennedy, the senior foreign correspondent for *The Times*, noted in his journal, '[Eden] told me that Sassoon had not told him a word about his visit the other day to the German Air Minister, Capt Goering. Nor had Simon* been told and apparently Sassoon had avoided the British Embassy. Disgraceful.'[17]

Philip held strong anti-Nazi feelings as a result of the party's policies towards the Jews, but he was due to appear at the Disarmament Conference in Geneva on 15 February and some personal insight into the position of the new German Air Minister would undoubtedly have been an advantage. There is no record of the meeting; Duff Cooper had lunch with Philip on his return from Germany and noted that he 'found it more military than before the war'.[18] Philip may have been able to discover whether Göring had any interest in cutting back or scrapping aircraft with military capabilities. Eden later recorded in his memoirs that 'As the months passed their chances faded.'[19]

---

* Sir John Simon, the Foreign Secretary.

On 14 March, Philip Sassoon would rise in the House of Commons to present the air force spending estimates once more, just two weeks after the burning of the Reichstag during the German general election campaign, and nine days after the Nazis' sweeping victory. However, the statement Philip delivered did not reflect these changes in Europe in any way. Churchill said of the debate in his memoirs, 'The British Air Estimates of March 1933 revealed a total lack of comprehension alike by the Government and the Oppositions, Labour and Liberal, of what was going on.'[20] Philip knew what was going on, though, and his speech reflects his concern about the 'risks' his own government was taking. There can seldom have been a presentation by a minister of government policy which did more to lay bare its failings for the benefit of those who wished to attack it. Philip gave more of a cry for help than a call to arms.

Opening the debate, he reminded the House of the 'unremitting' demands for savings that had been placed on the Air Ministry by the Treasury. Turning to the specifics of the estimates, he made sure that the House was fully aware of the scale of the cuts that were being made, pointing out that

the apparent rise of £26,000 in the net figure to a total of £17,426,000 actually conceals an approximate further reduction of £340,000. And I would remind hon. Members that this follows on a reduction of no less than £700,000 last year, which made the achievement of additional savings in expenditure this year a singularly difficult task. They have, indeed, only been rendered possible by such drastic measures as the decision to close down for the time being one of the four flying training schools . . .

Risks have had to be taken. As the House will have observed, no new units have been formed either at home or abroad during the past year, and no provision is made for new units in the present Estimates. The Home Defence Force remains at a total of 42 Squadrons, of which 13 are non-Regular, and 10 Regular Squadrons are still required to complete the modest programme which was approved as long ago as 1923, and which is already several years overdue for completion.

Philip made Britain's position relative to other countries very plain:

The Royal Air Force stands to-day only fifth on the list of Air Powers,* although, at the end of the late War, we could with justice claim to take, not fifth, but first place, when all the factors which go to make up air strength were taken into account; for in 1918 we had a larger number of trained flying personnel and a larger total number of aircraft than any other nation. The House will also remember that, while air expenditure in this country has shown a steady decline since 1925, other nations have very largely increased their outlay on air services over the same period.[21]

Responding, Churchill was generous in his praise for Sassoon personally, congratulating him 'upon his extremely lucid, interesting, and agreeably delivered statement on behalf of his Department. We all heard it with the greatest interest, and everyone knows how absolutely wrapped up in the work of the Flying Service the right hon. Gentleman is.'

He then turned his attention to the main thrust of the government's case: that cuts in air defences should be set against its broader objective for a general disarmament of military aircraft among the powers. Churchill continued:

Of course, if all the air forces of the world were to be reduced to our level . . . that would be a very great enhancement of our ratio of military strength; and they are bound to notice that . . . But I do not suppose that there would have been anyone more surprised

---

* The leading air powers were, in order of front-line aircraft numbers, France, Italy, USA, Russia and Great Britain.

than the Under-Secretary of State or his Chief if, when they had made these specious suggestions at Geneva, all the Powers had suddenly risen and, with loud acclamations, said, 'We accept them.' . . . I do not think there is any single man in any part of the House who thinks, or who has ever thought, that they had the slightest chance of being accepted.

He added, on the substance of Philip's presentation of the air estimates, and responding to the 'risks' that Sassoon himself had set out, 'I regretted to hear the Under-Secretary say that we were only the fifth air power, and that the ten-year programme was suspended for another year. I was sorry to hear him boast that the Air Ministry had not laid down a single new unit this year. All of these ideas are being increasingly stultified by the march of events, and we should be well advised to concentrate upon our air defences with greater vigour.'[22]

Philip took solace that evening in welcoming the Prince of Wales and his brother Prince George to Park Lane for the opening of his latest loan exhibition, 'Three French Reigns', which featured art and furniture from the time of Louis XIV, Louis XV and the monarch who met his end at the guillotine, Louis XVI. King George V and Queen Mary also visited the exhibition, on Sunday 26 March, and stayed for tea with Philip. The Queen noted in her diary, 'G was delighted with the French things.'[23]

There were certainly no hard feelings between Philip and Winston after the air force debate, and Churchill was back at Trent Park in May for a party with the Czech Ambassador, Jan Masaryk. Masaryk was the son of the Czech President, and a friend of Sir Robert Horne, who had business interests in the country. If the key question of the moment was whether Britain should rearm or disarm as the best way of securing peace, Philip was seen as belonging to the rearm camp. Over the summer at Lympne, he held a weekend party with T. E. Lawrence, Anthony Eden and the Permanent Under-Secretary at the Foreign Office, Sir Robert Vansittart, who also believed in the new threat from Germany and the urgent need for Britain to rearm. Vansittart would tell ministers, 'We are terribly weak. We must gain time for becoming stronger. Only military strength will stop Hitler and at present we do not possess it.'[24]

Siegfried Sassoon was another guest at that weekend party. He and Philip had met only once before, despite being second cousins and having numerous mutual friends, including Rex Whistler, who was also in residence to continue his painting at Lympne. Whistler's close friend Stephen Tennant had previously been Siegfried's lover, although the poet was now engaged to be married to Hester Gatty. The discussion of war may have alarmed the pacifist Siegfried, who later wrote to Hester, 'The whole thing is too depressing for words. To me it is as though the powers of darkness were winning . . . the French really believe that the Germans will bomb Paris as soon as they are strong enough. And Philip Sassoon playing Winston's game at the Air Ministry (did you see that he went to see Göring on his way to Geneva!) The only hope is that the idea of war is so much in the air that people are realizing what it will mean.'[25] Winston and Clementine Churchill would also be back at Lympne in September, for a house party with Bob Boothby, Brendan Bracken and Anthony Eden, who was now becoming an increasingly regular guest.

The winter of 1933 would prove Churchill's warning about the failure of the Disarmament Conference correct. Hitler announced that Germany would be withdrawing from the talks and issued new demands for increases in armaments. These demands included increasing the size of Germany's army from 200,000 to 300,000 servicemen, and the formal creation of an air force of around 700 front-line machines, which would make it greater in size than the equivalent British force for home defence. Eden noted in his memoirs that 'By November 1933 we knew that Hitler was starting to build military aircraft in quantity.'[26]

The British response was to offer a compromise that would allow a more limited German rearmament while still trying to resurrect the ideas of the disarmament talks, and in particular the abolition of military aircraft. This was debated in the House of Commons on 6 February 1934, with 'little enthusiasm',[27] and two days later Philip held a lunch at Park Lane with the Foreign Secretary Sir John Simon, the Air Secretary Lord Londonderry, Austen Chamberlain and the King's private secretary Sir Clive Wigram (a cousin of Churchill's informant Ralph). With British policy towards Germany lying in tatters, Chamberlain recalled of their discussion that the Foreign Secretary had 'no policy and is content to live from day to day . . . neither the officials at the FO nor our representatives abroad know what he is at or what they should try for . . . he has allowed the Germans to think they have got us on the run – indeed I fear they have – and nothing could be more dangerous'.[28]

At a cabinet meeting later that month, Londonderry, on behalf of the Air Ministry, urged his colleagues to consider that 'other powers, almost without exception, were pursuing a far more active policy of air development . . . I fear that in other than pacifist quarters the very limited extent of next year's programme will arouse considerable criticism.'[29]

It was in this febrile atmosphere that Philip Sassoon rose on 8 March 1934 to deliver the air estimates for the coming year. He was placed in the invidious position of knowing that a general rearmament in the air was necessary, with the House of Commons aware that it was what he believed, but offering up only £135,000 more to help achieve it, enough for just four more squadrons, and an increase in the budget of less than 1 per cent, which meant the Air Ministry's budget was still less than it had been spending two years previously.

Philip set out the dangers clearly to the House:

Last year I expressed the hope that, by the time the next Estimates came round, the Disarmament Conference would have come to some satisfactory agreement for the limitation and reduction of air armaments. That has not yet occurred . . . Far from accepting our proposals, and farther yet from following our example, other nations have increased their air armaments steadily, until they far outnumber ours . . .

In these circumstances His Majesty's Government feel that it is no longer possible to postpone further the 10-year-old programme of 1923, which is already so long overdue for completion. They feel that we cannot any longer accept a position of continuing inferiority in the air . . . if other nations will not come down to our level, our national and Imperial security demands that we shall build up towards theirs.[30]

Churchill's response was once more gracious to Philip, but merciless on the strategy of the government. He told the House that Philip Sassoon

has gained for himself a most important and agreeable measure of respect and good will from the mass of the serving officers and men in the Service to which he has devoted his main interest. There is nothing that I could say which in the slightest degree could in any way enhance the feeling, which I think is general in the House, that the Under-Secretary of State fills the important post which he occupies with efficiency, distinction, and success. I feel, however, that, confined as he necessarily is within limits prescribed by the office which he holds to recount the functions of his Department and to explain to us its projects and its administrative details, it would not be sufficient if this Debate ended without a declaration from some Cabinet Minister upon the great issues of policy upon which the Under-Secretary of State is not entitled to speak otherwise than he has been instructed . . .

It is not to be disputed that we are in a very dangerous position to-day. This is a very good White Paper. The opening paragraph sets forth a most admirable declaration, but what is there behind it? £130,000. Very fine words. It must have taken the Cabinet a long time to agree to them – with the Air Minister drafting them and putting them round. They give great paper satisfaction. But what is there behind them? £130,000.

There was general uproar in the House at the failure of the government to produce a cabinet minister to explain the strategy to meet the ambition that Philip Sassoon had set out. The Chief Whip hurriedly found Stanley Baldwin, who joined Philip on the front bench and made the highly unusual move of intervening in the debate with an impromptu speech after Churchill had sat down. Baldwin told the House,

It is quite true that the bomber will always get through any defence you can visualise to-day, but it is equally true that the greater the force there be to oppose it the greater the chance of casualties among the bombers, and therefore the more thought before invasion takes place . . . if all our [disarmament proposals] fail . . . this Government will see to it that in air strength and air power this country shall no longer be in a position inferior to any country within striking distance of our shores.

It was a telling intervention designed to try to buy the government some time, but it was still policy being made up on the hoof. While the Air Ministry could rejoice at Baldwin's statement, it was also possible that he hadn't really understood what he had committed himself to.

Following the pressure of presenting the air estimates for another year, Philip ran his usual extensive round of summer parties, with the high point coming on Sunday 27 May when he welcomed the King and Queen, along with their granddaughter Princess Elizabeth. Queen Mary recorded in her diary that 'we spent a delightful 2 hours seeing his lovely garden and having tea out'.[31]

Philip's other guests that summer reflected his sympathies with the anti-disarmament forces within the Conservative Party, with Churchill, Eden, Duff Cooper and Boothby all staying at Trent. On

30 June, Boothby was attending an air pageant at RAF Hendon with Philip when news started to arrive about the 'Night of the Long Knives' in Germany, when the Hitler regime carried out a series of arrests and murders of political opponents, purging many within the broader Nazi organisation itself. Boothby later noted that the conversation among Philip's guests at Trent that evening was devoted to the subject: 'One thing, we all agreed, had emerged from the shocking and squalid events of the day. The Nazis had been shown up for what in fact they were – unscrupulous and bloodthirsty gangsters. In future they should be treated as such. How true; and how right were our conclusions. Alas! in other more influential quarters, a different view was taken.'[32]

In August, Philip hosted a weekend party for Churchill and Victor Cazalet, another anti-appeasement MP, who had just returned from Germany, concluding that the people there were 'mad, and nothing will control or influence them except time alone. There are a good many anti-Nazis about, who say they must "just exist" until things change.'[33] Anti-Nazi sentiment should have brought Churchill and Cazalet together, but they had fallen out badly over Churchill's opposition to the government's policy of giving more self-government to India, and this initially made their stay together at Lympne rather awkward. Cazalet wrote in his journal, 'Winston is here – very disturbing. He refused at first to shake hands. I insisted. Then he mellowed. There was a long discussion as to whether there were any great men alive today. Winston takes the view that everyone is inferior, and there are no big men. India was avoided. Later at lunch on Sunday, he again mellowed. Finally we played Bezique and I took £5 off him for which I admit he bore no malice. He talks at times as well as ever.'[34]

At this time Churchill was engaged in correspondence with Desmond Morton, trying to get precise figures for the front-line strength of the German air force. Morton's best estimate was they would have attained around five hundred aircraft by 1935, and were continuing to rearm secretly but rapidly.[35] Churchill would return to Lympne in early September but between his visits that summer Ralph and Ava Wigram stayed there with Philip. Ralph was not yet working with Churchill, but later that year would start sending him documents containing secret Foreign Office reports on the real strength of German armaments.

In late September, Philip Sassoon set off on an inspection of air stations in the Far East, including Singapore, Kuala Lumpur and Rangoon, with Churchill sending him 'every good wish dear Philip for a safe and prosperous journey. What wonderful things you will see.'[36] Philip sent an airmail letter from India to the editor of the *Folkestone Herald,* reporting that 'So far my trip has gone marvellously. It has been very strenuous but I feel very fit and have had a good welcome from all the ranks of the Air Force wherever I have been.' The editor praised Philip's energy: 'It seems to me that whilst a good many people spend their time talking hot air, Sir Philip gets on with the job. I'm hanged if I should want to fly 600 to 800 miles a day for the best part of a month.'[37]

Philip was back in time for a further instalment of Churchill's campaign for increased expenditure on air defence. On 28 November, he had moved an amendment in the House of Commons to the debate on the King's Speech, stating that 'the strength of our national defences, and especially of our air defences, is no longer adequate to secure the peace, safety, and freedom of Your Majesty's faithful subjects'.

In his speech, he directly challenged the promise given by Baldwin in March that Britain could retain parity with the rapidly expanding German air force without a massive increase in its own defence spending. He told the House of Commons that the German air force was already 'approaching equality with our own' and added, 'If Germany executes her existing programme without acceleration, and if we execute our existing programme . . . without slowing down . . . the German military air force will . . . by the end of 1936 . . . be nearly 50 per cent stronger [than ours], and in 1937 nearly double.'[38]

Baldwin replied for the government, disputing Churchill's figures:

'Germany is actively engaged in the production of service aircraft, but her real strength is not 50 per cent of our strength in Europe today.' He also stated that 'of the regular units of the Royal Air Force to-day . . . 560 are at present stationed in the United Kingdom. There are also at home the Auxiliary Air Force and the Special Reserve Squadrons, with an establishment of 127 aircraft: making a total of just under 690 aircraft available to-day in the United Kingdom that could be put into the first line.'

Baldwin's statement reassured the House that Germany was not yet out in front, and in March 1935 Philip was for the first time able to present to Parliament a substantial increase in the air estimates, of over £3,000,000, to underline the government's commitment not to accept inferiority in the air to Germany. Philip opened the debate on 19 March with a startling comparison between himself and St Sebastian, the Christian martyr depicted in art for centuries as a near-naked, loinclothed youth strapped to a tree, his torso barbed with arrows:

> In past years I have regularly found myself in these debates on the Air Estimates in the unhappy position of a kind of modern St Sebastian, assailed indeed by arrows from all sides, but lacking the comforting assurance that I should in due course reap the rewards of martyrdom. From one side of the House have come the cloth-yard shafts of those hon. Members who considered our provision for the air defence of this country inadequate; from another side the barbed bolts of those who would like to see the immediate abolition of all armed forces.[39]

This description of his position was not unreasonable: on the one side he could expect pressure from Churchill for the government to be moving faster to rearm, and on the other side in the same debate Clement Attlee, leading for Labour, deplored the increase in spending on armaments, regretting that 'we are back in a pre-war atmosphere, we are back in . . . an armaments race'.

Philip set out his case: 'The failure to date of the Disarmament Conference to achieve agreement made necessary the statement by [Stanley Baldwin] when he announced last year that the Government had no longer any option but to proceed with our very long-delayed programme. We have stripped our defences to the bone, and the result has been that our weakness has not only become a danger to ourselves but a danger even to the cause of peace.'

He then turned to the specifics of the current strength of the air force: 'The first line strength of the Royal Air Force to-day is 890 machines* in regular squadrons, and 130 machines, approximately, in non-regular squadrons, which makes a total of 1,020 machines. At the end of this year, the figure will come up to 1,170, and the 1936 programme will bring it up to a figure of 1,310.'

Churchill responded with the usual courtesies to Philip:

The Under-Secretary always gives a very good account of the work of the Royal Air Force, and he is in the best position to do so because he has had long experience, and has intimate connection with so many of its activities. We are fortunate to have in this House a representative who takes such a great interest in his duties and is able to speak to us so agreeably about them. However, there are a certain number of aspects of this question on which the Under-Secretary can only speak as he is instructed. Nothing was more notable in his able review than what he left out. After all, we are deeply exercised in our minds about the relative strength of the British and German air forces, and over that vital and crucial part of our discussion, the most anxious and important part of the whole question connected with the air, my right hon. Friend drew, or was inclined to draw, a veil of impenetrable opacity.

---

* This number was consistent with the figures given by Baldwin in November 1934, but included aircraft stationed overseas. The size of the air force in the UK was still 690 front-line machines.

Churchill now made his comparison between the relative strengths of the two air forces, which showed they had reached near parity, based on his intelligence and the government's official figures, with around 1,000 military aircraft each. This refuted Baldwin's claim of the previous November that Britain had a 50 per cent superiority over Germany. Churchill told the House:

> a comparison between the British and German air forces at the end of November would appear to have been as follows: First-line strength, Great Britain 560, Germany 600; military aircraft, Great Britain 1,020, without training machines, and Germany 1,100. Beyond all question these are much the most favourable figures from our point of view which could possibly be cited, and I am sure that they will fall far short of the truth. But even taking them as they are, they altogether disprove the first assertion of the Lord President of the Council on 28 November, because they show the two countries virtually on an equality, neck and neck.

Philip rose to intervene:

> I do not pretend, and no one else can pretend, that the situation is one which does not give us all cause for grave anxiety . . . There has been great acceleration, as far as we know, in the manufacture of aircraft in Germany, but still, in spite of that, at the end of this year we shall have a margin, though I do not say a margin of 50 per cent. I would only say that as far as I know it is not the case that, as [Churchill] said, Germany at the end of this year will have a 50 per cent superiority over us.

Looking back on the debate in his history of the Second World War, Churchill considered that Philip had made a 'very confident reply'.[40] But the assurances that had been given by the government would barely last a week.

On 25 and 26 March the Foreign Secretary, Sir John Simon, along with Anthony Eden and Ralph Wigram, conducted two days of talks with Hitler and his officials at the Reich Chancellery in Berlin, on matters of European security and armaments. The timing of these meetings could hardly have been more unfortunate, as a few days before Hitler had publicly repudiated one of the chief restrictions on German rearmament in the Treaty of Versailles by announcing that he would be reintroducing conscription with the intention of creating an army of thirty-six divisions.

Eden noted of the final meeting on the afternoon of 26 March, 'Finally, Simon put last, as he had often told me a cross-examiner should, the question that to us mattered most: what was the present strength of the German air force? After a moment's hesitation, Hitler replied that Germany had reached parity with Great Britain.'[41] Or as the British Ambassador recorded the response: 'About the same as yours. I don't know how many aeroplanes Göring really has got, but that seemed about what there ought to be.'[42] Eden remembered that 'There was no triumph in his tone, but there was a grim foreboding in my heart.'[43]

The alarm was now well and truly sounded at the Foreign Office. On Monday 1 April, Wigram wrote to Sir Christopher Bullock, the Permanent Secretary of the Air Ministry, asking for the 'observations' of the Air Council* by the end of the week on Hitler's statement that he had achieved air parity with Great Britain. Four days later, Bullock responded with new figures showing the latest estimate of the relative strengths of the two air forces, which confirmed Wigram's worst fears. The statements that had been given by the ministry for Philip Sassoon to use in the debate on 19 March were completely wrong. The real front-line strength of the air force permanently stationed in the United Kingdom was

---

* The Air Council was the governing body of the Royal Air Force, comprising ministers, the Chief of the Air Staff and other senior officers. Its successor today is the Air Force Board at the Ministry of Defence.

not 880, or 690, but 453. More than 230 of the aircraft that the ministry had claimed to be 'front line' in March were in fact auxiliary planes or part of the Fleet Air Arm, with no guarantee that they would be available to use in Britain in an emergency. The Air Ministry also calculated that Germany now had 850 front-line aircraft. Wigram had appealed directly to senior officials within the ministry to get the true picture of British air strength, but the question naturally arises as to how the figures could be so different from those which had been presented to the House of Commons by Philip in March, and by Stanley Baldwin in November 1934. Throughout these debates, there was constant argument over what did or did not constitute 'front-line' aircraft, with the government always seeking to use numbers that gave a more favourable impression of the situation. By including the Fleet Air Arm and the auxiliary and training forces available at any one time, it might be possible to present the front-line strength of the air force as ahead of Germany's when in truth it was only around half. A memo prepared for ministers by the Air Staff in May 1935, after the truth had finally come out, shines a light on the nature of this debate within government. It stated, 'It is of course unnecessary further to elaborate the highly misleading nature of a system of calculation such as this, and it will clearly be necessary to formulate a precise definition of the term "first-line strength".'[44]

Churchill clearly did not blame Philip for the 'misleading' presentation of the front-line strength of the air force. In a lengthy memo on the air defence crisis he sent to Baldwin at the end of April, he stated that '[Philip Sassoon] was instructed to say that we still had a substantial superiority over Germany and that even in November 1935 we should have superiority.'[45] Winston had been staying with Philip at Trent Park earlier that April and perhaps Philip was able to convince him that he had been required to use a form of words that had been agreed in advance by senior members of the government.

In response the cabinet decided that the government had to

honour the commitment Baldwin had given the previous November: that Britain would not allow inferiority to Germany in the air. This agreement required additional finance for the Air Ministry to fund a large programme of expansion, and was announced in a debate in the House of Commons on 22 May. There Baldwin conceded the mistakes the government had made:

> First of all, with regard to the figure I then gave of German aeroplanes, nothing has come to my knowledge since that makes me think that that figure was wrong. I believed at that time it was right. Where I was wrong was in my estimate of the future. There I was completely wrong. I tell the House so frankly, because neither I nor any advisers from whom we could get accurate information had any idea of the exact rate at which production was being, could be, and actually was being speeded up in Germany in the six months between November and now. We were completely misled on that subject.

Later in his speech he blamed no one individual for the situation, stating, 'we are all responsible and we are all to blame'.[46] The speech was a clever Baldwin stunt, the eye-catching apology for misjudging the size of the German air force masked the fact that the government had knowingly overstated Britain's own air defences, a matter where 'accurate information' should have been easy for ministers to come by.

While no personal blame was attached to Philip for the statements he had made, it was nevertheless a wounding period. This was further compounded by tragedy, with the loss of another of his friends in a terrible accident. At the age of just forty-six, T. E. Lawrence died on 19 May following a motorbike crash near his home in Dorset. His life, in the words of his friend Noël Coward, was 'snuffed out in one blinding, noisy moment on that idiotic motor cycle'.[47] Churchill commented, 'I had hoped to see him quit his retirement and take a commanding part in facing the dangers which now threaten the country . . . In Lawrence we have lost one of the greatest beings of our time.'[48] Philip Sassoon said in his tribute, 'His death was a great loss, not only for literature but to the air force for whom he did so much.'[49] The Air Ministry had been hoping to persuade Lawrence to use his expertise in designing aeroplane engines to support the process of rearmament.

During these dark days in the first months of 1935, there was speculation that Ramsay MacDonald was about to retire, and a new national government formed under Stanley Baldwin. In March, the day before the great debate on the air estimates, Philip had hosted a golfing party at Trent with Duff and Diana Cooper and Chips Channon among the guests. Channon recalled in his diary,

> Trent is a dream of a house, perfect, luxurious, distinguished with the exotic taste to be expected in any Sassoon Schloss. But the servants are casual, indeed almost rude . . . I lunched with the Coopers en ménage, and we discussed politics and the effect of Hitler's dramatic repudiation of the Versailles Treaty, and his militaristic attitude generally. Duff thinks it is as well as we know where we are. Duff thinks that MacDonald will resign in the summer soon after the Jubilee celebrations [on 6 May].'[50]

Philip Sassoon also discussed the prospects for the new government with Anthony Eden during his convalescence at Trent in April. Eden had been under great physical and mental stress after months of shuttle diplomacy between the capitals of Europe and the Disarmament Conference at Geneva. This resulted in his suffering a minor heart attack on a flight back from Prague, as a result of a blood clot in one of his arteries. Sassoon thought that Baldwin would appoint a new Foreign Secretary to replace the now largely discredited John Simon and believed that Eden, despite his youth and lack of cabinet experience, could be preferred, telling him, 'I am sure you will get it.'

Churchill was also staying at Trent during part of Eden's

convalescence, at around the same time that he was preparing his great memorandum for the cabinet on the true deficiencies of Britain's air defences. Eden recalled that Churchill 'was kind enough to tell my wife of the telegram he had sent to Mrs Churchill, who had been abroad at the time, about my unhappy flight from Prague: "Now the only good member of the Government has had a heart attack in an aeroplane."'[51]

Chips Channon had known Eden since they were students at Oxford together after the war, and he wrote of him in 1935, 'I have never had an exaggerated opinion of his brilliance, though his appearance is magnificent.'[52]

Eden was emerging as one of the new stars of British politics, and he was now one of the most frequent guests at Philip's weekend parties; he had also in 1935 joined the board of trustees of the National Gallery, giving them a further area of common interest. In his memoirs, Eden recalled his frequent stays with Philip in the 1930s:

> Philip was a wonderful host and impresario. His gift was to get people together who wanted to see each other and then efface himself. The resulting performance was his pleasure. He once told me that he got all the news worth hearing that way without the trouble of reading what the press had to say. He was a rich man who liked to spend his money making his friends happy around him; there was a touch of the Arabian Nights in the wonder of his entertainments. He was kindly and unselfish, asking for nothing for himself . . . For me [at Trent] there was also the tennis court, with the patient professional, and the swimming pool in which to revel, to say nothing of our host's lovely pictures, furniture and porcelain to discuss and admire. No contrast could have been more complete from workaday London, yet Trent Park was so close that I would sometimes escape from Whitehall for an hour's tennis there even on a weekday.[53]

Ramsay MacDonald duly resigned on 7 June and Baldwin returned as Prime Minister and formed a new government. Philip's friend Sam Hoare would become the new Foreign Secretary, with Eden remaining at the Foreign Office as his deputy. The reshuffle would also lead to changes at the Air Ministry. Sir Robert Vansittart, the Permanent Under-Secretary at the Foreign Office, thought that 'The Air Ministry was weak, especially in its intelligence. Charlie Londonderry and Philip Sassoon were both my friends, but were not a strong enough combination to impress parliament.'[54] The combination would be brought to an end, with Philip retaining the Under-Secretary of State's position, while Londonderry was moved out of his ministry. J. C. C. Davidson, Stanley Baldwin's political fixer and a former chairman of the Conservative Party, had a scathing view of his abilities: 'Londonderry had the reputation of being a rather soft, Regency-beau type of man. Although he had a certain amount of cunning and capacity, he was not really equipped for thinking . . . He was never really fit for Cabinet rank, and his association with the Air Force was, although keen, rather on the social than the technical side.'[55] In truth, Londonderry's fall was a result not just of his own mistakes but of the whole government's failure to grasp the need to build up the strength of the air force rapidly. The new Secretary of State for Air was Philip Cunliffe-Lister, who would soon be ennobled as Lord Swinton. He was already a friend of Sassoon's and had been a regular guest at the weekly cabinet lunches at Park Lane.

The immediate foreign policy crisis that would command the attention of the new government was not German rearmament but Italian aggression in East Africa. Mussolini wanted to build on the special claim that Italy believed it had over Abyssinia (modern-day Ethiopia) by turning it into a colony and consolidating the standing that he believed his nation should have among the great powers. A skirmish involving a few hundred troops on the border between Italian Somaliland and Abyssinia in late 1934, in which Mussolini's colonial forces suffered significant casualties, threatened to bring the whole situation to a head. After a tit-for-tat diplomatic row between the two countries, Mussolini sent fifty thousand troops to the Italian garrison in Eritrea and made no secret of his intention to launch a full invasion of Abyssinia.

This emerging crisis would be the first great test for the new Foreign Secretary, Sam Hoare. Just over a week after his appointment he joined Anthony Eden and Sir Robert Vansittart at Trent Park to try to devise a solution. The dilemma that Hoare was trying to resolve at Trent he defined as being fourfold:

> First, Hitler's strength was becoming daily more formidable, and his intentions more unabashed. Secondly, Japanese aggression threatened us with war in the Far East when we were not strong enough to resist Hitler in Europe, and at the same time fight in the Pacific. Thirdly, it was essential to British security to have a friendly Italy in the Mediterranean that would both guarantee our lines of communication to the Far East and make it unnecessary for the French to keep an army on the Italian frontier. Fourthly, and as a favourable pointer towards the maintenance of Anglo-Italian co-operation, Mussolini was at that time on very bad terms with Hitler.[56]

Hoare felt that a deal could be struck if the British reached out to Mussolini. As they gathered amid the luxury and tranquillity of Trent Park, it was a seductive piece of logic. Philip Sassoon had also met Mussolini, and knew well his Air Minister, General Balbo, particularly from their numerous sporting encounters at the Schneider Trophy races. Looking back, however, Hoare concluded that 'Perhaps we were too optimistic. Perhaps we did not sufficiently realise the contrast between Mussolini's outlook and ours . . . Perhaps, also, I somewhat lightly flattered myself with the feeling that my past associations with the Duce* might still have some effect upon him.'[57]

---

* Mussolini used the title 'Il Duce': The Leader.

The solution they settled on at Trent was to offer the Abyssinians a narrow corridor of land through British Somaliland, which would give them access to a seaport, in return for making substantial concessions to the Italian demands for territory in Abyssinia. The cabinet, 'although somewhat taken aback by the suddenness of the move',[58] agreed that Eden should travel to Rome to put the offer devised at Trent to Mussolini. The offer was also leaked to a British Sunday newspaper, which caused uproar in the House of Commons when the purpose of Eden's mission became clear. Mussolini rejected it out of hand, claiming that the French government was prepared to give him a free hand in Abyssinia.

Over the summer there followed a series of failed attempts to achieve a negotiated settlement. Both Lloyd George and Churchill urged Hoare privately to try to find a common position with France, with Churchill reminding him, 'The real danger is Germany, and nothing must be done to weaken the anti-German front.'[59]

On 3 October, in a flagrant challenge to the League of Nations, Mussolini invaded Abyssinia. The League still wanted talks to continue, both to try to prevent a broader conflict between the European powers and to salvage its own reputation. There was, though, a further complication for the British negotiating team, as Stanley Baldwin had asked the King to dissolve Parliament for a general election on 14 November. The prospect of a new war would be a factor in the election campaign. Earlier in the year the results of the 'Peace Ballot', which was arranged by the League of Nations and in which over eleven million British people voted, had shown large majorities in favour of the League and international disarmament. In Philip Sassoon's constituency there had even been a public meeting in Folkestone's Fishmarket organized by local supporters of Oswald Mosley's British Union of Fascists, under the title 'Mosley for Peace'.

In a letter to the *Folkestone Herald*, Philip Sassoon entirely endorsed the approach of Sam Hoare to try to find a negotiated settlement on Abyssinia through the League of Nations. He admitted that 'The League is an experiment,' but added, 'If the League means anything, it means the birth of a new spirit in the sphere of international relations, the regeneration of the political consciences of the nations that belong to it. The views of Italy or the fate of Abyssinia, much as we may regret the former or sympathise with the latter, are secondary considerations beside the paramount question: Has international morality entered on a new and higher plane, or are treaties still mere scraps of paper, to be torn up at will?'[60]

Speaking at a packed Folkestone town hall during the election campaign, where every chair and every available inch of floor space were occupied, Philip was given a 'rousing' reception. He defended his record at the Air Ministry, and told his audience why it had been so important for the government to start the process of building Britain's military strength back up:

> If, in relation to our foreign policy, there is any one particular in which – in common with all other governments since the war – the national government is open to criticism, it is that we have allowed our defence forces to decline to a level which impairs the influence which Great Britain can exert in support of the League.
>
> If we are at fault in that, others must share the blame. The blame must be shared especially by those members of the opposition parties who throughout the past four years have strenuously opposed any increase in our fighting services. It must be shared by those who on every occasion have urged upon us to disarm still further.

In talking about the prospects of a future war in Europe, Philip used language that was very similar to the views consistently expressed in the House of Commons by Winston Churchill. He said, 'We are not preparing for war. But the events of the past few months have proved what some of us have for some time feared. I mean that the present weakness of Great Britain has become a danger to peace.'[61]

Philip Sassoon was once again safely returned in Folkestone and Hythe, and Stanley Baldwin secured a strong majority for the national government, but not on the enormous scale of 1931, swelled as it was then by the collapse of the Labour government and the economic crisis of that year. Although Baldwin's government was national in name, it was Conservative in reality. Ramsay MacDonald and John Simon, as leaders of the National Labour and National Liberal parties, retained seats in the cabinet, but of the 427 MPs who sat on the government benches, all but 41 were Conservatives.

On election night Philip Sassoon attended a party given by Harry Selfridge, where the guests included the cream of fashionable London society, as well as many media and political celebrities. Lord Beaverbrook and Winston Churchill were joined by Douglas Fairbanks Jr, Noël Coward, Ivor Novello and the actress Madeleine Carroll, who had just shot to international fame as the star of Alfred Hitchcock's screen adaptation of *The Thirty-Nine Steps*.[62] At the party Philip escorted Lady Houston, who was a great supporter of air racing and had donated £100,000 towards the staging of the 1931 Schneider Trophy races at Cowes after the government had withdrawn financial support. She was also an ardent admirer of Mussolini, and a supporter of his campaign in Abyssinia. Lady Houston's views placed her in a distinct minority of public opinion, but although people wanted Mussolini to be stopped, there were limits to how far they were prepared to go.

In early December, the Foreign Secretary Sam Hoare was preparing to hold talks with his French counterpart, Pierre Laval, on a new proposal to try to save Abyssinia from total destruction and to keep Italy in the anti-German alliance. Hoare's health had not been good, and at a cinema party hosted by Philip Sassoon at Park Lane, with Anthony Eden also among the guests, he collapsed and remained unconscious for a time before being revived. His doctors ordered an immediate rest, and with Baldwin's approval he agreed to take a two- or three-week break in Switzerland. He accepted a meeting with Laval in Paris on his way to Zuoz, carrying Baldwin's blessing and advice to 'push Laval as far as you can, but on no account get this country into war'.[63]

Hoare would later concede that to take on such a meeting, in poor health and without detailed guidance from the cabinet on the terms they would accept, was a mistake. His meeting in Paris produced what became known as the Hoare–Laval Pact, an accord that effectively went along with Mussolini's gains in Abyssinia and gave him an economic sphere of influence over another significant part of the country. After concluding his talks with Laval, Hoare went on to his Swiss skating holiday, and on the first morning on the ice suffered another blackout. When he came to, he found that he had broken his nose in two places when he fell. Meanwhile, the terms of the Hoare–Laval Pact had leaked first to the French and then to the English newspapers, before the cabinet had a chance to discuss them. The result was general uproar at the generosity of the terms towards Mussolini. For a few crucial days Hoare, under doctors' orders, was unable to return to England to face the storm, and when he did he was challenged by the cabinet to withdraw his support for the deal. He refused, and offered his resignation instead.

At the height of the crisis, on 19 December, Philip held a party at Park Lane, where the guests included the Prince of Wales and Wallis Simpson, Sir Robert Vansittart, Norah Lindsay and the millionaire art collector Sir Alfred Beit MP. It was the evening that Sam Hoare resigned as Foreign Secretary and, still with a bandage across his nose, gave a personal statement to the Commons setting out his position. Chips Channon recorded, 'Sam Hoare got up and in a flash he had won the sympathy of the House, by his lucidity, his concise narrative, his sincerity and patriotism . . . for 40 minutes he held the House breathless, and at last sat down, but not before he had wished his successor better luck, and burst into tears.'[64] Hoare wrote in his memoirs though that, 'Towards the end of my detailed argument I began to feel exhausted. I lasted out, however, until I sat down, when I felt a sudden pain in my broken nose. Instinctively I put up my hand to stop it. This trivial action started the story that I had broken down in tears at the end of my speech. I never felt less like tears.'[65]

Norah Lindsay remembered of the party later that evening, 'you never heard such a din. Vansittart, Philip and Alfred all talking hard, we in a circle round them, and the Prince in a coat with very short sleeves and long white cuffs over tiny red hands saying "Politics is a dirty game."'[66] The Prince had also been at the House of Commons earlier, where from the Peers Gallery he had listened to his 'friend, Sir Samuel Hoare, make his moving speech of resignation . . . Knowing much that had gone on behind the scenes, I was sorry that Sam Hoare has been made the scapegoat for what was, in the last analysis, Mr Baldwin's own policy.'[67]

Norah Lindsay also noted from the conversations at Philip's party that night:

It's inconceivable that such a momentous decision [the Hoare–Laval Pact] should have leaked immediately through and into the papers (even before the cabinet had seen it) . . . some say Baldwin left everything to Hoare and never took the trouble to go into the terms himself . . . I see in the morning's papers that Eden has been made Foreign Minister. This will surely placate our enraged House of Commons, as he stands for the League – but he is disliked by all the foreign nations because of his supercilious manner.[68]

Following his resignation, Sam Hoare recalled the final meeting to take his leave as a minister of King George V: 'I was greatly shocked by his appearance. He looked very ill, and spoke as if he was weighed down with anxiety. His voice sounded weaker and less confident than I had ever known it . . . Having said that he was sorry to lose me as his Foreign Minister, he then very tactfully turned the conversation to the tastes that we shared in Norfolk. "Now you are free, you will have more time for shooting. Go and shoot a lot of woodcocks in Norfolk."'[69] Hoare's concern over the health of the King was well founded. A month later, on 20 January 1936, he died at Sandringham.

• THE KING'S PARTY •

Where are the friends of yesterday
That fawned on Him,
That flattered Her;
Where are the friends of yesterday,
Submitting to His every whim,
Offering praise of Her as myrrh
To Him? . . .

That nameless, faceless, raucous gang
Who graced Balmoral's Coburg towers,
Danced to the gramophone, and sang
Within the battlemented bowers
Of dear Fort Belvedere;

. . . Oh, do they never shed a tear
Remembering the King, their martyr,
And how they led him to the brink
In rodent eagerness to barter
All English history for a drink?
What do they say, that jolly crew?
Oh . . . Her they hardly knew,

They never found Her really nice
(And here the sickened cock crew thrice):
Him they had never thought quite sane,
But weak, and obstinate, and vain . . .

Osbert Sitwell, 'Rat Week',
a survey of the abdication crisis of 1936[1]

On 21 January 1936, Philip Sassoon joined the long queue of MPs at
the Speaker's chair to take the oath of allegiance to the new sovereign,
King Edward VIII. Since they had met at General Headquarters during
the First World War, Philip had courted and indulged the Prince.
Together they had played golf with Walter Hagen, watched Georges
Carpentier box and danced with friends at the Embassy Club. Edward
had used Philip's parties to arrange assignations with Freda Dudley
Ward, his former girlfriend, as well as to maintain informal relations
with some of the leading politicians of the day. For Philip, his easy
access to Edward had helped to secure his position at the pinnacle of
the London social scene in the 1920s and 1930s.

Now the Prince with whom Philip had for twenty years played
sport and partied was the ruler of a quarter of the globe. There
was no change in style from Edward on his accession to the throne,
nor any losing of old friends. His social life would largely carry
on as before, only now without the occasional sign of displeasure
from King George, who had never approved of the London night-
clubs his son had frequented as Prince of Wales. Edward considered that as his father 'always started for bed at 11.10, it was
difficult for him to believe that anything but mischief could result
from staying up later'.[2] The royal household would also have to
adjust to a monarch who would rather spend August playing golf
in Biarritz than shooting grouse in Scotland, and was more likely
to enjoy his free evenings 'en petit comité with a few intimates
or at the Embassy Club, than in the great houses or salons of

London'.[3] As the Prime Minister Stanley Baldwin noted in his statement to the House of Commons to mark the new King's reign, 'He has the secret of youth in the prime of age.' Edward remarked of Baldwin's words that this 'exciting ingredient, or elixir . . . sounded fine – exactly the right thing for a King inaugurating his reign in an era that had put the highest premium upon youthful vigour and adaptability'.[4]

In the eyes of the world, the one thing this dynamic new King lacked was a queen. Now forty-one years old, he was the only one of his three surviving brothers not to have married, although he was secretly having an affair with Wallis Simpson, the wife of an American businessman.* Mrs Simpson had been the King's mistress for the last couple of years but, as Osbert Sitwell observed in his poem 'Rat Week', she was still something of a mystery to his friends. The King's relationship with Wallis had the same obsessive intensity as the one he had conducted with Freda Dudley Ward in the 1920s. Freda had remained a good friend of Edward's until his relationship with Wallis started in 1934. Then she was cut off completely and was even told by the switchboard operator at St James's Palace that the Prince would no longer take her calls.[5]

Philip Sassoon had known Freda and her family well for many years. She had frequently been a guest at Trent Park and Port Lympne, whereas Wallis was new on the scene. However, Philip's relationship with Edward was such that he would do anything for anyone who was important in the King's life. In contrast, his sister Sybil did not want to be under the same roof as Wallis and would not attend parties if she was present. Her views on the King's relationship with Mrs Simpson reflected those held by many establishment figures – that it was simply wrong for the King to conduct an affair with a married woman.

---

* Ernest Simpson was Wallis's second husband. An American-born but London-based shipping executive, he was a naturalized British citizen and had served as a captain in the Coldstream Guards during the First World War. Ernest and Wallis had married on 21 July 1928 and divorced on 3 May 1937.

On the day that King George V died, Duff Cooper – who two months previously had entered the cabinet as Secretary of State for War – was called in to see Stanley Baldwin at Downing Street, where the Prime Minister set out his concerns about the Prince of Wales's relationship with Mrs Simpson. Cooper's diary notes from that meeting give a good insight into the dilemma faced by Edward's friends, and how they failed to give him the advice he needed because of their desire to secure their relationships with him:

> The P.M. is very much disturbed about the Prince's relationship with Mrs Simpson. He thinks that if it becomes generally known the country won't stand it. 'If she were what I call a respectable whore' he said, he wouldn't mind, by which he meant somebody whom the Prince occasionally saw in secret but didn't spend his whole time with . . . Why the P.M. sent for me I don't know. He said that he knew I was a friend of the Prince's but he didn't suggest that I should take any action. I think he may have had it in his mind that I might advise Wallis Simpson to clear out – for a bit at any rate – because he said that that would be the best thing that could happen. I shall certainly do nothing of the kind. She would tell the Prince who would never forgive me.[6]

Fort Belvedere, Edward's beloved lodge on the southern edge of Windsor Great Park, would be the social epicentre for the new royal court. 'The Fort' was owned by the Crown Estate and had been in Edward's possession since 1929. When it became available, he asked King George if he might live there; he recalled that his father had replied with a smile, 'What could you possibly want that queer old place for? Those damn week-ends, I suppose . . . Well, if you want it, you can have it.'[7] The main house was a largely Victorian Gothic Revival building with a turreted tower from which you could see seven counties of England. On the north side the land sloped down to Virginia Water, but the gardens had become unkempt and the house itself also required substantial refurbishment and modernization. Edward remembered, 'I had a wonderful time fixing up The Fort, both inside and outside. It was a joy that I was loath to share with others; though I naturally sought professional advice, the final result in the main represented my ideas.'[8]

Philip was one of the friends Edward had turned to for help, as soon as he had taken possession of the Fort. In November 1929, the Prince wrote to tell him, 'I had M. Piperno down to The Fort on Friday, so that he should have the rooms and passages in his mind when collecting rugs for me to look at next spring. He also took measurements of the rooms and the passage ways as well . . . hope that his wares are really as cheap as you assure me they are. The trouble is that yours and my ideas of cheapness don't always quite tally. Perhaps you will come down to The Fort some day later on and advise a little.'[9] As well as being a guest at the Fort, Philip tried to guide Edward on replanting the gardens, and on one occasion brought one of his gardeners with him from Trent to carry out the work. Wallis Simpson later described the incident in her memoirs: 'A tall man with a slim figure and a handsome, intelligent face, was pacing importantly up and down the driveway. The motor and the gardener were not in sight.' She and Edward went out to join Philip, who, on seeing the Prince, exclaimed, 'Ah, I'm so glad to have found you at home, Sir. I've brought some of those delphiniums that you admired at Trent.'

Edward then said, 'That's very nice of you, Philip, but where are they? Philip replied, 'As a matter of fact my gardener must have just about finished putting them in . . . A little distance down the driveway. My gardener and I saw the right spot as we drove in.'

The Prince then exploded: 'Good God! What are you thinking? I'm the only one who could possibly know where I want them planted.' Wallis remembered that 'as if shot from a catapult David* took off down the drive with Sir Philip puffing and expostulating

---

* The King's full name was Edward Albert Christian George Andrew Patrick David, but he had been known from birth to his family as David.

at his flying heels'. Upon reaching the delphiniums, Edward insisted they were dug up and moved about a yard or so away to a place of his own designation. The Prince then whispered to Wallis, 'As a matter of fact, he picked about the best place but I couldn't resist being a little difficult all the same.'[10]

In the middle of February 1936, when the funeral commemorations for King George were over, Philip joined Edward and Wallis for a weekend party at Fort Belvedere, where the other guests included Duff and Diana Cooper and the American-born socialite Emerald Cunard, who were also part of the King's intimate circle. Philip used the occasion to ask for the King's support for the forthcoming art exhibition at his Park Lane mansion to raise funds for the Royal Northern Hospital. The 1936 show would focus on portraits painted by Thomas Gainsborough, and Philip asked Edward if he would loan some of the artist's works from the Royal Collection. The art historian Ellis Waterhouse, who was working on the exhibition, and also for the British School in Rome, where Philip was a trustee, noted in a letter to a friend, 'I had a long telephone conversation with Philip Sassoon yesterday and gather that he dined with his new Majesty the day before, who said he would lend any Gainsborough. P.S. Now proposing to have all the pictures from the present chamber in Windsor. I did not dissuade him, especially from encouraging Eddie VIII from having a democratic view about the Royal Collection.'[11]

The King was as good as his word and lent eight pictures by Gainsborough to Philip Sassoon's exhibition at Park Lane, seven of which were portraits of the children of George III and Queen Charlotte. These paintings had hung in Queen Charlotte's private rooms and were later arranged in Queen Victoria's audience chamber at Windsor. *The Times* reported that 'Nothing could be better calculated to quicken the interest in an exhibition which is proving a remarkable success. The Royal Portraits, which have never been seen by the public before, represent Gainsborough at the height of his powers.'[12]

The exhibition was reminiscent of the show of English 'conversation piece' paintings, including works by Gainsborough, that Philip had organized in 1930. Once again, standing in his beautifully appointed rooms, the viewer could be transported to the decorous and dignified world that Gainsborough had captured. It was escapism from the increasingly alarming events in Europe, where both Italy and Germany seemed intent on building up their military strength in defiance of the League of Nations.

In the early months of 1936, there remained growing concerns about the weakness of Britain's military defences and the war of conquest that Mussolini was pursuing in East Africa against Abyssinia. Following the public rejection of the Hoare–Laval Pact the previous December, Mussolini was sweeping all before him and in May would take the capital Addis Ababa, forcing the Emperor Haile Selassie into exile. It was a situation that the new King had closely followed the previous year, in part through his friendships with Sam Hoare and Philip Sassoon.

On 7 March 1936, encouraged by the inability of the League of Nations to stand up to Italy's aggression in Africa, Hitler sent Germany's armed forces into the Rhineland, in a further act of repudiation of the Treaty of Versailles, which stipulated that the region should be a demilitarized zone. With hindsight, we can look back at this action and say that, if Britain and France had stood up to Hitler at this point, the Nazi regime might have collapsed and war could have been averted. However, only Churchill and a few others at the time suggested such a course of action; many considered that Germany was only sending its army into its 'own back garden'.* Philip, however, thought that Hitler's actions said a lot about his general motivation. On the remilitarization of the Rhineland, he wrote, 'We have seen Germany choose deliberately to seize by the strong hand privileges which we believe she could have regained by negotiation.'[13]

---

* This phrase was famously used by Philip Kerr, the Marquess of Lothian, whom Philip Sassoon knew well from his time as PPS to Lloyd George.

The Germans regarded the new King as sympathetic to their grievances. Their Ambassador in London, Leopold von Hoesch, told Berlin that Edward VIII 'feels warm sympathy for Germany . . . I am convinced that his friendly attitude towards Germany might in time come to exercise a certain amount of influence on the shaping of British foreign policy. At any rate, we should be able to rely on having on the British throne a ruler who is not lacking in understanding for Germany and in the desire to see good relations established between Germany and Britain.'[14] Hoesch died only a few weeks later. When the new German Ambassador, Joachim von Ribbentrop, presented his letters to the King later that year, he also noted that Edward was 'most affable, enquired after the Führer and repeated clearly that he desired good Anglo-German relations'.[15] Ribbentrop was on good terms with Wallis Simpson, who had arranged in 1935 for him to meet Edward at a private lunch given by Emerald Cunard. Ribbentrop was then on a special mission to England on behalf of the German government, but the Foreign Secretary had specially requested that the Prince of Wales should not meet with any Nazi ministers. The lunch caused considerable resentment in the British government. Osbert Sitwell remembered overhearing Anthony Eden raising the issue with Philip at a party at Trent Park a few days later: 'He said that it made parliamentary government impossible, and that if he had been in place of his chief [Sam Hoare] he would have complained to the King, and then resigned his office.'[16] There is no evidence that Edward tried to exert influence over British foreign policy during his brief reign. The belief held by men like Ribbentrop, that the King was well disposed towards them, also needs to be balanced by the fact that he included in his close circle men like Winston Churchill, Duff Cooper and Philip himself who held strong anti-Nazi views.

In February 1936, Churchill had received further secret intelligence from Desmond Morton that Germany was maintaining a very high rate of armaments production. Following his successful campaign for increased spending on the air force, Churchill now advocated the creation of a new government position of Minister for Defence, to coordinate the requirements of Britain's armed forces, and for a new Ministry of Munitions to secure the supplies and convert existing factories for the production of armaments. To his friends such as Philip Sassoon and Austen Chamberlain, it was clear that Winston should take on these roles. Austen remarked, however, 'I don't suppose that [Baldwin] will offer it to him & I don't think that Neville [Chamberlain] would wish to have him back, but they are both wrong. He is the right man for that post & in such dangerous times that consideration ought to be decisive.'[17]

Austen Chamberlain was right. The Permanent Secretary of the Treasury, Sir Warren Fisher, supported the creation of this new Defence post but recommended to the Chancellor, Neville Chamberlain, that the chosen minister should be 'a disinterested type of man with no axe to grind or desire to make a place for himself'.[18] On 14 March they found that man in the shape of the Attorney General, Sir Thomas Inskip, an appointment which Churchill's friend and scientific adviser Professor Frederick Lindemann called the 'most cynical thing that has been done since Caligula appointed his horse as consul'.[19] The following day Philip conveyed his commiserations to Winston; he was also arranging for the head gardener at Trent to send some tufted Carolina ducks for Churchill's lake at Chartwell. Some drakes had already been safely transported to Kent, and Philip wrote to reassure Winston that he would dispatch 'two lady carolinas as soon as I can procure them – we must stop any abnormality on your part'. He then added, 'I am very disappointed you have not been made the co-ordinator [for the Ministry of Defence]. I am hoping you will be the Munitioneer which would be by far the most important job of the two.' Looking ahead to the forthcoming annual debate on the Air Ministry's estimates, he added, 'Don't be too hard on me on Tuesday.'[20]

Philip had no cause for concern. The great set-piece debate of the previous year was not repeated, as Churchill had already won the argument for substantial increases in the budget for air defence. As Philip was able to tell the House of Commons, with some satisfaction:

> The Estimates that I have the honour of introducing . . . at a gross total of approximately £43,500,000 and a net total of £39,000,000, are by far the largest that Parliament has been asked to vote to the Air Ministry since the War . . . As a result, the metropolitan squadrons will ultimately be increased to 129, with a first-line strength of approximately 1,750. The actual defensive and offensive power of the Home Defence Force will, however, have been augmented far in excess of this numerical increase. In addition, a further 12 squadrons are to be formed by 1939 for duties overseas. That will make a total of 37 squadrons outside these islands. All these figures exclude the Fleet Air Arm which is to be increased by 27 first-line machines in 1936 and on a much larger scale in 1937 and 1938. By the end of the financial year 1936 the first-line strength of the Force will have been doubled in the short space of two years. I do not think any Fighting Service has ever been set a comparable task in time of peace.[21]

The 'new types' of aircraft Philip referred to in his statement included the Supermarine Spitfire and Hawker Hurricane fighters that would play such decisive roles in the Battle of Britain in 1940. The speed and manoeuvrability of the Spitfire, which would make it such a potent weapon in the air, had no doubt benefited from its manufacturer Supermarine's technical developments in the course of the company's successful participation in the Schneider Trophy, the air racing competition that Philip had done so much to support.

Churchill's frustration, however, with the government's failure to create a Ministry of Supply, to ensure that Britain had the manufacturing production capacity it needed to rearm, would continue throughout 1936. In November, this culminated in a devastating attack in the House of Commons: 'The Government simply cannot make up their mind, or they cannot get the Prime Minister to make up his mind. So they go on in strange paradox, decided only to be undecided, resolved to be irresolute, adamant for drift, solid for fluidity, all powerful to be impotent. So we go on preparing more months and years – precious, perhaps vital to the greatness of Britain – for the locusts to eat.'[22]

Despite the darkening skies of international affairs, the spring and summer of 1936 were filled with the usual entertaining for Philip at Trent and Lympne. Winston Churchill, Anthony Eden and Duff Cooper were again guests, along with the Duke and Duchess of York, and in May the widowed Queen Mary made her annual visit for tea in the gardens at Trent. That summer Philip also attended a series of events where the King and Mrs Simpson socialized with groups of their supporters and friends. In June, Chips and Honor Channon gave a dinner at their house in Belgrave Square for Edward and Wallis. Channon noted that 'the King is Mrs Simpson's absolute slave, and will go nowhere where she is not invited, and she, clever woman, with her high pitched voice, chic clothes, moles and sense of humour is behaving well'.[23] The guests were from the 'King's Set', including again Philip, Emerald Cunard and Duff and Diana Cooper. Chips noted in his diary, 'Dinner proceeded well, and Philip Sassoon, who has not yet been given the job of Commissioner of Works,* which he longs for, asked Emerald to say a word for him to the King, which she did . . . The room was full of glamour and candle-light, everybody was gay and a little elated.'[24]

However, the most significant social event Philip attended that season was a dinner given by the King at York House, his residence in St James's Palace, on 10 July, with the Duke and Duchess of York also in attendance. This was the first occasion that Wallis Simpson was listed in the official published court circular as a guest of the King's. The dinner brought together many of the friends who had

---

* First Commissioner of Works was a cabinet-level ministerial post within the government with responsibility for public buildings and spaces.

joined parties with the King at Trent Park while he was Prince of Wales, including Winston Churchill, Sam Hoare (now back in the government as First Lord of the Admiralty), David Margesson (the Chief Whip) and Diana Cooper. The following day the King and Wallis joined Philip for a weekend party at Trent, where Dickie Mountbatten was also among the guests, along with Margesson (again) and General Franco's representative in London, the Duke of Alba.*

On 1 August Philip hosted a weekend party at Port Lympne, inviting Chips and Honor Channon and Norah Lindsay. Norah drove down to Lympne with the Channons and they 'gossiped madly all the way. The usual topics the King and his speech, the King and his yacht trip . . . The King . . . The King . . . The King.'25 When they arrived they found Ernest and Wallis Simpson at Lympne, and another friend of the King's, Helen Fitzgerald. It would not be until the end of October that Wallis would file for divorce from her husband, and until that moment the public pretence of their marriage continued. The MP Victor Cazalet was also there, along with Duff and Diana Cooper. The Coopers were on their way to the French Riviera, and then to join the King with Wallis, Helen Fitzgerald and Lord Sefton on board the yacht *Nahlin* for a cruise of the eastern Mediterranean. The King was holding a separate party at Fort Belvedere the same weekend, which would allow him to travel out to join the yacht independently of Wallis.

Lympne wasn't to the Channons' taste and Chips observed in his diary, 'The house is large and luxurious and frankly ugly. Honor said that it was like a Spanish brothel.'26 For Norah, though, the setting at Lympne was as magical as ever:

We had a lashing gale all day . . . Then came a fine interval and

---

* Jacobo Fitz-James Stuart, seventeenth Duke of Alba, had been Foreign Minister of Spain before the Civil War. He became the official Spanish Ambassador in 1939 when Britain recognized Franco's government.

we all rushed out to see the marsh lying so calm in the pale sunset
as if no storms had passed that way. And after dinner there was
a feast of beauty. A huge high moon rode in the sky with rags of
clouds racing still across her face and she was poised just between
a group of inky cypresses and again reflected in a silver radiance
in the pool below. It was as beautiful as any Italian garden. Then
as a last straw the big centre fountain was turned on and the frothy
silver creamy water gushed up in a vast plume, its edges where
the light didn't reach – tipped in ink. Far away the sea lay like a
plate of silver and lights twinkled here and there on a long stretch
of pansy velvet dark marsh.[27]

That evening they had been joined by a few members of 601
Squadron, stationed near by for their summer camp, and the discussion was far less tranquil than the moon-soaked garden. Channon
wrote that 'There was the usual German argument . . . with Philip
and Duff attacking the Nazis with the violence born of personal
prejudice . . . After dinner . . . a young R.A.F. pilot whispered to
me, "Is Duff Cooper off his rocker, or what?" Indeed he seems
obsessed at times.'[28]

Their discussion that evening coincided with the opening
ceremony of the Olympic Games in Berlin, which was attended by
Lord Beaverbrook, flown there by his son Max Aitken. Returning
his plane to England two days later, young Max joined the party
at Lympne. The Coopers had now left for France, and Channon
recorded that 'Someone referred to the Olympic Games, where we
ought to be now, and the opening ceremonies which are supposed
to have been stupendous. Max Aitken then proceeded to describe
the scene . . . Teenie [Cazalet] tactlessly flew at him (he hates the
whole Beaverbrook crew) and a dreadful discussion ensued during
which everyone lost their temper.'[29]

If Port Lympne had been something of a playground for princes
and their friends for over fifteen years, it received a more stately
visitor in September, when Queen Mary joined Philip for lunch

before visiting Sandgate and Folkestone. She noted in her day diary:

At 10.40 by train from Charing Cross for Port Lympne, Kent to pay a visit to Sir Philip Sassoon. He met me at Ashford with Sybil Cholmondeley and Hannah Gubbay and we drove to Lympne in a deluge. Went over the amusing modern house and had luncheon, luckily it cleared and we went out and saw the lovely gardens with fine yew hedges. The whole place created by Sir Philip – after having tea on the 'stope' we left for Folkestone via Hythe and Sandgate. Crowds of people all the way. Took leave of my kind hosts and we were back in London by 6.30 after a most enjoyable day.[30]

In Folkestone, Queen Mary was driven down the 'Road of Remembrance', where millions of servicemen during the First World War had marched to the harbour and the ships waiting to take them to France. She also visited the housing scheme that Philip had constructed after the war, at The Durlocks, above the harbour, to provide homes for fishermen and their families. At Sandgate she met the patients at the Star and Garter Hospital for disabled servicemen from the war, where Philip had also previously taken Charlie Chaplin, to give the men a boost.

In the autumn of 1936, Philip Sassoon's standing had never been higher. He was a close friend of the King's, as well as being intimate with other leading members of the royal family. He was heavily engaged with his work at the Air Ministry, which was at last starting to invest in the expansion of the air force in the manner that he had been pressing for, and he had maintained strong personal relationships not only with the leading members of the government, but also with Winston Churchill, who had become its arch-critic. He was recognized as a leading figure in the arts, which remained his great private passion, and his annual Park Lane exhibitions were as popular as ever. In late September, he embarked on another lengthy tour of the Empire's air stations, this time an 8,000-mile round trip across East Africa to Lake Victoria and back. In the notes made during his outward flight to Rome he wrote in the margin, 'Sophistication – to climb the hill of pleasure and experience and to find it rather flat on the top.'[31] This remark suggests a calm nonchalance at the position he held and the company he kept. Yet this was more of a reflection of how Philip wished to be seen than his true state of mind. There is no doubt that he took a great deal of care over the way he dressed, the style of his homes and the detailed preparations for his entertainments. Nothing was just thrown together, even if the effect was to produce an aura of easy charm and effortless luxury. Yet sophistication, for Philip, really meant the open rapport he enjoyed with royalty and leading celebrities, as well as his political friends. Familiarity may have made their company feel somewhat less exalted to him, but there was no doubt that he knew he was standing at the summit, even if he found the hill to be a little flat on top. That state of mind is also reflected in his travel journal when he recounts his audience at the Mombasa Palace with King Farouk of Egypt: 'The palace is beautifully situated on the sea but is quite monstrous – looks like a Riviera Hydro. The King is really charming – quite nice looking and really easy. He had on a pair of blue suede shoes and gave us some excellent coffee. Lots of Royal jokes.'[32]

Philip returned to London in October as royal affairs in England were about to take a more serious turn. Following her summer holiday with the King, Wallis had decided to file for divorce from her husband, and the petition was put down to be heard in Ipswich on 27 October. The King was rightly concerned that this would lead to public speculation about his relationship with Mrs Simpson, which was already attracting growing attention in the international media. The British press, which by convention would not then seek to invade the privacy of the royal family, had yet to report on the romance but it was only a matter of time. Edward called on the press baron Lord Beaverbrook, who was also the brother-in-law of his friend Helen Fitzgerald, to ask if he could persuade the other newspaper owners to respect Wallis's privacy and not report on her divorce hearing. Beaverbrook agreed and duly delivered, but the government was becoming highly agitated about the King's personal affairs.

At 10 a.m. on 20 October, Stanley Baldwin visited the King at Fort Belvedere to ask whether Edward could persuade Wallis to drop the petition for divorce. The King and the Prime Minister sat in front of the fire in the octagonal drawing room at the Fort, with Baldwin holding a stiff whisky and soda to calm his nerves, and began a conversation that would stretch out over the coming weeks. The Prime Minister started by saying, 'Well, Sir, whatever happens, my Mrs and I wish you every happiness from the depths of our souls.' This reduced both men to tears,[33] after which they began to discuss the simple question at the heart of this growing crisis: was the King intent on marrying Mrs Simpson, against the advice of his ministers, and even if this would mean giving up the throne?

The situation was unprecedented, but not unimaginable. George Bernard Shaw, a regular guest at Philip's Trent Park garden parties, where he would often be found arguing with Winston Churchill, had presented such a scenario in his 1929 play *The Apple Cart*. Here a popular king in his forties is under pressure from his cabinet to yield to their demands or abdicate. In the background, his mistress is pressuring him to marry her, urging him to 'Live a really noble and beautiful life – a kingly life – with me. What you need to make you a real king is a real queen . . . Everyone knows that I am the real queen. They cheer me in the streets. When I open one of the art exhibitions or launch a new ship they crowd the place out. I am one of Nature's queens; and they know it. If you do not, you are not one of Nature's kings.'[34]

In Shaw's play, the King uses his personal popularity with the people to face down his government and win the day. That November, Edward sought advice from the senior political figures he knew well from Philip Sassoon's circle, principally Sam Hoare, who was unsympathetic and thought he should drop Mrs Simpson, and Winston Churchill and Duff Cooper, who advised caution rather than confrontation with the government. Baldwin had brought matters to a head, but perhaps too soon. Wallis Simpson's divorce was not due to be granted until April 1937, and Edward's coronation had been scheduled for May. As yet there was no constitutional crisis, as it was not possible for the King to marry Mrs Simpson until she was divorced. If he could persuade Wallis to keep a low profile, and wait until after he had the crown on his head, he might be in a stronger position to negotiate with the government. The King's friends may also have thought, or hoped, that his relationship with Wallis would cool, as had his previous affairs.

Yet neither side would move. The government was adamant that the King could not marry Mrs Simpson, and that if their relationship was to continue it must be conducted out of the public eye. The King was equally determined that he would abdicate if he could not have his way. Throughout 1936, the King had become bolder in his association with Wallis, and until Baldwin confronted him about it in October, he had yet to be challenged over the constitutional minefield he was entering. His friends had prepared him badly for this moment. Philip, the Coopers and the Channons had all encouraged him, and had accepted Wallis as his partner in their relations with and entertainment for the King. On 17 November, Chips Channon noted in his diary that Emerald Cunard had shown him an anonymous note she had received, written in an 'educated handwriting', exclaiming, 'You old bitch, trying to make up to Mrs Simpson, in order to curry favour with the King.'[35] The Channons gave a further dinner for the King in Belgrave Square on 19 November, and later that month Philip Sassoon hosted a cinema party at Park Lane for Edward, where his friends tried to rally his spirits.

Osbert Sitwell remembered that there was a certain amount of enmity in society against the King's friends in the days leading up to the abdication. At a party given by Alfred Beit at 49 Belgrave Square, when Lady Mendl (an American interior designer and one of the friends identified by Sitwell in *Rat Week*) entered the ballroom, 'there followed a burst of hissing – the only time I ever recollect a demonstration of this kind in a private house in London'.[36]

The truth about Edward and Wallis became public knowledge in Britain on 3 December, and Channon noted in his diary that day, 'The King . . . is driving straight to the precipice; if he defies the Government and persists with his marriage plan the Cabinet will resign, and there is no alternative government . . . Only a possibility of Winston Churchill.'[37]

There were strong rumours in Westminster that a Churchill government, supported by a 'King's Party' in the House of Commons, was ready to take power, with Duff Cooper as Chancellor and Philip Sassoon as Secretary of State for Air. That speculation included Sassoon in this position underlines not only his close association with the King, but also a belief in Westminster that Churchill regarded him as a secret ally in his campaign for the expansion of air defence. However, the support was never there to make this project a realistic possibility. The Chief Whip, David Margesson, believed that the King's Party amounted to no more than around forty MPs, but warned Stanley Baldwin that this number could increase if there was clear public sympathy for the King's predicament.[38]

On 7 December, Churchill made a last-ditch and disastrous intervention in the House of Commons, one which Bob Boothby recalled was 'filled with emotion and brandy', to try to buy more time for the King.[39] Baldwin had given a statement to update Parliament on the situation, following which MPs had the opportunity to put short questions to the Prime Minister, but not to try to make speeches of their own. Churchill rose to ask the Prime Minister:

whether he could give us an assurance that no irrevocable step – [Hon. MEMBERS: 'No.'] – that no irrevocable step will be taken before the House has received a full statement, not only upon the personal but upon the constitutional issues involved? May I ask him to bear in mind that these issues are not merely personal to the present occupant of the Throne, but that they affect the entire Constitution? [Hon. MEMBERS: 'Speech,' and 'Sit down.']⁴⁰

The MPs clearly thought Churchill, who after all held no government position, was trying to insert himself into the drama of the King's decision whether or not to abdicate. Worse than that, he had allowed himself to get distracted by the barracking from other Members, and made a rambling statement with no question asked, and was eventually required by the Speaker to sit down. Afterwards, Boothby saw Churchill with Brendan Bracken in the Smoking Room,* where Churchill told them that he thought 'his political career was at an end. We told him that this was nonsense. But I wrote him a letter of bitter reproach that I later regretted.'⁴¹ In his letter Boothby complained to Churchill, 'I understood last night that we had agreed upon a formula, and a course designed to save the King from abdication if that is possible . . . But this afternoon you have delivered a blow to the King, both in the House and the country, far harder than any Baldwin ever conceived of.' This episode had not been Churchill's finest hour, but both he and Boothby were mistaken if they thought there had ever been a real opportunity to turn things in favour of the King at this late stage.

Boothby believed that there were now no more than seven MPs in the House of Commons who could be relied on to save the King, and nor was there support from the governments of the Dominions. The Canadian Prime Minister, William Mackenzie King, noted in his diary on 8 December that the King's 'sense of right or wrong has been largely obliterated by the jazz of life he has led for years, and the kind of friends with whom he has

---

* The Smoking Room is a Members-only bar near the chamber of the House of Commons. With its wood-panelled walls and leather chairs, it was a particular favourite of Churchill's and other Conservative MPs.

surrounded himself.'[42] On 10 December at Fort Belvedere, the King signed his abdication papers, witnessed by his brothers, including the new king, George VI.

The following day, at Edward's insistence, he made his farewell broadcast to the Empire, in preparation for which the Director General of the BBC, Sir John Reith, asked the royal household how he should be introduced. Reith himself suggested 'Mr Edward Windsor'. George VI's response was that since his brother had been born a son of the Duke of York, he was entitled to use 'Lord Edward Windsor'. The King also noted, referencing the same idea that Bernard Shaw had hit upon in *The Apple Cart*, that, unless he was given some other title, Edward would be entitled to stand for election to the House of Commons. It was settled by the King that his brother would keep his royal status and take the title of Duke of Windsor.*[43]

Edward arranged to dine with his family at Royal Lodge on 11 December before making his final broadcast from Windsor Castle. It had been agreed that he would immediately leave Britain and a Royal Navy destroyer, HMS *Fury*, was waiting at Portsmouth to take him to the continent. In his memoirs, he described his departure from Fort Belvedere for Royal Lodge that evening: 'As I drove off down the hill towards Virginia Water, I turned for a last look at the place I loved so much. The Fort was in sight for only a few seconds before the motor turned out of the gates and it disappeared. In that moment I realized how heavy was the price I had paid . . . The Fort had been more than a home; it had been a way of life for me.'[44]

Looking back on 1936, Philip reflected, 'We have mourned the death of one dearly beloved King and the abdication of another whose hold was scarcely less strong in our affections.'[45] In the wake of these testing events he held his usual Christmas and New Year

---

* In the broadcast, Reith introduced Edward as 'His Royal Highness Prince Edward'.

parties at Trent Park. Old friends like Gerald Berners, Rupert Belleville and Kenneth and Jane Clark were among the guests, along with Rex Whistler, Ronald Cartland* and Malcom Bullock. For the New Year, Winston Churchill, Brendan Bracken and Marie Belloc Lowndes, as had been her custom for many years, joined Philip at Trent.

Mrs Belloc Lowndes, or 'Bellocia' as Philip often called her, recalled sitting next to Churchill at dinner where there was much discussion about the abdication crisis. She asked him, 'We have heard everything you had to say concerning the King and all that has happened; but you have never once mentioned the person who seems to be all important in the matter.' He said, 'Who do you mean?' and she replied, 'I mean Mrs Simpson.'

Churchill answered, 'That . . . how der you [sic],' before observing in a 'scoffing' tone, 'I suppose you know very little of the King and his ways? If you knew much about the King, you would know that women play only a transient part in his life. He falls constantly in and out of love. His present attachment will follow the course of all the others.'[46]

A more telling epitaph on the whole sorry affair was uttered by Norah Lindsay's sister Madeline, written on the back of one of Norah's letters about the King: 'HM was so badly served by his friends who never told him the truth. So that he really did believe he could marry her and make her Queen and was shocked when he found he couldn't.'[47]

Yet, in walking out on England, Edward had left his friends behind as well, and the abdication certainly created a distance in Philip's friendship with the former King. The Windsors spent their initial period of exile at the Schloss Enzesfeld, near Vienna, which belonged to one of Philip's Rothschild cousins. After their marriage

---

* Ronald Cartland, who would turn 30 on 3 January 1937, had been MP for Birmingham King's Norton since 1935. He was also the younger brother of the novelist Barbara Cartland.

in June, Philip sent them a present with a formal note reading, 'Sir. It has taken me a long time to find a wedding present for you & the Duchess which would satisfy me. So I can wait no longer and hope that you may be able to find a corner for this old Irish Cup which brings to you and the Duchess my respectful and heartfelt good wishes for your health and happiness.'[48]

Sassoon would not visit them until September 1937, when a holiday trip to the Czech Sudetenland provided the opportunity for him to cross the border and join them in Austria. It was at a time when a private debate was in full flow between the King and his ministers over if and when the Windsors should be allowed to visit England and receive other members of the royal family. Philip would have only one further meeting with the Duke and Duchess, when he was shamed into visiting them after they had established themselves in Paris.[49]

With the abdication, a dividing line had been drawn, and for those in public life in particular allegiance to the new King and Queen had to be paramount. Of all the princes, Philip had been closest to Edward, but he counted the new King and Queen among his friends too. King George VI had been a regular guest at Trent Park for many years, and Philip had first met the new Queen Elizabeth before she had married. In March 1921, she had even written to her brother to say, 'I did not take what you might call a violent fancy to Sir P[hilip] Sassoon; he was merely rather amusing to talk to, and I like talking to people who have got quite different points of view to the usual run of men. Perhaps not very elevating ones, (points of view) but trs moderne (French).'[50]

Throughout his life, Philip had lost people he had been close to, from the premature deaths of his parents, through the casualties of the First World War, and most recently with the tragic accident that had killed T. E. Lawrence. He had learnt to carry on through all of these heavy burdens, and while Edward was gone if not departed, there was now a new King for Philip to serve.

9

• PHILIP SASSOON REVISITED •

> Anthony Blanche had not changed from when I last saw him; not, indeed, from when I first saw him. He swept lightly across the room to the most prominent canvas – a jungle landscape – paused a moment, his head cocked like a knowing terrier, and asked: 'Where, my dear Charles, did you find this sumptuous greenery? The corner of a hothouse at T-t-trent or T-t-tring? What gorgeous usurer nurtured these fronds for your pleasure?'
>
> Evelyn Waugh,
> *Brideshead Revisited* (1945)

The world of Philip Sassoon was clearly one of the inspirations for Evelyn Waugh's portrait of high society in his novel *Brideshead Revisited*. His central character, the painter Charles Ryder, is depicted at times as an artist in residence, working on murals during weekend parties, a portrayal that borrows from the example of Rex Whistler's work for Sassoon. Even the private-view art show, where Anthony Blanche casts a critical eye over Ryder's jungle landscapes, with its guests including a royal duke and society figures who care nothing for art and know even less, appears as something of a satire of Philip

Sassoon's annual exhibitions at Park Lane. It is no surprise, then, that in the novel Blanche suggests to Ryder that, rather than painting in the jungle, he has instead been hiding in the greenhouses at Trent Park.

Evelyn Waugh, like Beverley Nichols, was a novelist and a commentator on London society in the 1920s and 1930s, but he was kept at a distance from the upper echelon of society that Philip Sassoon inhabited, although he would have picked up insights into Philip's world from mutual friends, especially literary figures like Gerald Berners and Osbert Sitwell. He also became close to Diana Cooper after they met at a lunch given by Hazel Lavery, shortly after the great success of his novel *Vile Bodies*. Duff Cooper, on the other hand, took a particular dislike to Waugh, and once at a party told him to his face that he was just a 'common little man . . . who happens to have written one or two moderately amusing novels'.[1]

Unlike *Vile Bodies*, Waugh's satire of the bright young things of London society in the late 1920s, *Brideshead Revisited* wasn't written as the party carried on around them, but several years later, in the midst of the deprivations of the Second World War. Waugh created a fantasy memoir of that pre-1939 world of aristocracy and luxury that he thought had been lost for ever. It was a sentiment shared by Bob Boothby, when, towards the end of his life, he looked back on the era of Philip Sassoon as 'a dream of another world'.[*2]

In early 1937, there was already the strong feeling of an era coming to an end. The brief reign of King Edward VIII had passed, and along with it the social scene that had surrounded him both as monarch and as Prince of Wales for nearly twenty years. On 16 March Austen Chamberlain, the former Conservative leader from the years of the Lloyd George coalition, died suddenly. It was also well known in Westminster circles that Stanley Baldwin, the man who had outmanoeuvred them all, would soon retire as Prime Minister. In international affairs, Hitler's repudiation of the Treaty of Versailles, and Mussolini's

---

* Boothby used this expression in a letter to Queen Elizabeth the Queen Mother dated 11 December 1985, seven months before he died.

successful confrontation with the League of Nations, heralded the end of the post-First World War settlement.

Even for Winston Churchill this was a low point, despite his successful campaign to force the government to invest more in Britain's military defences. While spending New Year 1937 at Trent Park, Churchill had received news of the sudden death of Ralph Wigram, the senior official at the Foreign Office who had done so much to supply him with accurate intelligence about Germany's rearming. Churchill had told friends that he thought his political career was over after the failure of his last-ditch campaign to save Edward from the immediate threat of abdication. This was also the time when he seriously considered selling Chartwell, his beloved estate in Kent, because of the financial pressures he had been under constantly since the Wall Street Crash; the property agents Knight, Frank & Rutley were asked to test the demand for offers in excess of £30,000.[3] However, Winston told Clementine, 'If I could see £25,000 I should close with it. If we do not get a good price we can carry on for a year or two more. But no good offer should be refused, having regard to the fact that our children are almost flown, and my life is probably in its closing decade' (he was sixty-two).[4]

Philip Sassoon, however, was still a young man in the political world, even though he had been working among its leading figures for twenty years. Aged just forty-eight and in good health, he could have expected another twenty years of public life ahead of him. He was making progress at the Air Ministry, and in the estimates he presented to Parliament on 15 March 1937 was able to claim that they were the largest

that have ever been presented to this House. The net figure of £82,500,000 can be compared with an average figure of some £18,000,000 asked for by the Ministry in pre-expansion years. It exceeds by £32,000,000 the total Estimates of 1936. The magnitude of this figure gives rise to mingled feelings of disappointment and relief. All will feel regret that it should be necessary to expend so vast a sum on military preparations. All, on the other hand, must feel relief that proper steps are being taken to safeguard our country against attack and to fulfil our international obligations . . . Indeed, we think that a British Air Force, strong, ready and well-equipped, is the best contribution that this country can make to the peace of the world.[5]

While the financial resources were there to support the expansion of the air force, Philip shared Churchill's concerns about the lack of a practical strategy for delivering the weapons and munitions that the country needed. In May, following the successful birth of black swan cygnets at Chartwell, bred from birds sent there from Sassoon's collection at Trent Park, Philip wrote to congratulate Winston and added, 'your expansion scheme shows better progress than ours'.[6]

A week later Philip gave a speech to the Oxford University Air Squadron* to mark its tenth anniversary, and there he struck a more upbeat tone. He told the student air cadets that

Engaged as the Ministry is today upon a vast expansion scheme which will more than double the personnel of the Royal Air Force, the need for young officers of the highest quality is most urgent. We look hopefully to the Universities to supply some of them. In the air estimates which I announced in the House of Commons last March, the sum allotted to the Royal Air Force exceeded for the first time in history that allotted to the army. The figures . . . indicate the new place which this new service has taken in the defence policy of the Empire.

Philip then looked ahead to the crucial role that the RAF would play in future wars: 'Today many look to the independent use of

---

* The OUAS remains one of the longest-serving university air squadrons, and it supplied the RAF with numerous pilots who flew in the Battle of Britain.

air power as the factor most likely to decide any future war in Europe. This means that an air strategy has to be developed for Great Britain and the Empire.' He added, thinking not only of the advance of British aircraft design, but of new technology like radar which was being supported by his ministry, 'The war of the future is going to be a supreme test, not only of the courage and endurance of nations, but of their intelligence. The fiercest test of all will fall on the intelligence of the Staffs who control, develop and utilise a nation's resources by land, sea and air, and particularly by air.'

Philip turned to the vital question of the delivery of the expansion plan for the air force: 'Some of you may ask me, how is this development going on? Is the progress of expansion as rapid as was hoped for? Well, we have had difficulties. A big difficulty has come from the fact that we have had constantly to alter and extend our expansion programmes . . . We are now in the position when we can confidently expect to make more and more rapid progress with every month that passes.'[7]

Philip Sassoon had been a minister at the Air Ministry for ten of the previous twelve years, and this speech was a valedictory to mark his time in office there. He had done more than anyone to try to make the air force smart, and an attractive career for bright young officer cadets. Winston Churchill's son Randolph, for example, had approached him at this time to discuss joining the RAF's 601 Auxiliary Air Squadron.* Philip had also constantly championed investment in new aviation technology and the expansion of air defences.

Later that month Stanley Baldwin, as expected, resigned as Prime Minister and was succeeded, on 28 May, by Neville Chamberlain. Baldwin had been Conservative leader for fourteen years, and it is testimony to the extraordinary political control that he had built across the party that such a smooth transfer of power was possible.

---

* In the end Randolph Churchill joined not the air force but his father's old regiment, the 4th Hussars.

The old divisions of the early 1920s were long gone. While Winston Churchill remained critical of the party leadership, he did not have a big enough base of support to be a serious contender himself – a fact that he acknowledged, even to the extent of seconding Chamberlain's nomination for the party leadership.

In the immediate ministerial reshuffle, Philip Sassoon was offered the job he had long sought, as First Commissioner of Works. This new role gave him oversight of all the parks and palaces, squares and monuments which were owned by the nation, and he was also responsible for the commissioning of new government buildings. The First Commissioner of Works was a more senior ministerial position than Under-Secretary of State for Air, and frequently, although not in Philip's case, it had been a cabinet position. Winston Churchill wrote to his old friend on hearing the news, 'we are both delighted you have your wish'.[8] In his gratitude, Philip offered Neville Chamberlain the use of Trent Park for his first weekend as Prime Minister, as Chequers was not yet ready for him to move into.

Yet, while First Commissioner of Works was the job Philip wanted, Baldwin and Chamberlain had also decided to move him out of the Air Ministry. Thomas Jones, the Deputy Cabinet Secretary, had recorded in his diary the previous year a conversation with Baldwin about prospects for the reshuffle. Baldwin had told him that 'Margesson [the Chief Whip] wants to put Philip Sassoon at the Office of Works because he is not strong enough for the Air Ministry, but we can't do that now. We'll have to hold on.'[9] Margesson had been a regular guest at Trent and Lympne, and Philip would have had plenty of opportunities to lobby him for his desired move to the Ministry of Works. This idea of Philip not being 'strong enough' for the Air Ministry was more of a reaction by people like Baldwin to the continued scrutiny and pressure that the department had faced from Churchill's campaign on air force expansion. The problem was not a lack of vigour on Philip's part, but that more senior members of the government would not support the level of investment in the RAF that he and others thought was necessary. If Sassoon might have been more forceful, it would not have been with the staff in the Air Ministry, or on the floor of the Commons, but with senior ministers. Neville Chamberlain may also have thought that Sassoon was too close to Churchill, who continued to be a frequent guest at Philip's parties, and he therefore wanted him away from the departments that were responsible for the armed forces.

Alongside his ministerial responsibilities, Philip's social world in 1937 showed no signs of slowing. He held his annual spring exhibition at Park Lane to raise funds for the Royal Northern Hospital; this year it was a show of paintings by Sir Joshua Reynolds. He also had a full programme of parties at Trent Park and Port Lympne where many old friends returned. Queen Mary had visited Trent in early May, and on 26 June there was a garden party where the guests of honour were King George VI and Queen Elizabeth, followed by the great American aviator Charles Lindbergh. Winston Churchill and Lady Desborough came as usual, and the American golfer Walter Hagen returned to play at Trent, along with Gene Sarazen and Johnny Revolta, who also visited that summer. In August there were parties at Port Lympne around the annual summer camp for the young pilots and flying officers of 601 Air Squadron, where Philip remained an honorary Air Commodore.

The star political guest of that summer, though, perhaps reflecting the emergence as Philip saw it of a new generation of leaders, was the forty-year-old Foreign Secretary, Anthony Eden. It is notable that when the Prime Minister Stanley Baldwin spent Easter at Trent Park, which Philip often put at his disposal, Sassoon did not join him as he was hosting Anthony Eden and his family at Port Lympne. Sybil remembered that 'Anthony Eden was always there, he was [at Trent or Lympne] practically every weekend in the summer.' She also recalled how busy Trent was during those weekends: 'a great many people came, and foreign friends; seldom fewer than I should say 20 people sat down to lunch on Sunday'.[10]

Two other guests in the spring and summer of 1937 stand out in the visitors' books because of the frequency of their attendance. First there was the twenty-one-year-old society beauty Lady Elizabeth Paget, daughter of the Marquess of Anglesey. Chips Channon had met 'Liz' Paget along with two of her cousins, Isobel and Ursula Manners, at a dinner of Emerald Cunard's a couple of years previously and recorded: 'we saw three girls shimmering like goddesses . . . I have never seen such a beautiful trio.'[11] Duff Cooper thought Liz, who was his niece, 'very beautiful, and good and wise with a lovely sense of humour'.[12] She came three times to Trent Park in May and June 1937, and then for a weekend party at Port Lympne at the beginning of August. On three of these four occasions a handsome photograph of Liz graces the visitors' book to mark the occasion. If Philip had fallen a little in love with her, he was certainly in good company.

Ian Wilson-Young, a twenty-nine-year-old rising star at the Foreign Office, had also become a regular at Philip's parties over the previous year. Wilson-Young was unmarried, handsome and a fine golfer. He had spent Christmas 1936 at Trent with Philip, and from May to July 1937 he is recorded in the visitors' book a further seven times. Perhaps Philip was also a little infatuated with this promising young man, and wanted companionship from someone who shared his energy, interests and taste.

Wilson-Young and Liz Paget were both guests at Port Lympne at the beginning of August, but neither of them is recorded as being at one of Philip's parties thereafter. This raises the question of what could have happened at that weekend party to end both Philip's flirtation with Liz and his close friendship with Wilson-Young. The two had met before, and were in the same party when Liz first visited Trent in May that year, but perhaps this was the moment when they first appreciated Philip's interest in them both.

The other guests that weekend included Sybil Cholmondeley, Venetia Montagu and Venetia's partner the RAF auxiliary pilot and adventurer Rupert Belleville. Belleville was on his way to Spain to work as a freelance correspondent covering the Civil War, where he would befriend Ernest Hemingway through their mutual love of drinking and bullfighting. They were also joined at Lympne by Lord Berners and his twenty-seven-year-old boyfriend, the 'Mad Boy' Robert Heber-Percy. Venetia Montagu had previously had affairs, both romantic and platonic, with much older men, particularly Lord Beaverbrook and Herbert Asquith. Perhaps she was both a warning and an example for Liz Paget. Could Wilson-Young as well have been repelled by Berners' relationship with Heber-Percy, and have been concerned that it presented a vision for how his own friendship with Philip might develop? Whatever happened that weekend, all we can be sure of is that their lives moved on in different directions afterwards.*

Later in August 1937, a twenty-seven-year-old blond-haired and blue-eyed RAF officer called Anthony Wimbush also came to Philip's attention. Wimbush was stationed at the aerodrome at Hawkinge, close to Folkestone, and attended parties at Lympne in August and September. On 31 December, he accompanied Philip on a month-long holiday in the USA and the Caribbean, breaking Philip's usual habit of hosting New Year parties at Trent Park. Their journey home was perhaps not a good omen, as very bad weather delayed the crossing. It was reported that on board their ship, the Cunard White Star liner *Aquitania*, 'four heavy plate glass windows high up above the water line were smashed by the waves, and numerous tables and chairs and lamps were wrecked'.[13] For Philip, never a good sailor, this must have been torture.

Wimbush was not mentioned again in the visitors' books at Trent or Lympne after their return on 2 February 1938. Philip's friendship with him, like those with Liz Paget and Ian Wilson-Young, may

---

* In 1939 Liz Paget married the Austrian poet Raimund von Hofmannsthal, although Duff Cooper was worried that he would not be able to keep her in the style to which she was used: 'She is so accustomed to living surrounded by great wealth that she has no idea how much she would miss it' (*The Duff Cooper Diaries*, 16 January 1938). Ian Wilson-Young married in 1940.

have fallen victim to the often obsessive interest he could take in people who fascinated him. This was something which his older or more established friends knew how to cope with, but it could perhaps be overwhelming for others. The subject of Philip's interest could be showered with gifts and receive constant letters and requests to meet. As we have seen, it was a side of his personality that, years earlier, the Prince of Wales had detected when he told Freda Dudley Ward, 'We must try to somewhat loosen the ropes with which he has bound himself so tightly to us . . . I like a little of Philip very much but not too much.'[14]

Now approaching the age of fifty, there was also perhaps a sadness in Philip Sassoon which may have led him to desire more companionship as part of a happier home life. War, accident and illness had taken so many friends, of all ages, and he frequently complained that he did not see enough of Sybil and her family. Sybil's husband, George, Marquess of Cholmondeley, was not keen on their children staying with Philip, as he spoiled them by getting his chefs to prepare their favourite food, which they were often not allowed at home. Philip may also have had another motivation, beyond the desire for companionship, in seeking these relationships with young friends. Having lost both his parents before the age of twenty-four, he had formed close bonds with older men like Regy Esher and Louis Mallet, who acted as mentors to him, yet they were both now dead as well.* Without children of his own, Philip may have wanted to play a similar role for young people who interested him, and whom he wanted to support.

The legendary newspaper reporter Bill Deedes,† then a young parliamentary correspondent for the *Daily Telegraph*, remembered a day with Sassoon at this time. Both men were members of the Hythe Golf Club, and at Philip's suggestion Deedes joined him for a round

---

* Esher had died in 1930 and Mallet in 1936.

† The Deedes family had been in Hythe for generations, and had formerly owned Saltwood Castle.

on the course. Deedes offered a portrait of Philip pursuing his life with the same old vigour, but also suggested that the relentless pace was starting to catch up with him. He wrote:

It was a singular experience. Sir Philip had chartered four caddies, all of whom he paid for. Two carried clubs, two went to observe where our drives finished. Thus we were able to canter round this hilly course without ever pausing to look for a ball. We finished in not much over two hours. Turning our backs on any form of refreshment, we jumped into a waiting car and were driven fast to the sea, where Sir Philip kept an extensive beach hut. After five minutes in the water, we raced back to the hut and changed rapidly.

Philip rushed back to Lympne, and asked Deedes to follow on and join him for lunch. Deedes remembered that when he arrived,

Mrs Gubbay greeted me, 'What have you been doing to Philip? He has retired to bed exhausted.' My host recovered in time for our lunch, and then proposed a game of tennis. His cousin, a woman in her late forties, beat him soundly. 'He cheats so dreadfully,' she said, as if dealing with a small child. He then proposed a quick flip from Lympne aerodrome [which was] across the way [from his estate], where he kept a light plane. I pleaded another engagement. This was his style of life, and it did him no good at all.[15]

Philip also made a lasting impression at this time on another future politician, the nine-year-old Alan Clark, the son of his friend Kenneth Clark, director of the National Gallery, and his wife Jane. In 1936, Philip had lent Bellevue, the house that Louis Mallet had rented near the entrance to the Port Lympne estate and close to the aerodrome, to the Clarks. Philip would take Alan up for trips in his aeroplanes. Jane remembered on one occasion: 'Alan v pleased because when P flew them to Hawkinge it was v rough and he didn't mind a bit.'[16] Philip also arranged for the Clark family to be flown from Lympne to Trent Park if he was having a party there, and would give Alan and his brother a £5 note each when they left. Kenneth Clark noted in his journal that 'the children were all astonished by a platoon of footmen with red cummerbunds'.[17] Even years later, Alan Clark remembered Philip Sassoon and his 'smooth face . . . he looked incredibly young, walked on the tips of his toes and impressed one as being a person of importance'.[18]

Philip's friendship with the Clarks had grown from his work with Kenneth at the National Gallery, and from the genuine understanding of culture and creativity that they shared. Now his new ministerial position as First Commissioner of Works gave him a further outlet for these talents. As his sister Sybil remembered, 'He was an ideal person for that, because the other Ministers of Works had never so much built a bathing-hut, whereas my brother was a great collector and had great knowledge of everything to do . . . for building . . . When there were big things to repair – he would have been wonderful after the war.'[19]

During his two years at the Ministry of Works, Philip would be responsible for numerous high-profile schemes, including the restoration of the Painted Hall at the Royal Naval College at Greenwich, and substantial renovations in Downing Street and the Palace of Westminster. But his major project and legacy as First Commissioner of Works was the partial redesign of London's iconic Trafalgar Square. When he was appointed, Rex Whistler wrote to him in excitement, exclaiming:

I hope London will be transformed in a year or two into one of the loveliest and most elegant cities in the world. If only you had a completely free rein. But will you please dear Philip make the erecting of the two new fountains in Trafalgar Square one of the first things in your programme. Couldn't a great open competition be started for designs for them? The present ones are so unworthy of London and I'm sure can have no defenders . . . Very likely some now unknown Bernini would be discovered through this competition.[20]

Philip had inherited from his predecessor a plan for the creation of memorials for Admirals Beatty and Jellicoe to be placed in Trafalgar Square, but he was concerned about a profusion of statues, and supported an idea to make the two new fountains for the Square part of the memorials for Beatty and Jellicoe. Duff Cooper, who had been appointed First Lord of the Admiralty in Neville Chamberlain's new government, wrote to Philip stating that he could agree to this if it were part of a greater plan to refocus Trafalgar Square as a space of commemoration for the life of Lord Nelson and the work of the navy. He commented, 'If . . . the military statues were removed and their places taken by commemorative fountains, with a view to finally confining Trafalgar Square to Nelson and fountains, each in memory of a great sailor, then I think the views of the Navy would be met and Trafalgar Square would both be beautiful and would fulfil the function of a naval memorial.'[21]

The military statues in question were the memorials to Generals Gordon, Havelock and Napier, all heroes of colonial wars. It was also discussed whether the equestrian statue of King George IV should be moved to Windsor Great Park, although the Permanent Secretary of the Treasury, Sir Patrick Duff, who had been asked to find the funds for the improvements to Trafalgar Square, had a more specific recommendation: 'The best site at Virginia Water for the statue of George IV – as for so many other statues – would be the bottom of the Lake.'[22]

In an internal memorandum for the Ministry of Public Works, Philip instructed: 'We should without any delay proceed to remove Napier and Havelock to their newly appointed stations. We can then proceed to alter the existing fountains into appropriate memorials to Lord Jellicoe and Lord Beatty. From the First Lord's letter this will satisfy the Admiralty, as indeed it will please Parliament and the Public.'[23]

Philip commissioned the leading British architect Sir Edwin Lutyens to design the new fountains, which were completed on

10 September 1939. The statues of Havelock, Napier and George IV remained, however; only Gordon was eventually moved, in 1943, and now stands on Victoria Embankment. Sassoon had a further idea to introduce flower sellers to Trafalgar Square, but this was opposed by Westminster City Council on the grounds that it would increase rubbish and general untidiness.

Philip's other great public scheme was to replace all of the benches in London's Royal Parks* with a new design, based on his own at Trent Park. Writing in *The Times* to announce his plans, he remarked on the 'conventional ugliness of the old free seats . . . with their cast iron sides and dull green colour, they are in marked and unpleasing contrast to the occasional new seats of teak or oak which are also free . . . I have prepared a new design of seats which, besides being more attractive and more suitable than the old seats, will also be much more comfortable.'[24] There were no funds available at the Ministry of Works for this scheme, so Philip asked people to donate five pounds for a new bench to be placed in the Royal Parks to mark the Coronation year, and successfully raised the money for hundreds of new seats in this way.

As First Commissioner, Philip also oversaw improvements to the accommodation of the royal family and senior members of the government. At Buckingham Palace this included the creation of the swimming pool that is reserved for the private use of the royal family. Philip's recommendations to King George about its design have survived in the archives, including his suggestion that the lining and walkway around the pool should be made of vitreous mosaic tiles rather than glazed, as they are 'less harsh in appearance and less slippery'. Enclosing samples of the tiles for the King, Philip suggested that the edge should be marked in black mosaic with two bands of green, one below the level of the water and another near the bottom of the pool, to add 'sparkle and liveliness to the water'.[25]

---

* The scheme included Hyde Park, Green Park, St James's Park, Kensington Gardens, Greenwich Park, Regent's Park and Richmond Park.

Philip was again on hand to assist Duff and Diana Cooper with their move into Admiralty House, the magnificent grace-and-favour accommodation in Whitehall that was available for the First Lord of the Admiralty and his family. From the government art collection Philip found for Diana Cooper a bust of Nelson and a set of pictures illustrating Captain James Cook's voyages to decorate the dining room. He refused to indulge her request for a grand piano, writing to Duff Cooper in jest, 'I wrote to Diana and told her that if she mentioned the subject to me again I would immediately repaint Admiralty House the colour of Brünnhilde's [funeral] pyre. Which gave Lady Hoare so much trouble to produce and what you and Diana unaccountably fail to appreciate.'[26] Philip included in the same letter to Duff a note which gives some insight into Cooper's cautious and at times suspicious relationship with Anthony Eden: 'have just flown over to have lunch with Anthony – he said the nicest possible things about you – as per. So you have been misinformed there.'

Philip still made time for his own creative endeavours, and in February and March 1938 hosted what would be his final loan exhibition at Park Lane for the Royal Northern Hospital. The previous nine had raised a total of £30,000, the equivalent to approximately £1.5 million today. The show had the appropriately end-of-an-era theme of 'Old London' and featured paintings and tapestries of views and buildings from the city that no longer existed. King George VI, like his brother the Duke of Windsor two years before, loaned a number of works from the Royal Collection, including a large tapestry from Hampton Court depicting the Dutch fleet at dawn before the Battle of Solebay,* which had been commissioned by Charles II. From Windsor Castle, the King lent two Canalettos showing views from the garden terrace of the old Somerset House, one looking upriver to Westminster and the other

---

* Solebay, a naval battle between the British and Dutch, took place off the coast of Suffolk, near Southwold, in 1672.

downstream to St Paul's. Philip positioned Hogarth's great depiction of upheaval and social change, *Southwark Fair,* on the main staircase of 45 Park Lane.

Shortly after his exhibition on 'Old London' had opened in Park Lane, Philip was invited as First Commissioner of Works to give an address to the Royal Institute of British Architects on the future design of the city. In it he set out his views on the purpose and practice of architecture:

> Architecture reflects the spirit of its age . . . Certainly architecture has always been, I think I may say, the most permanent of man's social and historical records. Architecture in all places and at all times should do its best to take advantage of the materials which are available to it . . . Perhaps we have not yet discovered, for instance, how to achieve the happiest results with steel and concrete, to mention one example. Another basic problem is that a way should be found with the means available to us of combining utility with beauty. I am sure you will agree with me that ornament and embellishment by themselves are of little purpose. For instance I do not think they have ever made a bad building into a good one. On the other hand, if utility is the only end there is no place for art in architecture.[27]

He then set out the challenges for architecture and design that are in proportion and in keeping with the style of the city:

> Those of us who have seen for example the Doge's Palace in Venice, that top heavy superstructure on its little Dachshund legs, will realise that it is certainly not proportion which makes it one of the most beautiful and satisfying buildings in the world. I have just come back from a holiday in the United States, and there I must say that I did find those stupendous buildings in New York gave me a sense of proportion. Not only were they built with tremendous scale, but it seemed to me that they were built with

great taste; these big buildings were finished almost with the detail of a Cartier cigarette box. Now, I think that the great cities of the world have each their own individual architecture, and it seems to me that proportion should conform in each case to that individual atmosphere. I can admire skyscrapers in New York, but I cannot conceive them in our London streets . . . I have found the charm and character of London in those small Georgian houses too many of which unfortunately have been disappearing of late and which have been replaced, I think, with buildings which have no character of their own.

Philip's personal love of Georgian architecture was evident from his redesign of Trent Park, but he was not calling for all new buildings to become a pastiche of that period:

I do not for one moment say that modern architecture should copy the architecture of the Georgian period. The charm of our old buildings so largely depends upon the delightful combination of their architecture and the harmony which goes with it of the materials of which they are composed. The aim of our modern architecture, it seems to me, should be to produce new harmonies which should give full expression to the qualities of those new materials and methods which are now available to us and at our command.

This he could certainly claim to have achieved personally at Port Lympne, and it had been reflected in his approach to the reworking of Trafalgar Square.

While Philip's work as First Commissioner kept him interested and occupied, he maintained his close interest in the broader affairs of the government through his regular lunches for senior ministers at Park Lane. These gatherings, and Philip's close relationship with the Foreign Secretary Anthony Eden, gave him an insight into the tensions at the top of the government on international policy. In particular it was becoming clear that Eden and Neville Chamberlain had vastly different outlooks on Britain's rearmament and approach to dealing with Hitler and Mussolini.

In his diary on 8 November 1937, Eden noted a discussion with the Prime Minister about Britain's military defence: 'Told him of my conviction that rearmament must go faster . . . I know that some of my colleagues think we at the F.O. insufficiently insistent in our efforts to improve relations with Dictator Powers. This, however, not true position. It was thought unless it were known that we were rearming effectively our efforts in International sphere today useless. N.C. did not, I think, share my view.'[28] Eight days later Eden confronted Chamberlain over the government's approach to Germany. The Foreign Secretary wanted a strong warning to be sent to Hitler not to interfere in Austria and Czechoslovakia, and was then aghast to see a press report, following Lord Halifax's visit to Germany,* which suggested that Britain would give the Nazis a free hand in central Europe in return for a ten-year truce on the question of returning colonies that Germany had lost after the First World War. This resulted in a bad-tempered exchange between the two men, and ended with Chamberlain telling Eden to 'go home and take an aspirin'.[29] Eden's principal private secretary at the Foreign Office, Oliver Harvey, noted in his diary that 'A.E. complains bitterly of defeatist attitude of all his older colleagues . . . in matter of rearmament and of attitude towards dictators generally.'[30]

On 17 December both Eden and Chamberlain attended Philip Sassoon's lunch for ministers at Park Lane, where there was a discussion about an approach to the Italian Ambassador Dino Grandi with a view to arranging talks with Mussolini. Chamberlain regarded improving Anglo-Italian relations, at any price, to be of the greatest importance, whereas Eden wanted conditions attached

---

* Göring had invited Lord Halifax, the Leader of the House of Lords, to an international sporting exhibition in Berlin. While he was there Halifax also met Hitler.

to the talks, including the withdrawal of Italian forces from Spain, where they had been supporting General Franco in the Civil War. There had also been submarine attacks in the Mediterranean on British and French shipping, which were widely suspected to have been carried out covertly by the Italians. Eden saw the dictators as gangsters and bullies, and believed that unless you stood up to them, they would see you as weak and just come back for more. Chamberlain, on the other hand, thought he could deal with them, and was prepared to consider the recognition of almost any grievance they put forward as a price worth paying for peace.

Following his return from holiday in America, Philip hosted a lunch for cabinet ministers at Park Lane on 11 February 1938. There was further disagreement between Chamberlain and Eden. Sam Hoare, who was also in attendance, remembered that the Prime Minister set out his case, contrary to the advice of his Foreign Secretary, for urgently resuming formal talks with Mussolini's government without conditions attached. Eden remembered that 'during Philip Sassoon's lunch . . . I suggested to N.C. [Chamberlain] that he should let me see Grandi alone in the first instance. If anything important resulted I could always arrange a second interview for him. I failed however to convince N.C. who was clearly determined to see Grandi himself.'[31] The following day, after Chamberlain and Eden had met with the Italian Ambassador, the Foreign Secretary noted in his diary, 'N.C. made it clear to me that he knew exactly what he wanted to do. He wanted to tell Grandi . . . that we would open conversations [with the Italian government] at once.'[32]

Throughout this brewing cabinet crisis, Neville Chamberlain was much more adept at keeping other ministers onside and Eden isolated. For example, on 13 February, Philip Sassoon spent the weekend at Chequers, where Sam Hoare and William Morrison, the Agriculture Minister, were also among the guests. Matters would finally come to a head on 20 February, when Eden resigned as Foreign Secretary, as it was clear that the majority of the cabinet were united behind Chamberlain's approach. Two days later, Philip invited Eden and his private secretary Oliver Harvey to dinner at Park Lane to try and build Anthony back up. Harvey noted that they discussed Eden's forthcoming meeting in his constituency, where he would set out his reasons for resigning:

> We all think this should be held as soon as possible and A.E. decided to have this on Friday. A.E. said he was now in a very difficult position as he had to decide what his future attitude should be. I said he should make his speech, setting out his faith once more, and then wait and see . . . We discussed the disastrous effects which the P.M.'s speech may be expected to have on Central Europe and France: it was an open intimation that Great Britain would do nothing to protect the small nations from the dictators.[33]

Winston Churchill was also devastated by Eden's resignation and in his memoirs recalled receiving the news at Chartwell: 'I must confess that my heart sank, and for a while the dark waters of despair overwhelmed me . . . From midnight till dawn I lay in my bed consumed by emotions of sorrow and fear. There seemed one strong young figure standing up against long, dismal, drawling tides of drift and surrender . . . Now he was gone. I watched the daylight slowly creep in through the windows, and saw before me in mental gaze the vision of Death.'[34] Churchill would not have to wait long for further confirmation of how well founded his apocalyptic vision was: on 11 March 1938, German forces entered Austria to complete its annexation and 'Anschluss' into the Reich.

There would then follow what Churchill called 'anxious' summer months when attention turned to Czechoslovakia and the vexed question of the Sudeten Germans. The Sudetenland had been taken from Germany and incorporated into the new state of Czechoslovakia by the Treaty of Versailles. There had been persistent calls from the Sudeten Germans for self-government, either within a federal Czechoslovakia or by the return of this territory to Germany. Hitler was only too happy to agitate in support of their cause, bolstered as he was by his triumph over Austria. Philip, like other ministers, believed that while Germany should not be allowed to seize the Sudetenland, the German people who lived there had a right to call for self-government, in the same way that the Irish had successfully claimed home rule from Great Britain. This was no simple border dispute, however; as the British Ambassador to Berlin, Sir Nevile Henderson, recalled, 'Czechoslovakia was the keystone of the French alliance system and the potential bulwark against German expansion south-eastwards. But after the Anschluss she was left vis-à-vis Germany in a completely hopeless position, both strategically and economically, and it was clear that the integrity of her Versailles frontiers could only be upheld if France and Britain were prepared either to negotiate or to fight for their maintenance.'[35] Sam Hoare noted in his memoirs that, frankly, those two countries were not prepared so to do: 'The over-riding consideration with Chamberlain and his colleagues was that the very complicated problem of Czechoslovakia ought not to lead to a world war, and must at almost any price be settled by peaceful means.'[36]

By May 1938, the tensions in Czechoslovakia between the authorities and the Germans living in the Sudetenland were rising. Nevile Henderson recalled, 'The situation . . . was gradually deteriorating, incidents of a more or less serious nature had become matters of daily occurrence . . . All the materials for an explosion were thus present when rumours began to spread of a German concentration on the Czech frontier.'[37]

As the crisis grew, on 19 June Philip held what would be the last of his larger political weekends at Trent Park. At the centre of it, as he had been so many times before, was Winston Churchill, along with the Chief Whip David Margesson and James Stuart MP, who would subsequently be the Conservative Chief Whip for most of Churchill's wartime government. There too were other government ministers, including Euan Wallace and William Morrison, and Viscount Cranborne, who had resigned in February as a junior minister at the Foreign Office, alongside Anthony Eden.

Eighteen years previously, to the day, Philip had entertained the prime ministers of Britain and France at Lympne, as they discussed how to enforce the Versailles agreement in Europe; now in 1938 he and his friends were watching as it was dismembered. In the intervening years under Sassoon's roof, they had debated crises from Poland to Abyssinia, and vital questions of German reparations and British rearmament. At the heart of it all had been a desire to make Europe work again, and preserve peace. Now they were staring down the barrel at a new continental war.

Churchill's presence at Trent that summer underlines the strong personal commitment that Philip Sassoon felt towards old friends. With hindsight, we know that Churchill was on the brink of his finest years as a statesman, but in the summer of 1938 many thought he was finished. Yet Churchill was not downhearted about his own prospects, or about the prospects of peace in Europe. Writing in the *Daily Telegraph* a few days after his weekend at Trent, he declared, 'No one has a right to despair of a good solution.' He could see how difficult it would be for Germany to try to take the Sudetenland by force if its bluff was called, and he knew to despite Hitler's rhetoric 'the German military leaders are foremost in counselling caution and delay'.[38] Anthony Eden came to stay at Trent the following weekend, and, as the crisis in Czechoslovakia developed, Philip kept him up to date on the negotiations based on insights he gleaned from Sam Hoare.

In August as efforts were made to try to mediate and find a peaceful solution, Philip held his usual weekend parties at Port Lympne, with old friends like Lady Desborough and Marie Belloc Lowndes mixing with young RAF pilots from 601 Squadron. The threat of a new war must have weighed heavily on Lady Desborough, who had lost two of her sons, Julian and Billy Grenfell, on the Western Front in 1915. Among the airmen at Lympne that summer were Lord Beaverbrook's son Max Aitken and John Peel, who had both been regular guests in recent years at Sassoon's air force parties. Max was then twenty-eight years old, and John twenty-seven, similar ages to those of Philip's old schoolfriends who had been killed during the First World War, men like Patrick Shaw Stewart and Edward Horner, as well as Julian Grenfell.

Philip joined other leading members of the government at Heston Airport to see off Neville Chamberlain for his talks with Hitler at Munich, where the final agreement was made to give in to Germany's demands and hand over the Sudetenland. Faced with the prospect of fighting Germany alone, the Czechoslovakian government acceded to the Munich proposals. Churchill did not believe Chamberlain's claim that his agreement with Hitler meant 'peace for our time'. He regarded Munich as a 'tragedy', telling the House of Commons in the debate that was held following Chamberlain's return, 'do not suppose that this is the end. This is only the beginning of the reckoning. This is only the first sip, the first foretaste of a bitter cup which will be proffered to us year by year unless, by supreme recovery of moral health and martial vigour, we arise again and take our stand for freedom as in the olden time.'[39]

Philip's old friend Duff Cooper resigned as First Lord of the Admiralty in protest at the Munich agreement, telling Parliament, 'The Prime Minister has believed in addressing Herr Hitler through the language of sweet reasonableness. I have believed that he was more open to the language of the mailed fist.'*[40]

Philip shared Cooper's strong anti-Nazi sentiments, but did not consider resigning from the government. In fact he welcomed the Munich agreement and even sent Neville Chamberlain a silver tray with a note reading, 'In grateful admiration of your magnificent work for peace during these fateful weeks.'[41] He believed that the British military, and in particular the air force, was not yet ready for war. If he had resigned over Munich, he might have been compelled to accept some responsibility for this, even though he had consistently argued for increased spending on air defence.

---

* Cabinet ministers who resign can make personal statements of explanation in the House of Commons.

Resignation was also not in Philip's character. He wanted to be involved in the government and through his ministerial position continue to support the work he cared about. Leaving office would have placed him on the outside, and away from the action and intrigue of government. Yet this did not mean that Philip had become an out-and-out appeaser; he believed that Britain should build up its defences so that it could negotiate with the dictators from a position of strength. He was also concerned about whether the crisis in Czechoslovakia provided grounds enough for an all-out war on Germany.

Ian Fleming, later the author of the James Bond spy novels, but then working as a stockbroker in the City of London, wrote in a letter to *The Times* on the eve of the signing of the Munich agreement, 'Moral issues must be disentangled from the instinct of self-preservation and we must state what we would fight for and why.'[42] Two weeks after Munich Philip gave his answer to these questions in an open letter to his constituents in Folkestone and Hythe. 'It is to the lasting credit of Mr Neville Chamberlain,' he wrote, 'that he kept his sense of proportion. He remembered what so many of us had forgotten, that only a vital issue could justify this country going to war. So far as the issues at stake were issues concerning Czechoslovakia only, then deep as our sympathies with the Czechs might be, they were not sufficient.'[43] He then went on to define the grounds that would justify Britain going to war:

What would have been a sufficient issue would have been the knowledge that the German attack in Czechoslovakia was but the first step in an attempt to establish German hegemony in Europe. On that issue we would fight ... Any attempt by Germany to dominate Europe would be a threat to France and would bring in Great Britain on her side. Mr Chamberlain made that clear to Herr Hitler in plain terms. Peace was preserved because Herr Hitler denied any such German intention and backed up his denial by a modification of his demands upon the Czechs. Now it may be that Herr Hitler does not really intend to act up to that denial. Some in this country think he does not. But for the time being at least the denial stands. Are there any who think that doubt of Herr Hitler's word is a vital issue on which the Empire should go to war? I do not think that there are many.

Philip was clear that the moment might come when Britain would have to fight, and fight against Germany. He did not believe, however, that that moment had yet arrived. With hindsight, his statement about 'Hitler's word' appears naive in the extreme. Philip's friends such as Churchill, Eden and Cooper believed that there were already strong grounds to doubt it. Hitler had shown in the Rhineland, Austria and now the Sudetenland that he was prepared to act without warning and in contravention of old treaties and assurances if he thought he could. How could Britain on that basis accept his word at Munich?

Philip Sassoon's caution was understandable. For four years during the Great War he had served at General Headquarters alongside Douglas Haig. He knew what war meant, and his greatest wish was to avoid its return. Where he agreed with Churchill, Eden and Cooper was that the best way to prevent war was to make Britain strong, and show the dictators that it was prepared to use force to defend the peace of Europe. He added in his open letter to his constituents:

We have also learnt our lesson. We know that the common people of all Western Europe clamour for peace, because they dread war. But we know too, that while great nations in Europe are ruled by power politics, peace can only be preserved by strength . . . The weakness which the crisis discovered in our defence organisation, both civil and military, must be made good with all speed. It is not enough to be half prepared and to have plans in the making. By sea, land and air our plans must be tested and working and our civil military preparations complete. It is only in this way that the respite, which Mr Chamberlain has won for us, can become an enduring peace.

Winston Churchill noted in the first volume of his war memoirs, *The Gathering Storm*, perhaps with regard to the concerns of old friends like Philip Sassoon, 'Many persons in Britain who knew of our nakedness felt a sense of relief as each month our Air Force developed and the Hurricane and Spitfire types approached issue.' Yet Churchill did not believe that the Munich agreement had bought the Allies valuable time to prepare for war because German armaments production accelerated over the following year at a faster pace than it did in Britain and France. He did acknowledge, however, that there was 'one vital sphere in which we began to overtake Germany and improve our own position', and this was in the air. In setting out Air Ministry spending estimates in 1937, Philip had been well aware of the programme of modernization and expansion for the RAF that was in place, but he also understood how much there was still to do. As Churchill himself wrote in *The Gathering Storm*, 'In September of 1938 we had but five squadrons remounted on Hurricanes . . . In July [1939] we had twenty-six squadrons of modern eight-gun fighters . . . By July 1940, at the time of the Battle of Britain, we had on average forty-seven squadrons of modern fighters available.'[44]

Any hopes that the Munich settlement would lead to a lasting peace were shattered when Hitler's forces entered and occupied Prague on 15 March 1939. Four days later Nevile Henderson was recalled from Berlin as British Ambassador, and Herbert von Dirksen, his German counterpart, left London.

These events cast a long shadow over the state visit to Britain of the French President Albert Lebrun, which began on the 21 March and was designed to show the strength of the alliance between these two nations. Philip, as First Commissioner of Works, took personal charge of a series of set-piece events that ran over three days. There was a state banquet at Buckingham Palace on the first night and the following evening a special concert for the King and Queen and the President at the Royal Opera House in Covent Garden. There they were installed in a vast royal box that Philip had commissioned Rex Whistler to design for the occasion. 'Chips'

Channon, who was also in the audience, a little way along from the royal party, recalled that 'Covent Garden was breath-taking in its magnificence', though he thought the box was 'light, gay, pretty but a touch tinselly and night-clubbish'.[45]

On 23 March, President Lebrun was invited to address both Houses of Parliament assembled in Westminster Hall. This was the first time that a statesman other than the British monarch had been invited to give such a speech. This ancient hall's foundations date back nearly a thousand years, and it has witnessed coronation banquets and the lying in state of kings and queens before their funerals, as well as the trial and sentencing to death of Charles I. Philip would now create a new set piece to welcome the President of France.*

At 11 a.m. President and Madame Lebrun were received at the North Door of Westminster Hall by Philip and greeted by a fanfare of trumpets. They processed through the Hall, along with the Lord Great Chamberlain, to the steps at the southern end, where they were greeted by the Speaker of the House of Commons and the Lord Chancellor. The band of the Irish Guards played 'La Marseillaise' and then the Lebruns were seated on the landing halfway up the great stone staircase that leads to St Stephen's Hall. Behind them stood Philip, along with the Speaker and Lord Chancellor. Below, they would have seen Westminster Hall filled with over a thousand dignitaries and parliamentarians. To their left sat Neville Chamberlain and members of the British cabinet. On their right was the Foreign Secretary Lord Halifax with the representatives of France. Philip Sassoon was at the centre of it all; the stage director of this great occasion.

For the evening, Philip organized a farewell dinner for the President at the Foreign Office, which was again attended by the King

---

* It is still a rare honour for visiting dignitaries to be invited to give a speech to both Houses of Parliament in Westminster Hall. Since my election to the House of Commons in 2010, I have seen Pope Benedict XVI (2010) and President Barack Obama (2011) make such an address. The format for these occasions has changed little from that devised by Philip Sassoon in 1939.

and Queen. The dinner was held in the Locarno Room, which Philip dressed for the occasion with portraits of Kings of England lent by the National Portrait Gallery. Philip also asked the Goldsmiths' livery company in the City of London to lend their plate for the dinner, and the Duke of Buccleuch for the loan of tapestries to hang between the royal portraits. Thirty Louis XVI chairs were brought from Philip's dining room at 45 Park Lane to seat the guests, for a meal which was accompanied by eight different wines, including Château Palmer Margaux 1875 and the 1920 Château d'Yquem.[46] For after dinner Philip organised a theatrical performance in the Durbar Court, where masses of azaleas, roses and lilies were arranged around the pillars of the Foreign Office. The highlight was a performance from Peggy Ashcroft and John Gielgud enacting the balcony scene from Shakespeare's Romeo and Juliet.*

Neville Chamberlain wrote to tell his sister Ida that, Philip had 'excelled himself in the decorations which were simply superb. The stairs and corridors in the F.O. were lined by lifeguardsmen motionless & glittering in scarlet & silver. Between them were countless Japanese cherries, plums & other flowering shrubs. Even the waiters were for the first time arranged in a new & gorgeous livery of blue and gold with scarlet trimmings while the table was adorned with magnificent plate, some of it from Philip's own collections.'[47]

Leo Amery was also a guest for the performance in the Durbar Court and remembered that at the end 'the BBC had songs by a choir, including by a masterpiece of tactlessness "Come, cheer up my lads".† I only hope no Frenchman there knew either the theme or some of the verses.'[48]

---

* Peggy Ashcroft and John Gielgud were then aged thirty-one and thirty-four, and major stars of West End theatre. Their 1936 performance of Romeo and Juliet, which Gielgud also directed, was perhaps their greatest theatre work, and had been a huge hit both in London and New York

† The opening line of 'Heart of Oak', the official march of the Royal Navy, which originated from the time of Britain's triumphs over France in the Seven Years' War.

No offence would appear to have been taken, and after the state visit Pierre-Étienne Flandin, a former Prime Minister of France,* wrote that

Two nations, which have fought each other through the centuries were reconciled in the early years of the twentieth century. And, in the beginning this was perhaps a marriage of reason . . . But, little by little, it has become a marriage of true minds, of minds with the same hopes and fears, with the same joys and sorrows. And, because they have witnessed the emergence of a spectre which menaces their ideal of liberty, they henceforth rely upon one another, encouraged by their mutual remembrances of a glorious past.[49]

Yet the renewal of the vows of the Entente Cordiale did not mean that Britain and France were ready and equipped for a confrontation with Germany. On 10 March, five days before the German invasion of Prague, Sam Hoare had even suggested that Europe was about to enter a new golden age of peace. Sir Robert Vansittart, though, looking back on the state visit in his memoirs, remembered watching Lord Halifax dancing after the banquet at Buckingham Palace with Madame Lebrun and thinking that the golden age was well and truly over.

This living funeral for the old order, though, was a final great show from Philip Sassoon as well. He had been suffering from a throat infection and succumbed to a flu-like virus which forced him to take a break from his official duties. On 19 April 1939, *The Times* posted a bulletin stating, 'Sir Philip Sassoon is suffering from influenza and has been advised by his doctor to cancel his public engagements for at least a fortnight.' Philip was warned by his doctor, Alec Gow, that he must take proper rest or else there was

---

* Pierre-Étienne Flandin was a French conservative politician who had been Prime Minister between 8 November and 31 May 1935. He would later serve for two months as Prime Minister in the Vichy government between December 1940 and February 1941.

a danger that the virus would spread to his lungs. However, King George VI and Queen Elizabeth were about to depart for a visit to Canada and the United States, and Philip was determined to see them before they departed. On 20 April, he called on them at Windsor Castle and the same day wrote to Winston Churchill, 'I have recovered now and hope to see you soon.'[50]

On 22 April, Philip's old friend from the RAF staff, John Hawtrey, visited him at Trent Park, and two days later Sassoon even managed to answer a question on air-raid precautions in the House of Commons. However, his recovery had not been complete and, as his doctor had warned, the virus spread to his lungs. On 19 May, *The Times* reported that Philip had been confined to bed with a high temperature. He was only fifty, physically fit, and it seemed incredible that his life could have been put in danger in this way. Yet he had a very serious pneumonic (streptococcal) infection that, while treatable by modern medicines, was life threatening in 1939.

Philip's condition steadily worsened, and on the morning of Saturday, 3 June 1939, with his sister Sybil and Hannah Gubbay by his side, he died at home in Park Lane. That evening Sybil wrote to Dr Gow to thank him for

the devoted, wonderful and deeply human way in which you have helped darling Philip through these dreadful weeks and at the same time looked after Hannah and me . . . Now that the agony of waiting has been changed to the anguish of losing him one can take stock of what has taken place. I feel that he had touched the highest point of human interests & joy – & loved by his friends, adored by his family, keeping his own fine nature untouched by success and prosperity, before anything came to sadden or spoil life for him, he went – leaving a bright track in which we must try to follow him. He died with his hand in yours holding to you in the firm faith that all was going to be alright . . . We are unhappy beyond bearing, we have lost the most darling brother and cousin

. . . We are going now to take our leave of Philip for the last time as we know him.[51]

The King and Queen had requested regular updates on Philip's condition during their tour of North America, and sent a telegram to Sybil when they received the news of his death: 'We are deeply grieved to hear of the loss of our old friend and send you our heartfelt sympathy.'[52]

Queen Mary wrote to the King and Queen, 'Philip Sassoon's death is a real grief . . . so young to die . . . if only he had not gone about for so long with that high temp of 103.'[53] Prince George, the Duke of Kent, who had spent part of his honeymoon at Trent Park, wrote to his brother the King, 'My Dear Bertie . . . It was very sad about Philip – Hannah let me know every day – but I always thought it was hopeless – luckily he didn't suffer as he was really always "wandering". He will be a great loss.'[54]

The news of Philip's death quickly reached his constituency in Folkestone where flags were flown at half-mast on public buildings that same day. His passing was also soon known to his friends and colleagues in Westminster. Chips Channon recorded in his diary:

Sassoon died today – what a loss to the London pageant. No-one infused it with so much colour and personality. Philip was sleek, clever and amiable. Kindly yet fickle, gay yet moody, he entertained with almost Oriental lavishness . . . and exerted an enormous influence on a section of London Society. He was always pleasant and witty with me, talking in that clipped sibilant accent which has been so often imitated . . . He had a prolonged and hazardous friendship with the Prince of Wales whom he worshipped though their intermittent quarrels were famous. He was also intimate with the King, Queen and Queen Mary – royalties haunted his house always, and he was loyal to them as he was to no-one else. Politicians he dropped as soon as they fell from power. The Eden reign was the longest but of late he was inclined to drop him too, much to

Anthony's amused resentment. Philip was never in the Chamberlain racket and his power waned with Baldwin's retirement, but he never lost his thirst of life.[55]

Channon's diary tribute reflects many of the stereotypical attitudes held of Philip, which don't really do him justice. It is true enough that he was a leader of 'London Society' and he certainly lived up to the reputation his entertainments had earned for their 'Oriental lavishness'. Yet he was loyal to his friends, and not just those in the royal family. It was not true that he dropped Eden after the latter resigned from the Foreign Office; Eden continued to be a guest at Trent and Lympne until Sassoon's death. Philip's friendship with Winston Churchill throughout his wilderness years in the 1930s is another good example of how he stuck by people he liked and believed in. Chips Channon had been something of a rival of Philip's for the attention of the Prince of Wales, which may explain his description of their friendship as 'hazardous'. Philip had been loyal to Edward, and particularly helpful and discreet in the early years of his affair with Freda Dudley Ward. Yet he was not as close to Wallis Simpson as he had been to Freda, and in the year of the abdication crisis a new court of American friends like Emerald Cunard, Elsie Mendl and Channon himself came more to the fore. A group, disparagingly referred to by Osbert Sitwell in his essay *Rat Week*, as the 'riff-raff of two continents.'[56]

The official notice of Philip Sassoon's death was placed in *The Times* on Monday 5 June and stated 'Funeral strictly private. No flowers.' The funeral took place that same day at Golders Green crematorium, and was attended by just Sybil and Hannah. Philip's ashes were then scattered above Trent Park by his friend the RAF pilot James Hawtrey, flying with 601 Squadron. Hawtrey remembered that as they swooped and dived, flying low above the estate, Philip's ashes were released not from an ornate urn, but from a modest cardboard box marked 'Lipton's tea'.[57]

Obituary tributes from his friends appeared in the pages of *The*

Times over the next few days. Sam Hoare touched on Philip's great passion for art and entertaining his friends, referencing as well his famous 'conversation pieces' exhibition at Park Lane in 1930:

> There was no-one in my life-time like Philip Sassoon . . . It was no chance that made Zoffany one of his favourite painters. For there was no conversation piece that portrayed modern life better than the parties at Trent or Lympne. There was no posing or pretence about them, no grouping for show or effect. Lord Balfour playing tennis with Boussus,* Lawrence in his private's uniform, Bernard Shaw looking at the flowers or Sargent at the pictures, Charlie Chaplin talking to some young air force officer and a crowd of politicians and agreeable friends, men and women, young and old, at bridge or golf or in vivid talk together – these were the figures of Philip's conversation pieces.[58]

Osbert Sitwell, who had known Philip since they were at Eton together, reflected that 'Despite a successful career, I often thought that his character was more that of an artist than of a politician. And in Lympne and Trent he had indeed created two superb works of art. Lympne is perhaps the more imaginative, more truly representative of himself . . . But these things were only an exteriorisation of his own personality; he seemed to belong to some brilliant order of being . . . rare and unlike others, obedient to his own rules and logic.'[59]

Philip's old friend Evan Charteris, who had sat alongside him on the board of trustees at the National Gallery, as well as at the Tate and the Wallace Collection, made the personal observation that

> He spoke rarely from his innermost mind, still more rarely did he disclose the sense of tears that lay below his matchless gift for

---

* Christian Boussus was a French tennis player who reached the final of the French Open in 1931, and played in his country's Davis Cup team.

laughter, his high spirits and his boundless zest for life . . . He was above all things concerned with beauty, to evoke it when and where he could, to draw from 'the well amid the waste'* and with it at least adorn if he could not hide the 'waste'. And so it was that 'in this erring pilgrimage' beauty came to figure in his mind not, indeed, as an answer to life but to an unusual degree as a medium of reconciliation and acceptance . . . [B]y what will his friends best remember him? Not perhaps by his unique gifts as a host, nor by his entrancing hospitality, his vivid and amusing conversation, his taste, or the purple patches of his remarkable career . . . it would be none of these, but by the less spectacular qualities of humanity and kindness – qualities to which he was continually and without ostentation giving expression.[60]

At Philip's own request he had no memorial service, but the RAF garden party at Trent planned for later in June went ahead as he had intended, and on 26 July the gardens at Lympne were opened to the public for the last time, to raise money for the British Empire cancer campaign. For his friends and family these events would have provided a more fitting commemoration of his life.

There was also the matter of a parliamentary by-election in his constituency to settle. Neville Chamberlain, concerned about the prospects of the Conservative Party holding the seat given the growing public concern at the likelihood of war, asked Sybil if she would stand. She remembered that he told her, 'You don't realise that things are very serious and it would be very bad for the government if they were to lose the election, and you've been known for all these years, you would be certain to win.'

She replied, 'Oh, I couldn't possibly go into the House of Commons. First of all, perhaps I wouldn't always agree with the

* Yet another oriental allusion for Philip Sassoon. The reference to the 'well amid the waste' (meaning the brief period of life in the midst of the infinity of time) is a quotation from the eleventh- and twelfth-century Persian poet Omar Khayyám, as translated by Edward FitzGerald.

government.' She subsequently wrote to Chamberlain, telling him that she would 'fight the election for somebody else that you choose', and recalled that 'they found a very nice fellow, a man called Brabner. I spent six weeks down there, at Lympne, speaking practically every day, and he got in very well.'[61] Rupert Brabner was duly elected in the by-election on 21 July 1939, and served as a pilot with the Royal Navy during the war. He would be tragically killed in an aeroplane accident in March 1945, off the Azores, while flying to America for a conference.

In Philip Sassoon's bedroom at Park Lane, the room where he died, was a portrait of King Louis XV of France. In 1933, in the programme for the loan exhibition at Park Lane entitled 'Three French Reigns',[62] it was observed that the reign of Louis XV was the 'frontier between order and disorder'. Philip's premature death, falling exactly three months before Britain's entry into the Second World War, marked out his life on a similar frontier in history. He had been born in 1888 at the home of Baron Gustave de Rothschild in Paris as the heir of the two great Jewish families of the nineteenth century. Moving on from those rarefied salons in the Avenue de Marigny, his life had known the golden generation of Edwardian England, the agonies of the First World War and the great personalities who shaped the 1920s and 1930s. His death marked the end of the pre-Second World War world, the era before the Holocaust, the atomic bomb and the Iron Curtain. Death denied him the opportunity to see his beloved RAF triumph in the skies above Lympne during the Battle of Britain in 1940, when the freedom of the world he had known was hanging by a thread. Yet he was also spared living once more through a war which would take the lives of so many young men he had known. After the loss of his schoolfriends in the trenches of the First World War would come in 1940 the deaths in combat of the pilots who had frequented his parties at Lympne during those balmy Augusts in the 1930s – young men from 601 Squadron like Guy Branch and Tim Wildblood, as well as Roger Bushell, who was one of the prisoners of war executed by the Germans after being caught following the 'Great Escape'. Rex Whistler as well would be killed in action in Normandy in 1944.

Philip Sassoon had inherited great wealth, but he used it to fashion his own world. His estates at Trent and Lympne were his own creations, and the furnishing of his mansion in Park Lane entirely of his own planning. Without the great impresario who had made them, these stages on which prime ministers and Hollywood stars had performed fell into abeyance. Port Lympne, which he had left to Hannah Gubbay, was immediately put up for let after his death. It was then commandeered by the armed forces during the war and used as accommodation for airmen and Free Czech troops. In 1946, Colonel Arthur Waite, an Australian veteran of the Gallipoli campaign and the racing driver son-in-law of Lord Austin, of the Austin motor company, purchased the estate, but it remained largely uninhabited for the next thirty years.

The ownership of Park Lane fell to Sybil through the Sassoon family trust, but she had no use for it and sold the mansion at a knock-down price during the war. The house was subsequently demolished and the site became home to Hugh Hefner's Playboy Club, which in 1981 was the most profitable casino in the world. That building has in turn been replaced by the luxury hotel 45 Park Lane.

Trent Park was also commandeered during the war and used as a prison for high-ranking Nazi officers. Later, it became home to the University of Middlesex, and it is now owned by the property developer Berkeley.

Philip's great collection of art and treasures was divided with his property between Hannah and Sybil. Some remain as part of the Cholmondeley estate, but other pieces were sold over the decades. Philip left his own portrait by John Singer Sargent to the Tate Gallery. Yet, outside of his family, it is at Port Lympne, the estate he created and loved, that his legacy best lives on. It was here that I first began to appreciate his remarkable life and was inspired to write this book. The estate, which has been lovingly preserved and rejuvenated by the Aspinall Foundation, also owes its saving to a young man who held Philip Sassoon in high regard. It was Alan Clark who persuaded John Aspinall to buy the estate after returning to it in the 1970s, a visit he recorded in his diary:

[Port Lympne is my] favourite spot in the whole of East Kent – one of the most evocative in the world . . . I sit on the terrace where one would occasionally get tea limone, and indescribably thin cucumber sandwiches before being sent back to Bellers [that is, Bellevue]. Can still look through the glass doors at that marbled, Moorish interior, black and white floors and arched ceilings. Totally still outside, but trees now grown enormously, hemming it in, better even than in Philip's heyday. The place has *slept* for thirty years, no one lived in it since Philip died, nothing disturbed. At any moment Philip could come out and call – to this day I can hear his drawl.[63]

• ACKNOWLEDGEMENTS •

In 2010 I was first elected to represent the constituency of Folkestone and Hythe in the House of Commons, ninety-eight years after Philip Sassoon won the by-election that made him the MP for the same seat. I was aware of his story in general terms, and even made a passing reference to him in my maiden speech, but it was only a couple of years later after visiting Port Lympne and discussing the history of the estate with its current managing director, Bob O'Connor, that I was determined to discover more about Philip; to try to understand this fascinating man and his phenomenal world.

I am most grateful to Philip Sassoon's great nephew, David Cholmondeley, the Marquess of Cholmondeley, for his advice and insights, as well as for full access to his family's archives at Houghton Hall. I would also like to thank Lady Cristina Cholmondeley, Charles Cholmondeley, Lady Rose Cholmondeley and Lady Aline Cholmondeley, Philip Sassoon's niece, whom it was my privilege to interview before her death in 2015.

Whilst a good number of Philip Sassoon's letters and papers remain, the records of contemporary diarists and the memoirs of his friends have been an invaluable resource. In particular those of Bob Boothby, Henry 'Chips' Channon, Norah Lindsay, Kenneth Clark, Lord Riddell and Philip's sister Sybil. The prologue of this book is a tableau of one of Philip's famous summer parties at Trent Park in the mid-1930s, based on numerous different accounts by his friends.

Her Majesty Queen Elizabeth II has granted permission for the use of the materials in this book sourced from the Royal Archives at Windsor. I would also like to thank Pam Clark and her team at the archives for their help with my research.

I have been a grateful recipient of the excellent support from the members of staff of the House of Commons library and the Parliamentary Archives, which is the custodian of the Lloyd George papers, among other treasures.

Like so many writers of this period of history, I am indebted to Allen Packwood, the director of the Churchill Archives Centre, at Churchill College, Cambridge, for his great kindness and guidance on my work for this book.

Air Marshal Sir Baz North, who was awarded the Philip Sassoon Memorial Prize at Cranwell, was most helpful in providing information from the RAF and Air Ministry archives. I would also like to thank Charles Cator at Christie's for his insights on Philip Sassoon's influence as a collector of paintings, furniture and objets d'art in the 1920s and 1930s.

Oliver Leiva gave me an excellent introduction to and tour of Trent Park. Oliver was one of the founders of the Trent Park Open House programme led by Enfield Borough Councillor Jason Charalambous and they, along with the Save Trent Park Campaign, have done great work to promote awareness of this remarkable estate and its history, which is much loved by the community that surrounds it. I would like to thank Trent Park's current owners, Berkeley Homes, and particularly Glen Jones and Patrick Joyce for giving me access to the mansion. I am delighted that plans to create a museum there on the ground floor and basement are progressing so well.

Timothy Everest provided some fantastic insights into tailoring and the new Savile Row look of the 1920s. I am grateful to Anda Rowland for allowing me to view the archives at Philip Sassoon's tailors, Anderson and Sheppard, and to Eric Musgrave for making the introduction.

Since the publication of the first edition of this book, a number of people have shared with me interesting stories and anecdotes about Philip Sassoon. In particular Mark Seligman who has helped to correctly identify the car make and model that Philip is shown driving in the plate section of this book. I would also like to thank Radu Albu-Comanescu, the great nephew of Philip's friend Marthe Bibesco, Siân Evans, and my parliamentary colleagues in the House of Commons Keith Simpson, Kwasi Kwarteng, and Chris Bryant.

My friend and agent Diane Banks has been a great source of guidance and encouragement throughout this project. I would also like to thank Martin Redfern for believing in this book, and in Philip Sassoon. Likewise my former colleague at M&C Saatchi, Marcus Peffers.

Arabella Pike, Stephen Guise, Helen Ellis and the team at HarperCollins have done an amazing job in producing this book, and it has been a pleasure to work with them.

I am also fortunate that from an early age my parents Fearghal and Diane Collins encouraged my enthusiasm for the study of history. I would also like to thank in particular my history teachers at St Mary's High School in Herefordshire, Michael Fitzgerald and, at Belmont Abbey in Hereford, Gerard Boylan. My House Master at Belmont Abbey, the Rt Rev. Dom Antony Tumelty, also has a great love of this period of English history, and I am grateful that his health and God's grace allowed him to see the publication of this book. I hope as well that my tutor for this period of modern history at the University of Oxford, Professor Niall Ferguson, will take this book as some evidence that his efforts in my direction were not in vain.

I would also like to thank my wife Sarah, who has lived and breathed every dot and comma of this work. It would not have been possible without her love, ideas, enthusiasm and support. To our children Claudia and Hugo, I hope that in time the book makes up for some of the lost Sunday afternoons playing in the garden.

Winston Churchill was right, as in most things, with his observation that writing a book 'is like having a friend and companion at your side, to whom you can always turn for comfort and amusement, and whose society becomes more attractive as a new and widening field of interest is lighted in the mind'. I am certainly grateful to the numerous friends and colleagues who have taken an interest in and provided helpful thoughts and suggestions during my journey with Philip Sassoon.

• ILLUSTRATION CREDITS •

The photographs and artwork in the picture section are reproduced by the kind permission of the Marquess of Cholmondeley, with the exception of the following:

p. 3 (top), Private Collection/Bridgeman Images; p. 3 (bottom), Charles Cholmondeley; p. 4 (bottom), Max Beerbohm Collection, General Collection, Beinecke Rare Book and Manuscript Library, Yale University © copyright the Estate of Max Beerbohm, reprinted by permission of London Management; p. 5 (top), Imperial War Museums; p. 6 (bottom), Photo12/UIG/Getty Images; p. 7 (bottom), Mirrorpix; p. 8 (bottom), Austrian Archives/Imagno/Getty Images; p. 10 (bottom), National Portrait Gallery, London; p. 16 (bottom), Parliamentary Archives.

The author and publishers are committed to respecting the intellectual property rights of others and have made all reasonable efforts to trace the copyright owners of the images reproduced, and to provide appropriate acknowledgement within this book. In the event that any untraceable copyright owners come forward after the publication of this book, the author and publishers will use all reasonable endeavours to rectify the position accordingly.

• NOTES •

ARCHIVES CONSULTED

Chamberlain papers, University of Birmingham
Churchill papers, Churchill Archives Centre, Churchill College, Cambridge
Cooper papers, Churchill Archives Centre
Derby papers, Liverpool Record Office
Desborough papers, Hertfordshire County Archives
Eden papers, University of Birmingham
Esher papers, Churchill Archives Centre
Gwynne papers, Imperial War Museum
Haig papers, National Library of Scotland
Hankey papers, Churchill Archives Centre
Houghton Hall Archives, Norfolk
Lloyd George papers, Parliamentary Archives
Diaries of William Lyon Mackenzie King, Library and Archives of Canada
Mallet papers, Balliol College, Oxford
The National Archives, Kew (TNA)
Northcliffe papers, British Library
Royal Archives, Windsor
Strachey papers, British Library
Trustee papers, National Gallery Archive

CHAPTER 1: SON OF BABYLON

1. *Henry Wadsworth Longfellow Complete Works*, Delphi Classics, 2012
2. *'Chips': The Diaries of Sir Henry Channon*, ed. Robert Rhodes James, Weidenfeld & Nicolson, 1967, 29 January 1935
3. Kenneth Clark, *Another Part of the Wood: A Self Portrait*, John Murray, 1974
4. *'Chips': The Diaries of Sir Henry Channon*
5. G. E. Tindall, *City of Gold: The Biography of Bombay*, Penguin, 1982
6. Society column on the Sassoons, remembering Sir Edward, *Liverpool Daily Post*, 24 October 1916
7. Peter Stansky, *Sassoon: The Worlds of Philip and Sybil*, Yale University Press, 2003
8. Sir Lawrence Jones, *A Victorian Boyhood*, Macmillan, 1955
9. Ibid.
10. Errol Trzebinski, *Silence Will Speak: A Study of the Life of Denys Finch Hatton and his Relationship with Karen Blixen*, William Heinemann, 1977
11. Osbert Sitwell, *The Scarlet Tree*, Macmillan, 1946
12. Jones, *Victorian Boyhood*
13. *Spectator*, 20 November 1926
14. Oscar Wilde, 'The English Renaissance of Art', lecture first delivered in New York on 9 January 1882, in Richard Ellman, *Oscar Wilde*, Alfred A. Knopf, 1988
15. Jones, *Victorian Boyhood*
16. Stanley Jackson, *The Sassoons*, William Heinemann, 1968
17. Sir Lawrence Jones, *An Edwardian Youth*, Macmillan, 1956
18. Nicholas Mosley, *Julian Grenfell: His Life and the Times of his Death, 1888–1915*, Weidenfeld & Nicolson, 1976
19. Jones, *An Edwardian Youth*
20. Gertrude Atherton, *Adventures of a Novelist*, Blue Ribbon Books, 1932
21. Ibid.

22. Stansky, *Sassoon*

23. Philip Sassoon, *The Third Route*, William Heinemann, 1929

24. Frances Horner, *Time Remembered*, William Heinemann, 1933

25. Philip Sassoon letter to Lady Desborough, 24 June 1915, Desborough papers, Hertfordshire County Archives

26. Stansky, *Sassoon*

27. Transcript of Sybil Cholmondeley in conversation with her grandson David, 1984, Houghton Hall Archives, Norfolk

28. *Dundee Courier*, 25 May 1912

29. *Dover Express*

30. *Exeter and Plymouth Gazette*, 10 June 1912

31. *Dundee Courier*, 4 June 1912

32. Max Beerbohm, *Philip Sassoon in Strange Company*, 1913, Max Beerbohm Collection, General Collection, Beinecke Rare Book and Manuscript Library, Yale University

33. Lord Beaverbrook, *The Decline and Fall of Lloyd George*, Collins, 1963

34. Ronan Fanning, *Fatal Path: British Government and the Irish Revolution, 1910–1922*, Faber & Faber, 2013

35. *Evening Telegraph* (Angus, Scotland), 7 August 1912

36. Beverley Nichols, *The Sweet and Twenties*, Weidenfeld & Nicolson, 1958

37. Ibid.

38. Ibid.

39. Robert Graves and Alan Hodge, *The Long Week-end: A Social History of Great Britain, 1918–1939*, Faber & Faber, 1940

40. Ibid.

41. D. J. Taylor, *Bright Young People: The Rise and Fall of a Generation, 1918–1940*, Chatto & Windus, 2007

42. Jones, *An Edwardian Youth*

43. Lord Berners, *A Distant Prospect*, Constable, 1945

44. Robert Graves, *Goodbye to All That*, Jonathan Cape, 1929

45. Mrs Henry Dudeney, *A Lewes Diary 1916–1944*, ed. Diana Crook, The Tatarus Press, 1998, 17 July 1930

46. Philip Sassoon letter to 'Jack', undated, Philip Sassoon papers, Houghton Hall Archives

47. Bob Boothby, *Recollections of a Rebel*, Hutchinson, 1978

48. Clark, *Another Part of the Wood*

CHAPTER 2: THE GENERAL'S STAFF

1. Reprinted in E. B. Osborn, *The New Elizabethans: A First Selection of the Lives of Young Men Who Have Fallen in the Great War*, John Lane, The Bodley Head, 1919

2. Vladimir Dedijer, *The Road to Sarajevo*, Simon & Schuster, 1966

3. Niall Ferguson, *The World's Banker: The History of the House of Rothschild*, Weidenfeld & Nicolson, 1998

4. Jones, *An Edwardian Youth*

5. Philip Sassoon letter to Lady Desborough, 17 February 1915, Desborough papers

6. G. A. K. Uhani letter to Lady Juliet Duff, 27 August 1917, reprinted in Maurice Baring, *Dear Animated Bust: Letters to Lady Juliet Duff, France 1915 to 1918*, Michael Russell, 1981

7. Julian Grenfell letter to Lady Desborough, 24 October 1914, in Mosley, *Julian Grenfell*

8. Siegfried Sassoon, 'The General' (1917)

9. Julian Grenfell, 'A Prayer for Those on the Staff' (1915)

10. Philip Sassoon letter to Lady Desborough, November 1914, Desborough papers

11. Alan Houghton Brodrick, *Near to Greatness: A Life of the Sixth Earl Winterton*, Hutchinson, 1965, entry from Lord Winterton's diary, July 1919

12. From remarks recorded by Marie Belloc Lowndes after meeting Philip Sassoon on 26 January 1915, in *Diaries and Letters of Marie Belloc Lowndes, 1911–1947*, ed. Susan Lowndes, Chatto & Windus, 1971

13. Rupert Brooke, 'The Dead (IV)' (1914)

14. Philip Sassoon letter to Lady Desborough, 23 June 1915, Desborough papers

15. Jones, *An Edwardian Youth*

16. Philip Sassoon letter to Lady Desborough, 9 August 1915, Desborough papers

17. Cecil Roth, *The Sassoon Dynasty*, Robert Hale, 1941, from a letter dated 1 February 1917

18. The quotation from Sir Rennell Rodd is used by Osborn in the Introduction to *The New Elizabethans*

19. Jones, *An Edwardian Youth*

20. *The Duff Cooper Diaries*, ed. John Julius Norwich, Weidenfeld & Nicolson, 2005, 21 May 1920

21. Philip Sassoon letter to Lady Desborough, 13 October 1916, Desborough papers

22. Jeremy Paxman, *Great Britain's Great War*, Penguin Viking, 2014

23. Marie Belloc Lowndes, *A Passing World*, Macmillan, 1948

24. Ibid.

25. The Folkestone harbour visitors' books have been digitized by the Step Short project and can be found online at www.step short.co.uk. The collection amounts to over 43,500 names, including King George V, David Lloyd George and Field Marshal Haig

26. G.S.O. [Sir Frank Fox], *G.H.Q. (Montreuil-sur-Mer)*, Philip Allan, 1920

27. John Charteris, *Field-Marshal Earl Haig*, Cassell, 1929

28. Ibid.

29. Douglas Haig letter to Lady Haig, 16 June 1918, in *The Private Papers of Douglas Haig, 1914–1919*, ed. Robert Blake, Eyre & Spottiswoode, 1952

30. Ibid.

31. Ibid.

32. Winston Churchill letter to Clementine Churchill, 1 January 1916, in Martin Gilbert, *Winston S. Churchill*, vol. III: *May 1915–December 1916*, Heinemann, 1972

33. Philip Sassoon letter to H. A. Gwynne, 6 January 1916, Gwynne papers, vol. IV, Imperial War Museum

34. Stansky, *Sassoon*

35. Lord Esher letter to Philip Sassoon, 5 February 1916, Esher papers, Churchill Archives Centre, Churchill College, Cambridge

36. Winston S. Churchill, *The World Crisis*, vol. III: *1916–1918*, Thornton Butterworth, 1927

37. Lord Beaverbrook, *Men and Power, 1917–1918*, Hutchinson, 1956

38. Philip Sassoon letter to Lord Northcliffe, 11 August 1916, Northcliffe papers, British Library

39. Philip Sassoon letter to Lady Desborough, 12 June 1916 (following Lord Kitchener's death on 5 June), Desborough papers

40. Philip Sassoon letter to Lord Esher, 24 July 1916, Esher papers

41. Philip Sassoon letter to Lord Esher, 11 August 1916, Esher papers

42. Douglas Haig letter to Lady Haig, 23 July 1916, in *Douglas Haig: War Diaries and Letters, 1914–1918*, ed. Gary Sheffield and John Bourne, Weidenfeld & Nicolson, 2005

43. Lord Northcliffe letter to Philip Sassoon, 6 October 1916, Northcliffe papers

44. Martin Gilbert, *Churchill: A Life*, William Heinemann, 1991

45. Douglas Haig note, 1 August 1916, on letter received from the Chief of the Imperial General Staff, 29 July 1916, in *Haig: War Diaries and Letters*

46. Ibid., diary entry for 8 August 1916

47. Philip Sassoon letter to Lord Northcliffe, 11 August 1916, Northcliffe papers

48. Lord Esher letter to Philip Sassoon, 14 August 1916, Esher papers

49. *Haig: War Diaries and Letters*, diary entry for 12 August 1916

50. Ibid., diary entry for 17 September 1916

51. Philip Sassoon letter to Lord Northcliffe, 14 September 1916, Northcliffe papers

52. Warning given by Lloyd George's parliamentary private secretary, David Davies MP, in Jackson, *The Sassoons*

53. See Gilbert, *Churchill: A Life*

54. Lord Northcliffe letter to Philip Sassoon, 2 October 1916, Northcliffe papers

55. David Lloyd George, *War Memoirs*, vol. IV, Ivor Nicholson & Watson, 1934

56. Lord Northcliffe letter to Philip Sassoon, 8 December 1916, Northcliffe papers

57. Philip Sassoon letter to Douglas Haig, December 1916, Haig papers, National Library of Scotland

58. Philip Sassoon letter to Alice Dudeney, December 1916, Box 21, Houghton Hall Archives

59. *Birmingham Daily Post*, 16 January 1917

60. Lord Derby letter to Philip Sassoon, 22 July 1917, Derby papers, Liverpool Record Office

61. Philip Sassoon letter to Lord Esher, 16 March 1917, Esher papers

62. David Lloyd George, *War Memoirs*, vol. II, Odhams Press, 1933

63. Lord Esher, 'War Journals', 1 December 1917, Esher papers

64. Ibid.

65. Lord Derby letter to Douglas Haig, 12 December 1917, Haig papers

66. Lord Northcliffe letter to Philip Sassoon, 13 December 1917, Northcliffe papers

67. Douglas Haig letter to Lady Haig, 14 December 1917, in *Haig: War Diaries and Letters*

68. Philip Sassoon letter to Lord Esher, 18 December 1917, Esher papers

69. Georges Carpentier, *Carpentier by Himself*, trans. Edward Fitzgerald, Hutchinson, 1955

70. James C. Humes, *Churchill: The Prophetic Statesman*, Regnery History, 2012

71. Philip Sassoon quoted in Jackson, *The Sassoons*

72. George Riddell recalled Philip Sassoon telling this story to Lloyd George after the war in *Lord Riddell's Intimate Diary of the Peace Conference and After, 1918–1923*, Victor Gollancz, 1933

73. William Orpen, *An Onlooker in France, 1917–1919*, Williams & Norgate, 1921

74. Lord Esher letter to Philip Sassoon, 10 August 1918, Esher papers

75. Philip Sassoon letter to Lord Esher, 23 March 1918, Esher papers

76. Philip Sassoon letter to Lord Esher, 29 March 1918, Esher papers

77. Philip Sassoon letter to Lord Esher, 30 March 1918, Esher Papers

78. Philip Sassoon letter to Alice Dudeney, 17 July 1918, Houghton Hall Archives

79. General Ludendorff, *My War Memories 1914–1918*, vol. II, Hutchinson, 1919

80. Douglas Haig letter to Lady Haig, 8 August 1918, in *Haig: War Diaries and Letters*

81. Philip Sassoon letter to Lady Desborough, 23 October 1918, Desborough papers

82. *Folkestone Express*, 16 November 1918

83. Ibid., 23 November 1918

84. Meeting reported in ibid., 30 November 1918

85. *Folkstone Express*, 14 December 1918

86. Philip Sassoon letter to Alice Dudeney, 23 February 1919, Houghton Hall Archives

CHAPTER 3: BRAVE NEW WORLD

1. Registered G-AENN in his name in September 1919, this was the first of a series of private planes Philip would own over the next twenty years. Anthony J. Moor, *Lympne Airfield at War and Peace*, Fonthill, 2014

2. Reported in the *Derby Daily Telegraph*, 20 September 1919

3. Harold Macmillan, *Winds of Change, 1914–1939*, Macmillan, 1966

4. Evelyn Waugh, *Evening Standard*, 22 January 1929

5. See record of her conversation on this subject with Ernest Hemingway in his book *A Moveable Feast*, Arrow Books, 2011

6. Philip Sassoon journal, Madrid, 16 to 19 March 1919, Houghton Hall Archives

7. *The Outline of Art*, ed. Sir William Orpen, Newnes, 1957 (revised edition)

8. Kenneth Clark, *Looking at Pictures*, John Murray, 1960

9. Philip Sassoon, diary note for 2 April 1919, Houghton Hall Archives

10. Osbert Sitwell, Philip Sassoon's entry in the *Oxford Dictionary of National Biography*

11. Sybil Cholmondeley in conversation, Houghton Hall Archives

12. Philip Tilden, *True Remembrances: The Memoirs of an Architect*, Country Life, 1954

13. Ibid.

14. Port Lympne was the main feature in two successive editions of *Country Life*: 19 May (gardens) and 26 May (interior) 1923

15. Belloc Lowndes, *A Passing World*

16. Philip Sassoon letter to Sir Louis Mallet, 13 August (no year), Mallet papers, Balliol College, Oxford

17. Tilden, *True Remembrances*

18. Ibid.

19. *'Chips': The Diaries of Sir Henry Channon*

20. Tilden, *True Remembrances*
21. Dudeney, *A Lewes Diary,* 25 August 1919
22. *The Duff Cooper Diaries*
23. *Lloyd George: A Diary by Frances Stevenson*, ed. A. J. P. Taylor, Hutchinson, 1971
24. Ibid.
25. Beaverbrook, *Men and Power*
26. Ibid.
27. Hansard, 21 November 1919
28. *Dover Express*, 21 April 1921
29. *Architect*, 23 May 1919
30. Article 231 of the Treaty of Versailles
31. David Lloyd George, *The Truth about Reparations and War-Debts*, William Heinemann, 1932
32. Maurice Hankey diaries, 8 May 1920, Hankey papers, Churchill Archives Centre
33. David Lloyd George letter to Winston Churchill, 10 May 1920, Lloyd George papers, Parliamentary Archives
34. David Lloyd George letter to Andrew Bonar Law, 10 May 1920, Lloyd George papers
35. Andrew Bonar Law letter to Lloyd George, 11 May 1920, Lloyd George papers
36. Hankey diaries, 14 May 1920, Hankey papers
37. Ibid.
38. Thomas Jones, *Whitehall Diary*, vol. I: *1916–1925*, Oxford University Press, 1969
39. Hankey diaries, 14 May 1920, Hankey papers
40. *The Times*, 15 May 1920
41. *Lord Riddell's Intimate Diary of the Peace Conference*, 15 May 1920
42. *Daily Mail*, 15 May 1920
43. *Lord Riddell's Intimate Diary of the Peace Conference*, 15 May 1920
44. Tilden, *True Remembrances*

45. Hankey diaries, 14 May 1920, Hankey papers
46. Ibid.
47. *Daily Mail*, 17 May 1920
48. Maurice Hankey, note from 'The Conversations at Hythe', 17 May 1920, CAB 24/105/97,The National Archives, Kew (TNA)
49. *Daily Mail*, 17 May 1920
50. Philip Sassoon letter to Lloyd George (in relation to his meeting with Lord Derby on 2 June 1920), Lloyd George papers
51. Hankey diaries, Hankey papers
52. *Folkestone Herald*, 26 June 1920
53. *Lord Riddell's Intimate Diary of the Peace Conference*
54. *Folkestone Herald*, 26 June 1920
55. All recollections from the Spa conference in a letter from Philip Sassoon to Lady Desborough, 6 July 1920, Desborough papers
56. Cabinet memorandum on the presentation by the German delegation at the Spa conference, 11 July 1920, CAB 24/109/1, TNA
57. Philip Sassoon letter to Lady Desborough, 6 July 1920
58. See Jonathan Rose, *The Literary Churchill: Author, Reader, Actor*, Yale University Press, 2014
59. Ibid.
60. David Coombs with Minnie Churchill, *Sir Winston Churchill: His Life and his Paintings*, Ware House, 2011
61. Christine Sutherland, *Enchantress: Marthe Bibesco and her World*, John Murray, 1997
62. Winston S. Churchill, *The World Crisis*, vol. IV: *The Aftermath, 1918–1922*, Thornton Butterworth, 1929
63. Lord Esher letter to Lord Derby, 26 April 1918, in Randolph Churchill, *Lord Derby: King of Lancashire*, William Heinemann, 1960
64. *Lord Riddell's Intimate Diary of the Peace Conference*
65. Ibid.

66. In *Anderson & Sheppard: A Style Is Born*, Quercus, 2011

67. Carpentier, *Carpentier by Himself*

68. Philip Ziegler, *King Edward VIII*, William Collins, 1990. The Prince compares himself with Max Beerbohm's assessment that George IV was 'indeed still a child'

69. From *Letters from a Prince: Edward, Prince of Wales, to Mrs Freda Dudley Ward, March 1918–January 1921*, ed. Rupert Godfrey, Little, Brown, 1998

70. *Lord Riddell's Intimate Diary of the Peace Conference*

71. Prince to Wales letter to Philip Sassoon, 15 March 1920, RA EDW/OUT/MISC/63, Royal Archives, Windsor

72. Prince of Wales letter to Philip Sassoon, 9 April 1920, RA EDW/OUT/MISC/64, Royal Archives

73. Prince of Wales letter to Philip Sassoon, 11 June 1920, RA EDW/OUT/MISC/65, Royal Archives

74. Prince of Wales letter to Philip Sassoon, 9 September 1920, RA EDW/OUT/MISC/68, Royal Archives

75. *Letters from a Prince*

76. Prince of Wales letter to Philip Sassoon, 11 June 1920, RA EDW/OUT/MISC/65, Royal Archives

77. Ziegler, *King Edward VIII*

78. Prince of Wales letter to Philip Sassoon, 11 June 1920, RA EDW/OUT/MISC/65, Royal Archives

79. Prince of Wales letter to Freda Dudley Ward, 27 July 1921, Royal Archives

80. Prince of Wales letter to Philip Sassoon, 3 August 1920, RA EDW/OUT/MISC/67, Royal Archives

81. Reported in the *Folkestone Herald*, 13 November 1920

82. *Letters from a Prince*

83. Prince of Wales letter from York Cottage, Sandringham, to Philip Sassoon, 26 December 1920, RA EDW/OUT/MISC/69, Royal Archives

84. *Lloyd George: A Diary by Frances Stevenson*

CHAPTER 4: CENTRE STAGE

1. C. K. Scott-Moncrieff, 'A Servile Statesman', privately printed, 1923, in Stansky, *Sassoon*
2. *Lord Riddell's Intimate Diary of the Peace Conference*
3. Philip Sassoon letter to David Lloyd George, 2 June 1920, Lloyd George papers
4. Ibid.
5. Philip Sassoon letter to David Lloyd George, 11 January 1921 Lloyd George papers
6. Winston Churchill letter to David Lloyd George, 30 January 1921, Churchill papers
7. Beaverbrook, *The Decline and Fall of Lloyd George*
8. Sir Oswald Mosley, *My Life*, Thomas Nelson, 1968
9. *Blackwood's Edinburgh Magazine*, February 1921
10. Anne Olivier Bell, ed., *The Diary of Virginia Woolf*, Harcourt, Brace, Jovanovich, 1980, vol. III, 15 June 1929
11. 'Men and Women of To-day', *Dundee Courier*, 28 March 1921
12. *Lord Riddell's Intimate Diary of the Peace Conference*
13. Lord Derby letter to Philip Sassoon, 23 December 1920, in Randolph Churchill, *Lord Derby: King of Lancashire*
14. James Denman and Paul McDonald, *Unemployment Statistics from 1881 to the Present Day*, Labour Market Trends, Office of National Statistics, January 1996
15. Briand quoted in *News of the World*, 24 April 1921
16. Lloyd George, *The Truth about Reparations and War-Debts*
17. *Lord Riddell's Intimate Diary of the Peace Conference*
18. A. J. P. Taylor, *The Origins of the Second World War*, Hamish Hamilton, 1961
19. Beaverbrook, *Decline and Fall of Lloyd George*
20. *Lord Riddell's Intimate Diary of the Peace Conference*
21. Churchill, *Lord Derby*
22. Thomas Jones, *Whitehall Diary*, vol. III: *Ireland, 1918–1925*, Oxford University Press, 1971

23. Speech in Folkestone to members of the battalion, reported in the *Liverpool Echo*, 23 March 1914. (The following day, however, Sassoon denied having made the offer.)

24. R. F. Foster, *Vivid Faces: The Revolutionary Generation in Ireland, 1890–1923*, Allen Lane, 2014

25. Tim Pat Coogan, *Michael Collins*, Hutchinson, 1990

26. Beaverbrook, *The Decline and Fall of Lloyd George*

27. Hankey diaries, Hankey papers

28. Lord Esher letter to Prince of Wales, 13 November 1921, RA EDW/PRIV/MAINA/236, Royal Archives

29. James Fox, 'Sir Philip Sassoon, Bt', in exhibition catalogue *Works of Art from Houghton*, Christie's, London, 8 December 1994; Tilden, *True Remembrances*

30. Ibid.

31. *The World Crisis*, vol. IV: *The Aftermath*, cited in Roy Jenkins, *Churchill*, Macmillan, 2001

32. Jones, *Whitehall Diary*, vol. III: *Ireland*

33. Tim Pat Coogan, *Michael Collins*

34. Jones, *Whitehall Diary*, vol. III: *Ireland*

35. Nichols, *The Sweet and Twenties*

36. Ibid.

37. Charlie Chaplin, *My Trip Abroad*, Harper & Brothers, 1922

38. Charles Chaplin, *My Autobiography*, Simon & Schuster, 1964

39. Chaplin, *My Trip Abroad*

40. Sybil Cholmondeley in conversation, Houghton Hall Archives

41. Chaplin, *My Autobiography*

42. Chaplin, *My Trip Abroad*

43. *The Duff Cooper Diaries*

44. Austen Chamberlain letter to his sister Hilda, 13 November 1921, in *The Austen Chamberlain Diary Letters: The Correspondence of Sir Austen Chamberlain with his Sisters Hilda*

and Ida, 1916–1937, ed. Robert C. Self, Cambridge University Press, 1995

45. *Lloyd George: A Diary by Frances Stevenson*
46. Jones, *Whitehall Diary*, vol. III: *Ireland*
47. Ibid.
48. Sir Robert Bruce, *The House of Memories*, Royal Philosophical Society, 1946–7
49. Philip Sassoon memo to Lloyd George, 19 December 1921; Philip's cover note to Lloyd George is in the Lloyd George papers and Churchill's copy of the memo itself is in the Churchill papers
50. A. J. Sylvester, *The Real Lloyd George*, Cassell, 1947
51. Beaverbrook, *The Decline and Fall of Lloyd George*
52. Austen Chamberlain letter to his sister Hilda, 1 January 1922, in *The Austen Chamberlain Diary Letters*
53. Lloyd George, *The Truth about Reparations and War-Debts*
54. Sylvester, *The Real Lloyd George*
55. Lloyd George, *The Truth about Reparations and War Debts*
56. Sylvester, *The Real Lloyd George*
57. Ibid.
58. *Dover Express*, 5 May 1922
59. Austen Chamberlain letter to his sister Hilda, 4 March 1922, in *The Austen Chamberlain Diary Letters*
60. Philip Sassoon letter to Lord Esher, 6 March 1922, Esher papers
61. Philip Sassoon letter to David Lloyd George, 13 March 1922, Lloyd George papers
62. In *Darling Pussy: The Letters of Lloyd George and Frances Stevenson, 1913–41*, ed. A. J. P. Taylor, Weidenfeld & Nicolson, 1975
63. Philip Sassoon letter to David Lloyd George, 24 March 1922, Lloyd George papers
64. *Toronto Star*, 24 April 1922, in Ernest Hemingway, *By-Line*, Collins, 1968

65. Thomas Jones, *Lloyd George*, Oxford University Press, 1951
66. Hansard, 4 May 1922
67. Ibid., 29 May 1922
68. Sir Charles Holmes letter to Philip Sassoon, 11 October 1922, Trustee papers, National Gallery Archive
69. Philip Sassoon letter to Sir Charles Holmes, 14 October 1922, Trustee papers, National Gallery Archive
70. Winston Churchill letter to Clementine Churchill, 16 July 1922, Churchill papers
71. *The Austen Chamberlain Diary Letters*, diary entry for 20 November 1922 (referring to the meeting that took place on 19 July 1922)
72. Winston Churchill letter to Clementine Churchill, 5 August 1922, Churchill papers
73. Jones, *Lloyd George*
74. Ibid.
75. John Cross, *Sir Samuel Hoare: A Political Biography*, Jonathan Cape, 1977
76. *The Times*, 20 October 1922
77. Cross, *Sir Samuel Hoare*
78. A full breakdown of how members voted can be found in *Memoirs of a Conservative: J. C. C. Davidson's Memoirs and Papers, 1910–1937*, ed. Robert Rhodes James, Weidenfeld & Nicolson, 1969
79. Ibid.
80. Hankey diary, Hankey papers
81. Harold Nicolson, *King George V: His Life and Reign*, Constable, 1952
82. Note from King George V to Lord Stamfordham, 7 November 1922, RA PS/PSO/GV/C/M/1811/102A, Royal Archives
83. *Folkestone Express*, 28 October 1922
84. *Folkestone Express*, 11 November 1922

CHAPTER 5: FLYING MINISTER

1. William Orpen, 'November 1922', updated copy in Lloyd George papers
2. Austen Chamberlain letter to his sister Ida, 21 November 1922, in *The Austen Chamberlain Diary Letters*
3. Ibid.
4. *Lord Riddell's Intimate Diary of the Peace Conference*, 18 November 1922
5. Austen Chamberlain letter to his sister Ida, 21 November 1922, in *The Austen Chamberlain Diary Letters*
6. Robert Blake, *The Conservative Party from Peel to Thatcher*, Methuen, 1985
7. Philip Sassoon to David Lloyd George, 1 February 1923, Lloyd George papers
8. Philip Sasson letter to Sybil Cholmondeley, 31 January 1923, in *Letters to Sybil*, privately published, 1923, Houghton Hall Archives
9. Philip Sasson letter to Sybil Cholmondeley, 2 February 1923, in ibid.
10. Philip Sasson letter to Sybil Cholmondeley, 13 February 1923, in ibid.
11. Philip Sassoon letter to Sybil Cholmondeley, 22 February 1923, in ibid.
12. Philip Sassoon letter to Sybil Cholmondeley, 24 February 1923, in ibid.
13. *Folkestone Herald*, 24 March 1923
14. Philip Sassoon letter to Lord Beaverbrook, 20 May 1923, Parliamentary Archives
15. Philip Sassoon letter to Lord Beaverbrook, 22 May 1923, Parliamentary Archives
16. *Memoirs of a Conservative*
17. Beverley Nichols, *All I Could Never Be*, Jonathan Cape, 1949

18. Michael Holroyd, *Lytton Strachey: A Critical Biography*, vol. II: *The Years of Achievement, 1910–1932*, William Heinemann, 1968

19. Ibid.

20. London society press article, 6 April 1924, in Robert Wainwright, *Sheila: The Australian Ingenue Who Bewitched British Society*, Allen & Unwin, 2014

21. Mosley, *My Life*

22. *Folkestone Herald*, 1 December 1923

23. *Dover Express*, 30 November 1923

24. *Folkestone Herald*, 1 December 1923

25. Philip Sassoon letter to Winston Churchill, 4 March 1924, Churchill papers

26. This letter was sent on 7 March 1924 and signed by the following MPs: Austin Hopkinson, Esmond Harmsworth, Murray Sueter, Henry Chilcott, Sir Martin Conway, Sir Philip Sassoon, J. S. Rankin, Oliver Locker-Lampson and Sir Burton Chadwick

27. Sir William Tyrell (civil servant and friend of Sir Louis Mallet), letter to Stanley Baldwin, 1 November 1924, in Martin Gilbert, *Winston S. Churchill*, vol. V: *The Exchequer Years 1922–1929*, Heinemann, 1979

28. Richard Toye, *Lloyd George and Churchill: Rivals for Greatness*, Macmillan, 2012

29. Philip Sassoon diary note, 24 November 1924, Houghton Hall Archives

30. Letter of 3 December 1924 noted in Philip Sassoon diary note, Houghton Hall Archives

31. Letter of 16 November 1924 copied into Philip Sassoon diary note, Houghton Hall Archives

32. Philip Sassoon letter to Winston Churchill, 17 November 1924, Churchill papers

33. Philip Sassoon diary note, 10 December 1924, Houghton Hall Archives

34. Philip Sassoon letter to Winston Churchill, 13 December 1926, Churchill papers

35. Profile of Trent Park, *Country Life*, January 1931

36. Ibid.

37. Sitwell, *The Scarlet Tree*

38. In Allyson Hayward, *Norah Lindsay: The Life and Art of a Garden Designer*, Frances Lincoln, 2007

39. Dudeney, *A Lewes Diary*, 10 July 1925

40. Robert Rhodes James, *Victor Cazalet*, Hamish Hamilton, 1976, diary entry for 18 December 1927

41. Trent visitors' book entry, 9–11 June 1927, Houghton Hall Archives. *Lady, Be Good* was the last stage performance at the Empire before the theatre was remodelled to show films

42. *The Neville Chamberlain Diary Letters*, vol. II: *The Reform Years, 1921–1927*, ed. Robert Self, Ashgate, 2000, 19 March 1927

43. Alexandre Dumas, *The Count of Monte Cristo*, Vintage, 2009

44. Sybil Cholmondeley in conversation, Houghton Hall Archives

45. *The Leo Amery Diaries*, vol. I: *1896–1929*, ed. John Barnes and David Nicholson, Hutchinson, 1980, 4 July 1928

46. Michael Bloch, *Closet Queens: Some 20th Century British Politicians*, Little, Brown, 2015

47. Hansard, 11 March 1924

48. Viscount Templewood, *Nine Troubled Years*, Collins, 1954

49. Sybil Cholmondelely in conversation, Houghton Hall Archives

50. Stansky, *Sassoon*

51. Sassoon, *The Third Route*

52. This and all subsequent quoted relating to the trip to India are from ibid. unless otherwise stated.

53. Bob Boothby, *Recollections of a Rebel*

54. The Earl of Birkenhead, *Halifax: The Life of Lord Halifax*, Hamish Hamilton, 1965

55. T. E. Lawrence letter to H. S. Ede, 30 June 1928, in *T. E. Lawrence by his Friends*, ed. A. W. Lawrence, Jonathan Cape, 1937

56. Philip Sassoon in ibid.
57. *Yorkshire Post*, 14 November 1928
58. *Folkestone Herald*, 24 November 1928
59. Ibid.
60. T. E. Lawrence letter to Philip Sassoon, 15 May 1929, Houghton Hall Archives
61. Thomas Jones, *Whitehall Diary*, vol. II: *1926–1930*, Oxford University Press, 1969, March 1929
62. See Bloch, *Closet Queens*
63. Robert Rhodes James, *Anthony Eden*, Weidenfeld & Nicolson, 1986
64. Bloch, *Closet Queens*
65. Jones, *Whitehall Diary*, vol. II: *1926–1930*, 6 March 1929
66. In Cross, *Sir Samuel Hoare*
67. *Folkestone Herald*, 18 May 1929
68. Bloch, *Closet Queens*
69. Jones, *Whitehall Diary*, vol. II: *1926–1930*, 21 June 1929
70. Clark, *Another Part of the Wood*
71. Jones, *Whitehall Diary*, vol. II: *1926–30*, 21 June 1929

CHAPTER 6: CAVALCADE

1. Tom Moulson, *Millionaires' Squadron: The Remarkable Story of 601 Squadron and the Flying Sword*, Pen & Sword Aviation, 2014
2. Ibid.
3. Prince of Wales letter to Philip Sassoon, 10 November 1929, RA EDW/OUT/MISC/73, Royal Archives
4. Mary Soames (ed.), *Speaking for Themselves: The Personal Letters of Winston and Clementine Churchill*, Black Swan, 1999
5. *Folkestone Herald*, 14 September 1929
6. Sassoon, *The Third Route*
7. Wainwright, *Sheila*

8. Dr G. C. Williamson, *English Conversation Pieces of the Eighteenth and Nineteenth Centuries*, B. T. Batsford, 1931

9. Ibid.

10. Philip Sassoon memo, 31 March 1930, Trustee papers, National Gallery Archive

11. From the Crawford papers, in Andrea Geddes Poole, *Stewards of the Nation's Art: Contested Cultural Authority, 1890–1939*, University of Toronto Press, 2010

12. Ibid.

13. Lytton Strachey letter to Dora Carrington, 10 June 1930, Strachey papers, British Library

14. A. J. P. Taylor, *English History, 1914–1945*, Clarendon Press, 1965

15. Philip Sassoon letter to Lytton Strachey, 5 August 1930, Strachey papers, British Library

16. In *The Journals of Woodrow Wyatt*, vol. II: *Thatcher's Fall and Major's Rise, 1989–1992*, ed. Sarah Curtis, Macmillan, 1999, 9 July 1991

17. Boothby, *Recollections of a Rebel*

18. Cole Lesley, *The Life of Noël Coward*, Jonathan Cape, 1976

19. Ibid.

20. Boothby, *Recollections of a Rebel*

21. Lesley, *The Life of Noël Coward*

22. Tom Clavin, *Sir Walter: The Flamboyant Life of Walter Hagen*, Aurum Press, 2005

23. *The Bradman Albums: Selections from Sir Donald Bradman's Official Collection*, Queen Anne Press, 1988

24. Laurence Whistler, *The Laughter and the Urn*, Weidenfeld & Nicolson, 1985

25. Hugh and Mirabel Cecil, *In Search of Rex Whistler: His Life and His Work*, Frances Lincoln, 2013

26. Letter from Rex Whistler to Edith Olivier, 12 August 1932, Edith Olivier Correspondence, Wiltshire and Swindon Archives, Chippenham

27. Ibid., 2 October 1932

28. 'Chips': The Diaries of Sir Henry Channon, 1 August 1936
29. Clark, Another Part of the Wood
30. Nichols, The Sweet and Twenties
31. Harold Nicolson, Diaries and Letters, 1939–39, Collins, 1966, 1 June 1931
32. Philip Sassoon letter to Winston Churchill, 17 November 1924 (following his appointment as Minister for Aviation), Churchill papers
33. T. E. Gregory cited in Lloyd George, The Truth about Reparations and War-Debts.
34. Philip Sassoon letter to the Folkestone Herald, 29 August 1931
35. Folkestone Herald, 10 October 1931

CHAPTER 7: THE GATHERING STORM

1. Ellen Wilkinson, Peeps at Politicians, Philip Allan, 1930
2. Templewood, Nine Troubled Years
3. Hansard, 10 March 1932
4. Ibid.
5. Yorkshire Post, 11 March 1932
6. Templewood, Nine Troubled Years
7. Winston S. Churchill, The Second World War, vol. I: The Gathering Storm, Cassell, 1948
8. Hansard, 23 November 1932
9. Sutherland, Enchantress
10. Churchill, The Second World War, vol. I: The Gathering Storm
11. Ibid.
12. Lloyd George: A Diary by Frances Stevenson, 22 November 1934
13. Churchill, The Second World War, vol. I: The Gathering Storm
14. Austen Chamberlain letter to his sister Hilda, 18 December 1932, in The Austen Chamberlain Diary Letters
15. Anthony Eden, The Eden Memoirs: Facing the Dictators, Cassell, 1962

16. Boothby, *Recollections of a Rebel*

17. Ian Kershaw, *Making Friends with Hitler: Lord Londonderry and Britain's Road to War*, Allen Lane, 2004

18. *The Duff Cooper Diaries*, 8 February 1933

19. Eden, *The Eden Memoirs: Facing the Dictators*

20. Churchill, *The Second World War*, vol. I: *The Gathering Storm*

21. Hansard, 14 March 1933

22. Ibid.

23. Queen Mary's diary, 26 March 1933, RA QM/PRIV/QMD, Royal Archives

24. Templewood, *Nine Troubled Years*

25. Jean Moorcroft Wilson, *Siegfried Sassoon*, vol. II: *The Journey from the Trenches, 1918–1967*, Gerald Duckworth, 2004

26. Eden, *The Eden Memoirs*

27. Ibid.

28. Austen Chamberlain letter to his sister Hilda, 10 February 1934, in *The Austen Chamberlain Diary Letters*

29. Secretary of State for Air memo to the cabinet, 22 February 1934, CAB 24/247/57, National Archives

30. Hansard, 8 March 1934

31. Queen Mary's diary, 27 May 1934, RA QM/PRIV/QMD, Royal Archives. David Burrowes, MP for Enfield Southgate, the constituency in which Trent Park is located, told me that he once asked the Queen if she remembered visiting the estate in her childhood, to which she replied that she did, and in particular the chocolate cake that Philip Sassoon had served

32. Robert Rhodes James, *Bob Boothby: A Portrait*, Hodder & Stoughton, 1991

33. Robert Rhodes James, *Victor Cazalet*, diary entry for 7 August 1934

34. Ibid., diary entry for 14 August 1934

35. Desmond Morton letter to Winston Churchill, 17 August 1934, Churchill papers

36. Winston Churchill telegram to Philip Sassoon, 22 September 1934, Churchill papers

37. *Folkestone Herald*, 13 October 1934

38. Hansard, 28 November 1934

39. Hansard, 19 March 1935

40. Churchill, *The Second World War,* vol. I: *The Gathering Storm*

41. Eden, *The Eden Memoirs*

42. British Ambassador in Berlin memo, 2 April 1935, Air Ministry papers, AIR 8/186/7A, National Archives

43. Eden, *The Eden Memoirs*

44. Air Staff memo, 28 May 1935, AIR 8/186/, National Archives

45. Winston Churchill memo to Stanley Baldwin, 29 April 1935, CAB 21/419, National Archives, in Martin Gilbert, *Winston S. Churchill*, vol. V: *The Wilderness Years (1929–1935)*, Heinemann, 1981

46. Hansard, 22 May 1935

47. Lesley, *The Life of Noël Coward*

48. *New York Times*, 19 May 1935

49. *Western Morning News*, 20 May 1935

50. *'Chips': The Diaries of Sir Henry Channon*, 18 March 1935

51. Diary entry, 11 May 1935, Eden papers, University of Birmingham

52. *'Chips': The Diaries of Sir Henry Channon*, 23 December 1935

53. Eden, *The Eden Memoirs*

54. Robert Vansittart, *The Mist Procession: The Autobiography of Lord Vansittart*, Hutchinson, 1958

55. *Memoirs of a Conservative*

56. Templewood, *Nine Troubled Years*

57. Ibid.

58. Ibid.

59. Ibid.

60. *Folkestone Herald*, 26 October 1935

61. Ibid., 9 November 1935

62. Lindy Woodhead, *Shopping, Seduction and Mr Selfridge*, Profile Books, 2012
63. Templewood, *Nine Troubled Years*
64. *'Chips': The Diaries of Sir Henry Channon*, 19 December 1935
65. Templewood, *Nine Troubled Years*
66. Hayward, *Norah Lindsay*
67. *A King's Story: The Memoirs of H.R.H. the Duke of Windsor, K.G.*, Cassell, 1951
68. Hayward, *Norah Lindsay*
69. Templewood, *Nine Troubled Years*

CHAPTER 8: THE KING'S PARTY

1. Osbert Sitwell, *Rat Week: An Essay on the Abdication*, Michael Joseph, 1986
2. *A King's Story*
3. Ibid.
4. Ibid.
5. Mitchell Owens, 'Fractured Fairy Tale: An Archive of a Royal Romance', *New York Times*, 8 June 2003
6. *The Duff Cooper Diaries*, 20 January 1936
7. *A King's Story*
8. Ibid.
9. Prince of Wales letter to Philip Sassoon, 10 November 1929, RA EDW/OUT/MISC/73, Royal Archives
10. Wallis, Duchess of Windsor, *The Heart Has Its Reasons: Memoirs*, Michael Joseph, 1956
11. Ellis Waterhouse letter to Harold Isherwood Kay, written at Café des Deux Magots, Paris, 19 February 1936, Trustee papers, National Gallery Archive
12. *The Times*, 3 March 1936
13. *Folkestone Express*, 26 December 1936
14. Ziegler, *King Edward VIII*
15. Ibid.

16. Sitwell, *Rat Week*
17. Austen Chamberlain letter to his sister Hilda, 15 February 1936, in *The Austen Chamberlain Diary Letters*
18. Gilbert, *Churchill: A Life*
19. Ibid.
20. Philip Sassoon letter to Winston Churchill, 15 March 1936, Churchill papers
21. Hansard, 17 March 1936
22. Hansard, 12 November 1936
23. *'Chips': The Diaries of Sir Henry Channon*, 10 May 1936
24. Ibid., 11 June 1936
25. Norah Lindsay letter to Madeline Whitbread, 2 August 1936, in Haywood, *Norah Lindsay*
26. *'Chips': The Diaries of Sir Henry Channon*, 1 August 1936
27. Norah Lindsay letter to Madeline Whitbread, 2 August 1936, in Haywood, *Norah Lindsay*
28. *'Chips': The Diaries of Sir Henry Channon*, 1 August 1936
29. Ibid., 3 August 1936
30. Queen Mary's diary, 10 September 1936, RA QM/PRIV/QMD, Royal Archives
31. Philip Sassoon travel journal, 27 September 1936, Houghton Hall Archives
32. Ibid., 30 September 1936
33. Ziegler, *King Edward VIII*
34. George Bernard Shaw, *The Apple Cart*, Penguin, 1956
35. *'Chips': The Diaries of Sir Henry Channon*, 17 November 1936
36. Sitwell, *Rat Week*
37. *'Chips': The Diaries of Sir Henry Channon*, 3 December 1936
38. Ziegler, *King Edward VIII*
39. Boothby, *Recollections of a Rebel*
40. Hansard, 7 December 1936
41. Boothby, *Recollections of a Rebel*
42. Diary entry, 8 December 1936, Ref. Item 17479, diaries of

William Lyon Mackenzie King, Library and Archives of Canada

43. Ziegler, *King Edward VIII*
44. *A King's Story*
45. *Folkestone Express*, 26 December 1936
46. *Diaries and Letters of Marie Belloc Lowndes*, diary entry for 28 January 1937 (looking back to the New Year)
47. Haywood, *Norah Lindsay*
48. Stansky, *Sassoon*
49. Ziegler, *King Edward VIII*
50. William Shawcross, *Counting One's Blessings: The Selected Letters of Queen Elizabeth the Queen Mother*, Macmillan, 2012

CHAPTER 9:PHILIP SASSOON REVISITED

1. Philip Ziegler, *Diana Cooper*, Hamish Hamilton, 1981
2. Robert Rhodes James, *Bob Boothby: A Portrait*, Hodder and Stoughton, 1991
3. David Lough, *No More Champagne: Churchill and His Money*, Head of Zeus, 2015
4. Winston Churchill letter to Clementine Churchill, 2 February 1937, Churchill papers
5. Hansard, 15 May 1937
6. Philip Sassoon letter to Winston Churchill, 14 May 1937, Churchill papers
7. *Folkestone Express*, 29 May 1937
8. Winston Churchill letter to Philip Sassoon, 29 May 1937, Churchill papers
9. Thomas Jones, *A Diary with Letters, 1931–1950*, Oxford University Press, 1954, diary entry for 22 May 1936
10. Sybil Cholmondeley in conversation, Houghton Hall Archives
11. *'Chips': The Diaries of Sir Henry Channon*, 6 February 1935
12. *The Duff Cooper Diaries*, 16 January 1938
13. *Western Daily Press*, 3 February 1938

14. See above, p. 113
15. W. F. Deedes, *Dear Bill: W. F. Deedes Reports*, Macmillan, 1997
16. Ion Trewin, *Alan Clark: The Biography*, Weidenfeld & Nicolson, 2009
17. Ibid.
18. Ibid.
19. Sybil Cholmondeley in conversation, Houghton Hall Archives
20. Peter Stansky, *Sassoon*
21. Ibid.
22. Ibid.
23. Ibid.
24. *The Times*, 23 July 1937
25. *Daily Mail*, 11 August 2014
26. Philip Sassoon letter to Duff Cooper, 17 August 1937, Cooper papers, Churchill Archives Centre
27. *Folkestone Express*, 26 February 1938
28. Rhodes James, *Anthony Eden*
29. *The Diplomatic Diaries of Oliver Harvey, 1937–1940*, ed. John Harvey, Collins, 1970, 16 November 1937
30. Ibid.
31. Anthony Eden diary note, 17–24 February 1938 (which recorded all of the events leading up to his resignation, including those that occurred prior to the 17th), Eden papers, University of Birmingham
32. Ibid.
33. Ibid., 22 February 1938
34. Churchill, *The Second World War*, vol. I: *The Gathering Storm*
35. Sir Nevile Henderson, *Failure of a Mission, Berlin 1937–1939*, Hodder & Stoughton, 1940
36. Templewood, *Nine Troubled Years*
37. Henderson, *Failure of a Mission*
38. Winston Churchill article for the *Daily Telegraph*, 23 June 1938,

in Winston S. Churchill, *Step by Step*, Thornton Butterworth, 1939

39. Hansard, 5 October 1938
40. Hansard, 3 October 1938
41. Philip Sassoon note to Neville Chamberlain, September 1938, Chamberlain papers, University of Birmingham, in Stansky, *Sassoon*
42. *The Times*, 28 September 1938
43. *Folkestone Express*, 15 October 1938
44. Churchill, *The Second World War*, vol. I: *The Gathering Storm*
45. *'Chips': The Diaries of Sir Henry Channon*, 22 March 1939
46. Anne de Courcy, *1939: The Last Season*, Weidenfeld & Nicolson, 2003
47. Neville Chamberlain letter to his sister Ida, 26 March 1939, in Robert Self (ed.), *Neville Chamberlain Diary Letters*, vol. IV: *The Downing Street Years 1934–1940*, Ashgate, 2005
48. *The Leo Amery Diaries*, vol. II: 1929–1945, ed. John Barnes and David Nicholson, 23 March 1939
49. *Sunday Times*, 26 March 1939
50. Philip Sassoon letter to Winston Churchill, 20 April 1939, Churchill papers
51. Sybil Cholmondeley letter to Dr Alec Gow, 3 June 1939, Houghton Hall Archives
52. King George VI telegram to Sybil Cholmondeley, Houghton Hall Archives
53. Queen Mary letter to King George VI and Queen Elizabeth, June 1939, RA GVI/PRIV/RF/11/501, Royal Archives
54. Duke of Kent letter to King George VI, June 1939, RA GVI/PRIV/RF/08/03, Royal Archives
55. *'Chips': The Diaries of Sir Henry Channon*, 3 May 1939
56. Sitwell, *Rat Week*
57. Peter Coats, *Of Generals and Gardens*, Weidenfeld & Nicolson, 1976
58. *The Times*, 5 June 1939

59. Ibid., 6 June 1939
60. Ibid., 9 June 1939
61. Sybil Cholmondeley in conversation, Houghton Hall Archives
62. 'Three French Reigns', 21 February–5 April 1933
63. Alan Clark, *Diaries: Into Politics, 1972–1982*, ed. Ion Trewin, Weidenfeld & Nicolson, 2000, 3 June 1976

• INDEX •